BRITISH VOLUNTEERS FOR LIBERTY:
SPAIN 1936-1939

BRITISH VOLUNTEERS
FOR LIBERTY:
SPAIN 1936-1939

by

Bill Alexander

LAWRENCE and WISHART
LONDON

Lawrence and Wishart Limited
39 Museum Street
London WC1A 1LQ

First published 1982
© Bill Alexander 1982

Photoset in North Wales by
Derek Doyle & Associates, Mold, Clwyd,
and printed in Great Britain by
Camelot Press Limited, Southampton.

Contents

15   The Fight Goes On in Franco's Gaols   183

16   Across the Ebro: The Last Offensive   197

17   The British in Other Roles   217

18   The Medical Services   225

19   Getting Home   237

20   At Home – But Not to Rest   245

21   Was It All Worth-While?   257

     Roll of Honour   261

     Select Bibliography   277

     Selected Name Index   283

     Index of Spanish Place-Names   287

Illustrations

13a British nurses in Spain

13b Hospital in a cave near the Ebro river, August
      1938

TEXT ILLUSTRATIONS

MAPS

Chronology of Main Events

1936

16 February	Popular Front win majority in General Election.
18 July	Army revolt begins.
25 July	French Government forbids arms for Republican Spain.
1 September	Franco declared head of Spanish state.
4 September	Largo Caballero becomes Prime Minister of the Republican Government.
9 September	'Non-Intervention' Committee meets in London.
12 October	Formation of International Brigades.
6 November	Government leaves Madrid for Valencia.
8 November	XIth International Brigade in action in Madrid.
24 December	No. 1 Company British Battalion leaves for Lopera on Cordoba front.

1937

9 January	British Government threatens volunteers with Foreign Enlistment Act.
31 January	XVth International Brigade formed, including British Battalion.
13 February	British Battalion in action at Jarama.
4 May	Uprising in Barcelona by POUM and Anarchists.
17/18 May	Negrín replaces Caballero as Prime Minister.
6 July	British Battalion in action in Brunete offensive.
24 August	British Battalion in action at Quinto in Aragon offensive.
15 December	Government opens offensive against Teruel.

1938

19 January	British Battalion moved to the defence of Teruel.
16 February	British Battalion attack on Segura de los Baños.
9 March	Major rebel offensive against Aragon front.
2 April	Base of International Brigades moved from Albacete to Barcelona.
15 April	Rebels reach Mediterranean – Republic cut in two.
25 July	British Battalion crossed Ebro in offensive.
27 July	First British assault on Hill 481 near Gandesa.
21 September	Negrín announces withdrawal of all foreign volunteers.
22 September	British Battalion fights its last battle in Sierra del Lavall.
24 September	Chamberlain meets Hitler and Mussolini and signs Munich Agreement.
29 October	Farewell parade of International Brigades in Barcelona.
7 December	British volunteers arrive back in London.

1939

26 January	Franco takes Barcelona.
15 March	Hitler occupies all Czechoslovakia.
28 March	Franco occupies Madrid and Republic defeated.
1 September	Germany invades Poland – the start of the Second World War.

INTRODUCTION
Why Another Book on Spain?

I have fought in two wars – the war in Spain (1936-1939) and the Second World War (1939-1945). No one asks me today about my experiences in the world war; but my service in Spain in the International Brigade brings continuing questions and an interest as marked among young people as among older. Much of the interest centres on those who volunteered to fight in the International Brigades of the Spanish Republican Army, putting their ideals and beliefs before comfort, security and even life itself.

The interest in the events of the Spanish war has brought continuing studies. The number of published books runs into many hundreds, and there have been innumerable pamphlets and articles.

The British volunteers in the International Brigades have never prepared their own official history though nearly every other national grouping has done so.

Bill Rust, correspondent of the *Daily Worker* in Spain from November 1937 until June 1938, was commissioned to write a history and was given access to the records of the British in the International Brigades. His book, *Britons in Spain* (Lawrence & Wishart), was published in January 1939 and is an excellent record, written at very short notice, giving an essentially correct and moving account of the British volunteers. But it was written while the war was still going on, when many volunteers had not yet returned from Spain, and while it was impossible to check many facts. Some inaccuracies and mistakes were inevitable.

Republican held areas

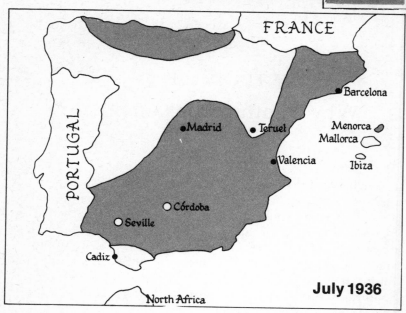

FRANCE

PORTUGAL

● Barcelona

● Madrid   ● Teruel

Menorca
Mallorca

● Valencia

Ibiza

○ Córdoba

○ Seville

● Cadiz

North Africa

July 1936

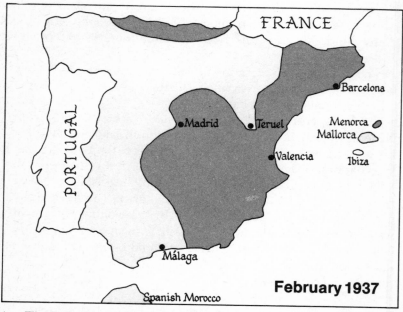

FRANCE

PORTUGAL

● Barcelona

● Madrid   ● Teruel

Menorca
Mallorca

● Valencia

Ibiza

● Málaga

Spanish Morocco

February 1937

1.   The Division of Spain, July 1936–July 1938

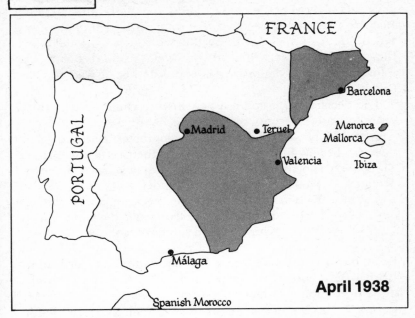

April 1938

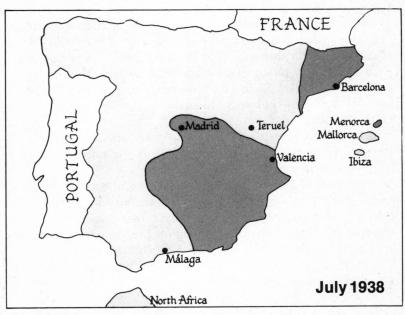

July 1938

Nearly forty years later the Committee of the International Brigade Association realized the urgency of commissioning a full account of such an important episode in the history of the British people. Any further delay would mean that information and reminiscences could be lost. I was asked to undertake it.

The decision to prepare a new history came at least thirty years too late. The only reason – it is not an acceptable excuse – for the delay was that most of the volunteers became deeply involved in new forms of activity after their return to Britain. Many were shortly to be soldiers again, in a war which we had prophesied would result from the defeat of the Spanish Republic. The delay was regrettable, because, by default, the writings of those who distort the truth and detract from the role of the volunteers have gained some currency.

In preparing this book I have had access to the records of the British Battalion, of the Dependants' Aid Committee, and of the International Brigade Association, as well as to letters written by Brigaders in Spain to such men as Harry Pollitt, Clement Attlee and D.N. Pritt; and to the many letters, documents and unpublished writings by British volunteers. One document I have not been able to use is the official Diary of the British Battalion, prepared for long periods, at the front on a day-to-day basis, mainly by Ted Edwards, the Battalion Secretary, and Bob Cooney. It was sent home to help Bill Rust prepare his book but was taken from the Dependants' Aid Office in 1940.

I have received invaluable help and advice from many people in preparing this history; however any estimations and opinions are my own.

A number of serious military histories of the war have now been published in Spain, and I have used these where relevant. For individual battles I have made use of my own experiences where possible, backed up by subsequent visits to specific locations. However, by far the most valuable part of my preparation have been interviews with very many of the volunteers alive today. Personal memories are sometimes faulty as to dates, places and movements, but collectively they have been invaluable.

Some Brigaders are by now reluctant to speak freely or even to answer quite simple questions about their experiences in Spain, because too many authors and interviewers have distorted and misrepresented what they said. I had the advantage of knowing personally the volunteers I interviewed, and of their knowing my connection with the International Brigade Association, so that I did not experience this reluctance, either with regard to the high points or the darker episodes of the war.

In any account limited to the activity of the British volunteers, it cannot be stressed too often or too strongly that they were but part of the International Brigades, and the International Brigades were only a small part of the Spanish Republican Army, the overwhelming majority of whose personnel, officers and men, was Spanish. That army fought with skill, bravery and tenacity, and was led by men of high military ability, and it continued fighting after the volunteers were withdrawn. Spanish soldiers joined the International Brigades and indeed, in time, became the majority in every unit.

I have confined my history to those who played a part actually in Spain itself: the soldiers, medical personnel, the few factory workers, writers and broadcasters. Those who worked in Britain in the 'Spain movement', organizing support and supplies for the Republic, made an invaluable contribution; but theirs is a separate story. I have not dealt with the group of volunteers organized by the Independent Labour Party (ILP) who went to Spain, except when they came in contact with the Brigades, because their story is quite separate from those who joined the International Brigades.

At the first, or first substantive, mention of an individual I have given – if known – his or her first name, home town and occupation, but have generally used the surname only after that. I have mentioned military rank only when it was significant at the time. Official promotion was often haphazard, depending on a rapidly changing situation and the administrative organization in the Brigade and Division; for instance, in No 2 Company of the British Battalion during the Ebro offensive in July 1938, casualties necessitated four command changes in one day, when it was held successively by two lieutenants, a sergeant, and a corporal.

I have tried to tell the real story. Not every volunteer was a hero; not everyone retained faith and pride in the cause for which they volunteered. But the overwhelming majority were ordinary men and women who showed enormous resources of talent and ability under stress, and emerged stronger, and willing and able to support those less tempered. Since their return, the great majority have in various ways continued the democratic and anti-fascist struggle. Their faith in the strength of the British working class, in the Spanish people, and in the ultimate defeat of world reaction and fascism has not wavered.

To them the greeting
Salud, camaradas!
Bill Alexander

London 1982

Chapter 1
Background, Myths and Realities

The war in Spain from 1936 to 1939 had its origins in, and was decisively influenced by, events far outside the country itself. In addition, the presence and motivation of the foreign volunteers who fought there depended, primarily, on their experiences outside Spain.

After the check to the wider revolutionary wave which followed the 1917 Revolution in Russia, reactionary regimes took power in many countries. The capitalist world suffered a series of crises of varying degrees of intensity and duration. Industries and land stood idle and unused alongside poverty and unemployment. Every ruling class tried to find a way out of its own crisis by lowering the conditions of the working people, which could only be done when their democratic rights, political parties and trade unions had been weakened or destroyed. Germany and Italy, defeated in the 1914-18 war, planned to expand their areas of exploitation, and rearmed. Living standards were attacked; the fear of war grew.

Fascism, the open dictatorial rule of the most reactionary groups, made spectacular advances: it seemed irresistible, almost inevitable. In Italy, Eastern Europe, and Austria, fascism and reaction were triumphant. In 1933 Hitler, backed by the big German industrialists, began the destruction of the workers' political parties and the trade unions, and to establish the Nazi regime. These successes encouraged and stimulated reactionary groups in other countries to follow the same path. However, at the same time, the exposure of the character and methods of fascism aroused strong feelings of horror and alarm among progressive, democratic people.

For centuries Spain had in some ways stood apart from the main social currents and changes in Europe. The impact on Spain of the bourgeois and industrial revolutions, and of the world war of 1914 had been limited. Industrial development was slow and largely confined to Catalonia and the north. Much of the land was owned by an aristocracy whose vast estates were worked by day-wage labourers, living in villages in primitive and miserable conditions. The Church was in the hands of a very wealthy hierarchy, set apart from the people, controlling the limited education system and promoting obscurantism and bigotry. The ruling groups maintained their power partly through the influence of the Church, but mainly through the large professional army based in the towns and officered by their own class.

In the countryside the militarized Civil Guard ruthlessly suppressed all popular resistance to exploitation and oppression. Any moves towards progressive, liberal changes, or improvement in the people's conditions, were strongly resisted, often by force. Though different groups in the ruling class formed political parties, their differences concerned tactics, share of influence and power. The ruling class was responsible for the long stagnation of Spanish society.

The professional people, the small businessmen, and the middle classes generally were frustrated; they saw their opportunities limited by the control of the semi-feudal, aristocratic groups. They wanted changes which would open out society, and − seeing the monarchy as an important barrier to change − supported the Republican parties.

Two main trade unions developed to protect the interests of the working people. The largest was the Confederación Nacional de Trabajo (CNT), drawing its strength from the industrial workers of Catalonia and Aragon and the rural day-labourers, and largely controlled and influenced by the Federación Anarquista Ibérica (FAI). The other, the Unión General de Trabajadores (UGT), was orientated towards the Socialist Party, with its main base among the workers in the smaller and service establishments.

The majority of the workers, in industry and on the land, were influenced by anarchist ideas, spread by the FAI. This, itself, was small and semi-secret, but through the CNT and other social organizations its influence was wide. Although refusing to work with other organizations it inspired and led many local actions, often violent, against the ruling class.

The Socialist Party was influential among the workers in Madrid and the north, but was deeply divided between right and left. The right, based mainly on the middle class and professional people, wanted only liberal, progressive changes in Spanish society, whereas the left wanted socialist changes.

The Communist Party (PCE) was small, with only a few thousand members. Its influence was mainly in the cities. When the Republic came into being in 1931 a group broke away from the PCE and formed the Partido Obrero de Unificación Marxista (POUM) which was deeply critical of the Soviet Union and in general shared Trotsky's views.

From 1923 General Primo de Rivera had imposed a military dictatorship on Spain, influenced and helped by Mussolini and with the connivance of King Alfonso. Rising opposition to reaction forced Rivera to resign in 1929. Two years later a republic was proclaimed when the King abdicated.

Alarmed at these developments, and encouraged by Hitler's victory in 1933, the reactionaries redoubled their efforts to check the popular movements. Efforts were made, not very successfully, to establish a fascist party, the Falange. Many other right-wing groups were formed but their main organization emerged as the Confederación Española de Dérechas (CEDA). In September 1934, the Republican Government moved to the right, the Socialists and Left Republicans were forced out and CEDA took their place. The working class opposed this by a general strike in 1934 which in the mining areas of Asturias developed into an armed uprising. This was bloodily and savagely crushed by units of the Spanish Army, mainly Moors, and the Foreign Legion, under the command of General Francisco Franco. The viciousness of his repression of the Asturian miners and steelworkers shocked the civilized world and led to angry protests, especially from miners in many countries.

After this experience of defeat, the Republican and working-class organizations came closer together and extended their activity. This united action, beginning at local level, developed in strength and momentum, and led to the formation, in January 1936, of the Popular Front ('Frente Popular')* This embraced the parties of the Republican Left, the Republican Union, Socialists, Communists and some smaller groups, and had the general support of the General Workers' Union (UGT).

The Popular Front agreement gave new impetus to the popular movement. In February 1936, in a freely-held general election, the parties of the Popular Front won a notable victory, taking 269 seats out of 480. The result had an impact far beyond the borders of Spain. It showed that fascism was not inevitable, and that the united democratic forces could develop new strengths. Events in Spain were studied closely, not only by anti-fascists everywhere but also by the fascist powers, who saw this victory as a potential menace to their own position.

The new Republican Government drawn from the Popular Front released political prisoners and took a few limited steps towards the implementation of its programme. Some land was handed over to the day-labourers and peasants, some concessions were made to Catalan nationalism; however, no decisive steps were taken to restrain the army officers and other reactionaries already plotting rebellion.

The reactionaries were alarmed at the growth of unity but were encouraged by the Government's hesitancy. They deliberately fomented civil disorder – rich young men drove around in fast cars firing pistols indiscriminately into the crowds – then proclaimed the Government incapable of governing, and made the customary Spanish ruling-class demand for the army to restore order.

---

* 'Frente Popular' is correctly translated as 'People's Front', but 'Popular Front' has now come into general use and I have used it throughout.

In fact, the conspiracy had been initiated almost immediately after the elections, but it was on 17 July 1936 that the military coup took place. In the minds of the generals and their supporters, there was no doubt that such a coup would be fully successful within a very few days. After all, the small professional army, whose large officer corps was drawn from rich and aristocratic families, had its barracks in every city; the well-armed Civil Guard, long employed to suppress any sign of revolt in the countryside, could be trusted to break its oath to the new government at the smallest excuse. And in support, if needed, the Army of Africa in Spanish Morocco might be glad of a chance to deal with the Spanish people. Against all these, what hope had the unarmed workers and peasants in the cities and villages?

However, in many of the main towns and areas of the countryside the people defeated the military coup. Often without weapons – the government delayed giving arms to the people – the people stormed the barracks. Despite casualties, their numbers and heroism thwarted the generals' plans. In Madrid dense crowds, joined by a few loyal Assault Guards, went to the Montaña barracks dominating the centre of the city. Almost unarmed, fired on by machine-guns, they smashed down the gates by sheer weight of numbers and took control.

The fighting was even more intense in Barcelona. The rebel army commanders moved their troops to take control of the important centres, but the people went onto the streets, building barricades, fighting with the few weapons they possessed, and then assaulting the barracks. In the two days fighting, 500 people were killed and 3,000 wounded before the rebels were finally defeated. In Seville, Cadiz and Spanish North Africa the people's resistance was overcome; however in the first fortnight the rebels failed to make more significant progress. It looked as though the insurrection would be defeated.

As soon as it became clear to the generals that their coup had failed disastrously in many of the chief cities, they launched open war on the people. Within six days of the rebellion, troops were being ferried from Morocco into Spain using German and Italian planes sent for the purpose. However, it was evident that they would not be enough to overcome the resistance, so a direct appeal was made to the fascist states for arms and men.

Hitler and Mussolini were already planning the expansion of their territories by war; indeed Mussolini's armies were fresh from their victory in Abyssinia, and were ready for further adventures. Hitler wanted a friendly government in Spain which would give him access to its minerals and raw materials, at the same time increasing his influence in the Mediterranean area then dominated by the British and the French. At the same time he recognised the value of the practice and experience to be gained by his forces in a war against a weaker opponent.

Neither Mussolini nor Hitler, however, could have forseen the demands which that war would make on them before its end. The scale and character of the help given to Franco by the fascist countries and by others have since been freely admitted, and indeed boasted about. Hitler sent armed units which he replaced at intervals so that as many as possible should gain experience of battle. It is said that some 50,000 German troops fought against the Republic, mainly in the airforce, the artillery and armoured units (26,113 German military personnel were decorated by Hitler for 'meritorious conduct' in the Spanish war). Mussolini mainly sent infantry – regular divisions complete with arms, amounting to 150,000 men. From Italy alone came 1,000 aircraft, and Italian submarines and naval vessels operated in the Mediterranean, sinking merchant ships on the supply routes to the Republic. In addition, Franco's troops had access to nearly 13,000 American trucks running on petrol supplied by Standard and Texaco Oil.

The British and French governments gave Franco even more decisive assistance: the device known as the 'Non-Intervention' Agreement. Under international law, the Spanish Republican Government had every right to use its funds to buy arms; the rebels, the generals who had broken their oaths and had revolted, had no such right. For the first few weeks of war, France sold some arms to the legitimate Republican Government, but the British and French governments then announced, after considerable secret British pressure, that the war was an internal affair which must not be encouraged or permitted to spread by the intervention of any other power. The sale of arms to either side would be intervention; a pact must be signed by all peace-loving nations restraining them from sending military men or material either to the rebels or to the Republican Government.

Hitler and Mussolini agreed that this was a good idea; but neither then nor at any other time had they the slightest intention of adhering to such a pact. It was sufficient for their purpose that everyone else should do so, for if the Republican Government had no source of arms, Franco's victory was certain.

The governments of Britain and France knew this very well; so did the rest of the world. No newspaper reporter could visit Republican Spain without having to take cover from German or Italian air bombardment. Captured German airmen, Italian prisoners taken at the front, and material of all kinds were exhibited, proving large-scale military aid for the rebels. But the Republic was still denied its legal right to buy arms.

Despite irrefutable evidence that Germany and Italy were, from the very first, providing large-scale military help to Franco, the Committee to supervise 'Non-Intervention' did nothing to stop it; the system of controls, developed later, was only effective in limiting aid to the Republic.

The Soviet Union exposed the fascist intervention in the Committee. Seeing it continued, it decided to help the Republic. In all, about 2,000 Soviet military personnel served in Spain, though there were never more than six to eight hundred at any one time. The Republic received a total of about 800 aircraft, 360 tanks, 1,555 artillery pieces and half a million rifles, together with ammunition, and also equipment and food from the *USSR*.

The Republic faced overwhelming odds: against it were ranged the wealth of the aristocracy, the great majority of army officers, and the power and influence of financiers and big business, together with the armed might of fascist Germany and Italy. Nevertheless, it took thirty-two months of bitter struggle before it was defeated.

Because of the continuing interest in the war and of its fundamental lessons about unity, there have been many attempts to denigrate or explain away the struggle for Republican Spain. Emphasis is often therefore put on the chaos, confusion and shortcomings of the Republic. However, the surprising thing was not the chaos and the difficulties, but the speed with which the Republic organized itself in such circumstances. Its government had to build an almost entirely new structure to run the country, while at the same time beating back a powerful fascist military machine: Its achievements and advances on the military, economic and social fronts is therefore the really striking feature of the period.

It has been often said that the Republic was defeated because of disunity and internal conflicts among its supporters. However, it is a striking fact that, unlike the Popular Front in France, unity in Spain actually developed in extent and strength and, despite severe external strains, only broke in the last few months of the war. The Popular Front brought together political parties of very dissimilar views and philosophies but only on a limited programme, on immediate issues. The Anarchists, a strong influence, especially in Catalonia, were not part of the Popular Front; they were opposed to unity and decried the organisation and discipline essential for modern warfare.

The bitter experiences of the war led to rapid changes in the political views of the people generally and of the political parties. Some forfeited their leadership by their failure to respond to such changes, even trying to hold back the people's movements. Largo Caballero, Prime Minister from September 1936 to May 1937, was opposed to forming a regular army: already by the end of 1937 the Defence Minister, Indalecio Prieto, was openly saying that the Republic was defeated.

They and others were replaced as popular pressure for unity grew.

The CNT́ leaders agreed to join the Government in late 1936. In August 1937 the Socialist and Communist parties agreed on a common programme. A month later all the youth organizations, including the Anarchists, came together. In April 1938 the two big trade union bodies, the CNT and the UGT, agreed on united action and entered the Popular Front and the Government, making it broader than it had ever been.

These developments of unity at the top were the result of pressure from below: the strengthening of the Popular Front in the localities, the growth of unity in the factories, and unity in action in the armed forces. The influence of extreme Anarchist ideas melted in the crucible of war. Anarchist soldiers accepted leadership and discipline, 'libertarian' experiments were incorporated into the war effort, and the people of Barcelona – the heartland of anarchism – did not support the POUM revolt against the Republic in May 1937. Not until 1939, when the Republic was reeling after the loss of Catalonia but still able to resist, did unity falter and break at the top.

The impression is sometimes given that the Spanish Civil War was not a war against fascism but an attempt to establish communism in Spain. This can only be done by grossly neglecting the active commitment of Hitler and Mussolini to Franco, and by exaggerating the strength of the Spanish Communist Party, which initially represented a minority in the Popular Front, with very limited influence. This influence grew sharply during the war because, by advocacy and example, the Communists advanced policies which the majority of the people recognized as practical and sound; and because the Soviet Union was the only state to provide substantial aid to the Republic. However, although the Communists in the course of the war probably achieved majority support in the main centres and among the armed forces, they argued that the struggle should remain within a broad, anti-fascist, popular-front framework. The

Communists therefore limited their representation in the Government, and opposed measures – like the forcible collectivization of land and small businesses in Aragon – which threatened unity. This Communist insistence on the democratic, popular-front character of the Republic has brought the criticism from the ultra-left that it was a betrayal of socialism and of the revolution. However it must be remembered that, in the February 1936 general election, the Spanish people had voted for a Popular Front government: the Socialist and Communist deputies constituted less than half its supporters. If the Communists and some of the Socialists had tried to implement a social revolution during the Civil War, the unity necessary to defeat fascism would have been splintered, and the Republic would have been completely isolated.

However the conduct of the war brought many steps towards socialism, for instance the expropriation of factories and property owned by Franco's supporters, and the formation of a police force, army and a state machine based on a broad popular government. Further progress towards socialism was dependent on the defeat of fascism.

Another continuing criticism is that Stalin and the Soviet Union betrayed and abandoned the Republic. This argument ignores the massive supplies of aid of all kinds supplied by the Soviet Union, virtually alone in its support. Geography, and fascist attacks on ships in the Mediterranean, made the supply of this aid difficult. At the same time, the British, French and US governments were trying to isolate the USSR and to incite the fascist powers to prepare to attack it.

The Soviet aim was to expose the realities of Hitler's and Mussolini's policies and to end the 'Non-Intervention Agreement' from inside the Non-Intervention Committee. 600 Soviet planes, 500 guns and many machine-guns were blocked in France by the 'Non-Intervention' control, and eventually ended up in fascist hands. The betrayers of the Spanish Republic were thus the appeasers in the British and French governments and those who supported 'Non-Intervention', not the Soviet Union.

Several historians have written venomously about the supposed reign of murder and terror in the Republican rear, although they are often more restrained about the well-authenticated record of Franco's imprisonments and executions during the war and for forty years afterwards.

The Republic had reason to be vigilant. When Franco was advancing from four directions on Madrid he boasted of the 'Fifth Column' of his supporters inside the city. Besides the Spanish supporters of fascism, every state had its intelligence services operating in the Republic; Britain was not the least active. The Republic had to safeguard itself against internal enemies. Injustices and mistakes were inevitable, but the Government erred, if anything, on the side of complacency and lack of vigilance.

After the first few weeks, during which anger at past misdeeds and the treachery of the generals and reactionaries led to executions and killings, the Republic treated Franco supporters with considerable, and dangerous, leniency.

It is claimed that the alleged reign of terror in the Republic extended into the International Brigades. For instance, André Marty, French Commander of the International Brigade Base, has been described as a 'mass murderer', a 'psychopath' and a 'butcher'.

Marty is remembered for his drive, determination and single-mindedness as one of a leading group – which included Luigi Longo ('Gallo'), Hans Kahle, Karol Swierczewski ('Walter') – who were required to turn a collection of individuals into a military unit, or units, within days. British volunteers who worked with Marty at the Base found him irascible, suspicious, unpredictable and a little nationalistic, but paid tribute to his drive and determination. The British who met him at the front at Gandesa and Mora, organizing the retreat from Catalonia, were greatly impressed by his courage.

Nevertheless, given the character of the war, there were inevitably some unjust arrests, imprisonments and even executions on the Republican side. However they were rare, untypical, and had a very limited impact on the Brigades.

Above all they should not obscure the heroism and bravery of the Spanish people and the volunteers who fought alongside them.

Chapter 2

'What's Spain to Do With You?'
The Volunteers Who Went and Why

From the first days of the generals' revolt in July 1936, progressive people everywhere began to realize the international significance of the fate of the Spanish Republic. At first spontaneously, as individuals or in small groups, later in larger numbers and organized, volunteers went to Spain to fight for the Republic, forming the basis for the International Brigades.

There is, and can be, no exact figure for the number of international volunteers in the Republican Army. At the time of the disbanding of the Brigades in October 1938, the Military Commission of the League of Nations which inspected them at the time stated that there had been 32,109 volunteers in all, of whom only 12,144 remained. But the more probable figure, based on the Brigade's own records, is a total of some 42,000 of whom 20,000 were killed, reported missing or were totally disabled. At any one time the number of volunteers actually in the Republican Army was from twelve to fifteen thousand, incomparably fewer than the organized military formations sent to the rebels by Hitler's Germany and Mussolini's Italy.

The exact number of British volunteers is not known; in the early days some arrived in Spain unrecorded, while during the war the continuous fighting made precise documentation impossible. The records of those who went through London to the fighting units contain 2,010 names, with some details of origin and subsequent fate in Spain. However, during the writing of this book forty-one more proven volunteers have been traced, and doubtless still more names will be added. There are no records of the dates of departure for Spain, let alone of arrival; but the dates of return were recorded by the Dependants' Aid Committee, set up in London to look after the interests of the volunteers and their families.

There were at least 170 volunteers in the medical services – ambulance drivers, administrators, nurses and doctors. In addition there were a few – never more than half a dozen – British who worked directly for the Spanish Republican Government propaganda services.

Why should over two thousand young people leave their homes to fight a war in a country they knew little about?

The dynamic force which drove volunteers from Britain to Spain and welded them into an effective fighting unit was a deep hatred of fascism. The brutalities of Italian fascism had been detested and condemned, but the rise and the success of Hitler's fascism in Germany – with its barbarities against workers, trade unionists, socialists, and communists, its bestial treatment of the Jews, and its attacks on culture and liberties – aroused a further widespread wave of antagonism. The realities had been exposed in meetings and demonstrations, in books and pamphlets, and even in some newspapers. The early thirties in Britain saw a rising hatred of fascism and an understanding of the need to stop it.

It was not only from abroad that the menace came. Oswald Mosley was actively trying to build a fascist movement in Britain, and sent disciplined, uniformed groups of Blackshirts to beat up Jewish people in London's East End. British fascists also attacked unemployed workers in Merthyr Tydfil, Aberdeen and elsewhere; any hecklers or interrupters at Mosley's rallies were treated with extreme brutality. It was clear that British fascism had the same ugly face as its German counterpart.

Despite some leaders of the labour movement, and some 'liberal' and religious groups who argued that active opposition to the Blackshirts only gave Mosley publicity, there was a growing understanding that fascism had to be actively stopped. Working people, intellectuals, and progressives of a wide variety of views were drawn into activity of all kinds to oppose it.

The understanding that fascism meant war was sharpened as the fighting in Spain began. The bombing of civilians in Madrid and Barcelona, the military intervention by Germany and Italy, and the speeches of the fascist leaders, made it clear that to them war was not only a necessary instrument to extend their influence but a glorious and welcome feature of their programme.

Dolores Ibárruri, the Spanish Communist deputy who was to become famous throughout the world as 'La Pasionaria', warned the peoples of Western Europe with the words: 'Stop the bombs on Madrid and Barcelona or they may fall on London and Paris.' Her warning crystallized the understanding that to oppose fascism was to defend not only freedom but peace as well.

The writer Ralph Fox, later to become a political commissar in Spain, wrote in *The Novel and the People* (published in 1937 after he had been killed in Spain):

> Our fate as a people is being decided today. It is our fortune to have been born at one of those moments in history which demand from each one of us as an individual that he make his private decision ... he cannot stand aside, and by our actions we shall extend our imagination, because we shall have been true to the passions in us (quoted by Dona Torr in 'Ralph Fox and our Cultural Heritage' in *Ralph Fox. A Writer in Arms*, edited by John Lehmann and others [Lawrence & Wishart, 1937] pp. 215-16).

Fox was performing the poet's function of speaking for 'those who have no voice'. He spoke for the volunteers.

The British volunteers went to Spain because they understood that fascism must be checked before it brought wider repression and war. These motives have attracted considerable misrepresentation, then and since. The *Daily Mail* specialized in stories that men had been recruited by promises of good jobs and high wages, having been picked up as 'down-and-outs' on the Embankment in London, or that they were just adventurers. There is not a scrap of evidence that anyone went to Spain without being told that they were going to fight as a soldier. If any adventurers or destitute people joined for an easy life, the reports of the casualties and the harsh conditions soon acted as an effective deterrent. In the early days, a very few enrolled for purely eccentric motives – a search for excitement or a love of military life – but they quickly made their own way out of Spain or, in the intense political and moral atmosphere of the International Brigades, became effective soldiers of the Republic. One such volunteer, who had been in prison for blowing safes, became a brave and stalwart member of the Anti-Tank Battery of the XVth Brigade.

In *The Spanish Civil War* (Eyre & Spottiswoode, 1961; revised Penguin edn, 1965, p.382), Hugh Thomas has alleged: 'Many of the British volunteers ... desired some outlet through which to purge some private grief or maladjustment.' Certainly they grieved – for instance for their German comrades and for all who had suffered under fascism. And certainly they would not have called themselves well adjusted to a British society which condemned two million to unemployment; but to envisage the volunteers as driven largely by private neuroses, or – according to another theory – by a 'death wish', is very far from reality. All such theories ignore the fact that some injured volunteers in Spain actually 'deserted' from hospital to the front, and that volunteers undertook dangerous missions and fought on in isolated positions, knowing the probable end – not to find death but to fulfil their beliefs.

They did not shirk death but, like all sensible soldiers, tried to avoid it if possible; and they had good reasons for living. On August Bank Holiday 1938, during the destruction and the slaughter of the Ebro offensive, members of the British Battalion were discussing the beer, the food, and the fun they would enjoy on the next Bank Holiday, in Britain. Money was sent to keep union cards paid up, ready for the resumption of work after their return. The future, whether with the family, at work, or just as the prospect of enjoying a meal of ample and accustomed food, was a general topic of conversation, but always with the proviso – 'When that bastard Franco is finished off'.

When recruiting became organized, the aim was to select volunteers between twenty-five and thirty-five years old. It was found that men below eighteen years, usually brought up in the harshness of mass unemployment in Britain, lacked the physical reserves to stand up to the strain and the inadequate diet. After February 1937 no one under eighteen was accepted, and those already in Spain were urged to go home. Not all did so. Charlie Hutchinson, a London lorry-driver, refused, but after fighting with one of the first International units at Córdoba in December 1936, he was transferred to the Fifth Army Corps Transport Regiment, serving till the end of the war. He drove trucks, lorries, and vehicles of every kind all over Republican Spain but mainly servicing the International Brigades. Ronnie Burgess was only seventeen and still at school when he fought at Córdoba in December 1936 and at Jarama in February 1937, only being finally persuaded to go home in September 1937. There were others similar to these two.

At the other end of the scale, men over forty found it difficult to keep going in the almost continuous fighting and movement in the harsh conditions of Spain; but many subtracted ten years or so from their real age in order to be accepted, and stood up to the strain with the best. Joseph May, a London printer, later admitted to being sixty-three, though he did not look it. After the first few days of the battle of Jarama, he commandeered a horse, which he used to bring barrels of welcome water from a farmhouse to the front lines. But whatever his real age (he was well over the age limit), he was repatriated. Bert Neville, a London taxi-driver, was fifty-three when he joined one of the first groups of volunteers; Tom Picton, a miner from Treherbert (South Wales), was fifty-two when he was shot dead as a prisoner of the fascists in April 1938.

One of the main tasks of the Dependants' Aid Committee was to collect money from supporting organizations and individuals in order to ensure that families and the returning

wounded volunteers received some income. Though donations
came from many quarters and were generous, the Committee
always faced a shortage of funds to help the wives and
families. There was therefore a preference for volunteers
without family commitments. However, many with families
demanded to be accepted, usually – though not always – with
the proud support of their wives. Life was not easy for the
families, but since most of them lived in class-conscious
working-class areas they were helped by neighbours and
workmates.

Since the Republican medical services were strained to the
limit with military and civilian casualties, volunteers who
were unfit and could not be active fighters would have been an
unwarrantable burden. After volunteering for Spain became
illegal in Britain in January 1937, the check in London could
be no more than a cursory look at physique and a few
questions. In Paris, where an organization, though illegal, was
receiving volunteers from many countries, and where British
volunteers had to report in order to make their way to the
frontier, there was a slightly more thorough check, and a few –
suffering from clearly disabling conditions such as diabetes or
tuberculosis, or from defective vision – were turned back.

In Albacete, the Spanish town where the base for the
International Brigades was established, there was some
medical examination, but nothing very searching.
Considering the primitive living conditions, often in the open
in extremes of heat and cold, and bearing in mind the
inadequate food and the often contaminated water, the British
volunteers remained remarkably fit and healthy.

Every volunteer who went to Spain from Britain went as a
result of their own decision. Only in a few cases, to meet some
special need, were individuals asked to volunteer by
Communist Party leaders. G. 'Mac' McLaurin, a Rhodes
Scholar from New Zealand, was asked by Harry Pollitt,
General Secretary of the British Communist Party, to leave his
Cambridge bookshop and to offer his expertise with a
machine-gun. He was killed in November 1936, covering a
withdrawal in the defence of Madrid. On Merseyside four

men with service in the Royal Navy were asked to exercise their expertise in the Republican Navy. A few capable political leaders, like Bill Paynter, miners' leader from South Wales, Billy Griffiths, from the Rhondda, and Eric Whalley, a leader of the unemployed in Mansfield, were asked to go to meet a political need.

On the other hand, there were political leaders who had to pester the Communist Party before they obtained permission to go to Spain. Bob Cooney, a leading Aberdeen Communist, Wally Tapsell, circulation manager of the *Daily Worker*, David Guest, the mathematician and writer on Marxist philosophy, were typical of the many who had to make special representation before they were allowed to volunteer.

The name 'British Battalion' or in Spanish, 'Batallón Inglés', was a misnomer, since the unit was initially formed of all the English-language speakers – and of others as well. In January 1937 the few Americans, and later the Canadians, left the British and joined their own national units. Forty-four Australians served, many of them from the very early days of the fighting around Madrid. Of their twenty-five dead, ten were drowned in May 1937, when the Spanish vessel *City of Barcelona*, bringing volunteers from France, was torpedoed in the Mediterranean.

Thirty volunteers came from Cyprus: in the American units there were other Cypriots who had been working in the USA. A Cypriot cultural club in Berwick Street, London, was the centre where those who were already working in London, mainly in the catering and clothing trades, or who had made their way there – having no direct route to Spain – were recruited. The size of their contingent, from a very small country, the scale of their casualties – fourteen were killed – and the senior positions held by such men as Mike Economides, Hercules Avgherinos, and Nicolaides show a deep grasp of the link between fighting against fascism and fighting for their own national independence.

From Eire there were as many as one hundred and five volunteers, and from Northern Ireland twenty-nine. In the British Battalion there were New Zealanders, Jamaicans,

Egyptians, South Africans and men from Hong Kong, showing how anti-fascist feeling was evident throughout the Empire and Commonwealth. In addition Finns, Dutch and one Chinese found a welcome from the British and stayed with them.

In Scotland and Wales the nationalist movements were then little developed and without much impact on the working-class. So English, Scots, Welsh and all other nationalities mixed, with some chaffing and jokes, and without thought to their label 'British'.

Little attention was paid to religious or cultural background, and no one thought of keeping any special record of Jewish volunteers. Figures which have been quoted can be no more than approximations. From the very unsatisfactory basis of Jewish-sounding names and personal knowledge, one may say that there were about 180 to 200 Jews in the Battalion. Against the background of Nazi atrocities against the Jewish people, and of street battles in London as Mosley tried to spread fascism in Britain, it is understandable that Nat Cohen and Sam Masters, clothing workers from Stepney, were among the first to join. They were followed by substantial groups from Hackney, Stepney and Manchester, and from other areas with large concentrations of Jewish people. Harry Bourne, Sam Lesser, Ben Glaser, Jeff Mildwater, George Nathan are typical of the many men of Jewish origin who fought in the Brigades.

The first small groups who joined in the first few months of the war contained a high proportion of intellectuals, students and professional people; indeed there is still some vague notion that everyone in the Brigades was a poet or a writer. At that time few workers commonly travelled abroad, and few had passports, money or knowledge of the routes to take them to Spain. These first groups, as we shall see, fought as members of a variety of units.

By the time the British Battalion was formed early in 1937, the overwhelming majority of the volunteers were industrial workers. There are no complete records of their jobs and backgrounds, but their home addresses show that a large majority came from areas of heavy industry. From Scotland came 437, from Wales 122, from the North-East coast 86, from Lancashire 308, from Yorkshire 69 and from the industrial Midlands 71. From Greater London came 514, while ones and twos joined from the South.

When, early in 1937 Walter Citrine, Secretary of the TUC and strongly hostile to doing anything to help the Republican cause, contemplated means of stopping unions from giving funds to the Dependants' Aid Committee, the Base at Albacete was asked to compile a list of trade-union membership among the Battalion, to counter this hostile attitude. The Battalion moved into action before a complete list could be made, but the partial record shows that, almost without exception, every British trade union – craft, general, and professional – was represented. A high proportion of union members joined when young and in work for the first time, showing high trade-union and class-consciousness in those days of unemployment and in the aftermath of the 1926 General Strike.

There are no complete records of Union offices and positions held by volunteers before going but, of the thirty-two men from the Rhondda, a third held official positions in the union or in the Unemployed Workers' Movement. This high rate of trade-union commitment was not untypical.

Since in Britain in 1936 there were two million unemployed, it is not surprising that many of the volunteers had at some time been without work, and that a number of these had been leaders of the protests and the activities of the unemployed. Peter Kerrigan, a leading member of the Communist Party and one of the leaders of the Scottish contingent of the 1936 Hunger March on London, came to Spain within a few weeks of the end of the march. John Lochore, leader of the youth on that march, recruited twelve others from Glasgow and reached Spain at the end of 1936. Nearly all the 117 South Wales miners had experienced unemployment, and many had led protests against it, and suffered arrest, fines, or imprisonment as a result.

No attempt was made to list the volunteers' political

affiliation: indeed on the *carnet militar*, the identity card, everyone was listed under 'Partido Politico' simply as 'Anti-fascista'. On the 6 January 1937, when there were just over 400 men at the British Battalion's training base at Madrigueras, near Albacete, the Political Commissar, David Springhall, reported that just under one third were in the Communist Party or Young Communist League, and fifteen in the Labour Party. But on orders from the Base at Albacete no records of political affiliation were kept. A number of people did join the Communist Party of Spain and the proportion of Communists recruited increased as political conviction rather than military experience became the chief criterion. But in and out of action, little attention was paid to party affiliation. The political commissars at Battalion level, and usually at company level, were Communist Party members with a record of activity in Britain. But this was by no means the case with the military leadership, for which there was one qualification alone: tested and proven in battle ability.

In November and December 1936 military experience was held to be essential for volunteers. Here the British were at a disadvantage compared with the French or Germans who had conscription. A few Brigaders, such as Aitken, Wintringham, McCartney, Nathan and Kerrigan, had fought in the First World War, but that experience had been a long time ago and was not always relevant. However, unemployment and hunger had been important recruiting sergeants in Britain, and many class-conscious men had joined the British forces to ensure regular meals. Their experiences in India, Egypt, and indeed in Britain reinforced their class-consciousness. Jock Cunning-ham, Jack Brent, George Fletcher, Bobby Walker, Tom Murphy, are examples of Brigaders who acquired their military knowledge and their political beliefs in the British army. Paddy O'Daire, from the Irish Free State Army, and Joe Hinks, from both the British Army and the Chinese Eighth Route Army had special experience and knowledge.

These ex-servicemen were of immense value, especially in the early stages when training often lasted no more than a few days. There were a few incidental problems. Those still on Reserve were concerned about their inability to report to their units; many of the Royal Navy men wanted to join the Republican Navy rather than the International Brigades. For some, the chaotic, confused character of the war, with inadequate weapons and inadequate food, put their understanding and patience under severe strain.

However, despite all the differences of nationality, background, experience and opinion, the British Battalion retained a remarkable cohesion and unity of purpose which — even put to the most appalling tests — never broke, for it was a unity based on the conviction of ideas.

Chapter 3

Getting to Spain

The first British volunteer to fire a rifle at Franco's rebelling troops was, almost certainly, Felicia Browne. An artist, a graduate of the Slade School, and a Communist, she had gone to Spain to draw and paint. She joined the militia in Barcelona on 2 August 1936, went with a group to Aragon, and was killed on 25 August when rescuing a comrade who had been wounded on patrol.

John Cornford, the poet and Communist student organizer in Cambridge, made his own way to Barcelona on 8 August, as he said 'to find out what was happening'. He enrolled in the POUM militia and his companion, Richard Bennett, a fellow student from Trinity College, went to work on Barcelona radio, sending news and information to the rest of Europe.

Nat Cohen and Sam Masters were near the French border, cycling to Barcelona for the Workers' Olympiad, when the rebellion began. On arriving in Barcelona they joined the militia there. There was also a group of the British Workers' Sports Federation in Barcelona at the time; all returned to Britain, but George Hardy, a London printer, and a few others returned to Spain later as volunteers for the Brigade.

Ralph and Winifred Bates, who knew Catalonia and Spain well, were walking in the high Pyrenees when fighting began. They made their way to Barcelona and used their knowledge of Spain and their abilities as writers to help in the Government's propaganda and information services. By September the number of British fighters had grown, as

Spanish trade unionist, 1936 (*drawing by Felicia Browne*)

individuals or small groups made their own way there. Cornford returned to Britain early in September 1936 and encouraged others to return to Spain with him.

At this time there was no organization to help those volunteers who wanted to get into Spain. A passport, the fare of £5-8-0, and determination were enough for the first few.

Harry Addley and Bert Ovenden, catering workers from Folkestone, wanted to find out what was happening in Spain. They travelled to Paris and made their own way, through Port Bou, a small town on the frontier, to Barcelona, where they met an English-speaking Spaniard in a café who invited them to join a group going to fight in Madrid. This and similar stories indicate both the lack of organization in Republican Spain at the time, and the spontaneous understanding that help was needed.

Personnel and supplies for medical aid started arriving very soon after the war began; in the first week, in July 1936, the Republican Government made a world-wide appeal for medical help. A Spanish Medical Aid Committee was set up in London to organize recruitment and the dispatch of supplies; medical personnel, drivers, nurses and doctors, were able to travel freely in and out of Spain throughout the war.

By September 1936 the world's working-class movements recognized the dangers of the large-scale help being given by Hitler and Mussolini to the rebels. Within six days of the generals' revolt, German planes were transporting Franco's troops from Africa into Spain. Leaders of the Communist International, the Argentine Communist Victor Codovilla and the French Communist Jacques Duclos, discussed forms of aid to the Republic with the Prime Minister Largo Caballero, and set up an organization for engaging volunteers to fight.

There were many political, financial and logistic difficulties in getting volunteers to Spain from all over the world. However, by the end of October 1936 recruiting and transport were organized, though arrangements naturally had to be flexible and were at the mercy of sudden vicissitudes.

In Britain recruitment was controlled by the Communist Party. Would-be volunteers who contacted the *Daily Herald*, the *New Statesman* or the Medical Aid Committee, were sent to Communist Party headquarters in King Street, Covent Garden. At first all the Party's national officials were actively involved in the detailed work. Harry Pollitt, Willie Gallacher, MP, J.R. Campbell, and Bob Stewart helped in buying and handing out tickets, checking travel details, clothes and so on. However by November 1936 R.W. Robson, always known as 'Robbie', was put in charge. He was an experienced, efficient Communist official with military experience in the First World War. Later he was to work from 1 Litchfield Street, London, on the floor above the office of the Dependants' Aid Committee. In each of the main Communist Party Districts a single official was given responsibility; he was never the District Secretary and did not operate from Party offices.

Would-be volunteers heard about recruiting through the labour movement or read about it in the *Daily Worker*. Speakers at the numerous meetings calling for support for Spain – often recently returned members of the Brigades – told potential recruits how to find their local, or the London, recruiting centre.

Those known in the working-class movement and in good health had few difficulties. The procedure varied according to circumstances, but simple information was compiled about a volunteer – motives for going to Spain, dependants, physical fitness and any special experience. Robson had the very difficult task of distinguishing adventurers and romantics from those who were genuine volunteers but whose political affiliations were not known. Anyone who tried to volunteer but was without credentials would be sent away. If they returned, as many did, this was taken as evidence of their sincerity and they were invariably accepted.

Since few of the volunteers had any money, the fares from the provinces to London were paid. If several had volunteered together they would travel as a group, but many came alone. Paddy O'Daire, an ex-Eire army man from Donegal who had been a farm worker in Canada and a labourer in Britain, cycling from Norwich into a fierce head-wind, left his bicycle in a railway-station, telling the porter he would collect it later.

It was two years before he got back to Britain.

Until 9 January 1937 groups were assembled in London, given a ticket to Paris and £1 for emergencies. Dave Springhall (Secretary of the London District of the Communist Party), who had arrived in Spain to become the Political Commissar of the British volunteers, protested strongly that £1 was too much and would encourage drinking. The volunteers travelled, quite openly, in groups from London to Paris and, after a meal and a check-up, went on by ordinary train to the Spanish frontier.

The railway crosses the border through a tunnel, under the Pyrenees, from Cerbère to Port Bou in Spain. Sometimes the train went through the tunnel, sometimes the parties walked through to Spain. The first depot and collecting point was the old fortress-like barracks overlooking Figueras, just south of the border. From there the journey continued by train, through Barcelona, to Albacete, south-west of Valencia, which became the Base of the International Brigades on 20 October 1936.

On 9 January 1937 the British Government threatened anyone going to fight in Spain with prosecution under the Foreign Enlistment Act of 1870. In fact, not a single volunteer was prosecuted although, according to Fenner Brockway, the Independent Labour Party stopped recruiting in face of this threat. Recruiting in Britain for the International Brigades continued as vigorously as before, though the arrangements and travel became more difficult and more discreet. The difficulties sharpened when, in February 1937, the Non-Intervention Committee imposed a ban on volunteers and set up a system of controllers on the French frontier.

However, the British railways were advertising weekend trips to Paris, leaving Victoria Station on Friday nights. Passports were not required. Volunteers were given a weekend ticket by 'Robbie' or by a helper, and were told to travel individually to Paris. At the Victoria platform barrier they were often questioned by plain-clothes' police, but they asserted that their only intention was to see the bright lights of Paris. Their luggage, which often consisted of a brown paper parcel containing toothbrush, clean shirt and socks, seemed improbable for a traditional Parisian weekend and did little to add conviction to the story, but the police, however strong their suspicions, could take no action.

Despite instructions to travel as individuals, groups inevitably formed, as bleary-eyed volunteers waited for the reception centres to open next morning in Paris. There, in cafés and in trade-union and Co-operative premises, changed from time to time for security reasons, they were checked and sorted into groups.

Volunteers of all nationalities made their way to Paris, where they underwent a rudimentary medical inspection and a check on identity. Everyone was given some French money as evidence that they were *bona fide* tourists. There were stern warnings of the dangers of drink and brothels. At various times, when there was a big flow of volunteers, someone from Britain worked in the Paris organization. Charlotte Haldane (wife of Professor J.B.S. Haldane), Bert Ovenden (who served in Spain before working in Paris) and Josh Francis (who later joined the Battalion and was killed commanding a company in Aragon) all helped in this way.

In each group one man was made responsible. Then, with strict instructions to behave like tourists and not to coalesce into big groups, they were sent by train to the South of France and Spain. The French people knew what was happening and the vast majority were far more interested in the rights of the Spanish people than in the restrictions imposed by their own Government. The instructions for caution were rather undermined when a British group saw a brass band playing off a party of French volunteers. Jim Ruskin, waiting with a group of 'tourists' at the Gare d'Austerlitz, was somewhat put out when a porter said: 'You Brigaders are waiting on the wrong platform.'

Popular feeling in France was strongly on the side of the Republic, despite the French Government's support for 'Non-Intervention, and the volunteers could generally rely on the sympathy and help of the French to get them safely through France.

However, every so often the authorities made an almost ritual arrest of a group. Tom Jones, a Wrexham miner, had a typical experience in April 1937 when the car taking his group of six from Béziers towards the frontier was stopped by police, and the group were taken in handcuffs to Perpignan where they were welcomed by a cheering growd. The local Anti-Fascist Committee sent in food while they were in custody awaiting trial. They were sentenced to twenty-one days' imprisonment for having broken 'the international law on Non-Intervention'. On their release they went to the local Anti-Fascist Committee. Two decided to go home and were given tickets to Paris; the other four were given tickets and a contact in Marseilles. There they were put on a ship bound for Barcelona, with 250 other 'tourists'. The skipper, fearful of submarines, hugged the coast so closely that the ship ran aground before finally reaching Barcelona.

Bert Ovenden, returning to Spain with others in 1937, was sleeping in a barn when a gendarme marched in. They were all handcuffed to a chain behind the gendarme's bicycle, charged with vagrancy, but released next day and went on over the border.

Three weeks or a month in gaol was the common fate of those unlucky enough to be arrested in France. On their release the local 'underground' set them on their way again to the frontier.

The land route over the Pyrenees was most generally used. The small parties were collected into larger groups in Sète, Ceret, Perpignan and other towns within easy reach of the frontier. The francs given in Paris were taken back; with some volunteers the appeal of the wine had overcome scruples and they had less than 200 francs left. Some groups were given a pair of rope-soled slippers – *alpargatas* – soon to become common footwear in Spain. Then, at night, in buses, lorries and taxis, the groups were taken to the foothills of the Pyrenees. In darkness, with no smoking and no talking, the march began, in single file, up the mountains.

It was believed that the guides who led these columns were local smugglers but no one asked questions. The paths were very difficult, at times almost precipitous, often had to be negotiated in rain or snow. Those who could not keep up with the rest had to be left behind. Some parties were fired on by French frontier troops; the British were lucky suffering no casualties in this way. The trip made a deep impression on everyone. Archi Cook, a Rhondda miner, remembered the nightingales singing. Harry Bourne, a clerical worker from London, remembered his tired irritation when for the hundredth time he bumped into the man in front. Everyone had vivid memories of the excitement and exhilaration as the white painted border rocks came into sight, and aching limbs were forced to run the last few yards.

The incoming groups were mustered at Figueras. Here the realities of Spain in wartime began to be felt. The diet contained plenty of beans and olive oil; coffee was a rarity and tea unknown. The water was of doubtful purity, and the wine, while plentiful and safe to drink, proved to be much more potent than British beer or even the French wine.

The journey, through Barcelona, to the Base at Albacete was in a packed, slow-moving train. But the cheering welcome at every station, and the oranges and fruit passed through the carriage windows, showed the popular enthusiasm for the Republic and for those who were coming to help.

Other groups were taken from Sète, Marseilles and other ports in Southern France by sea, some in small fishing-boats and coasters, and a few in sizeable vessels taking supplies to Barcelona and Valencia. They faced danger of a different kind. Hitler and Mussolini's navies paid no more attention than their other forces to the 'Non-Intervention Agreement' to which they were nominally committed. Submarines prowled the seas attacking any boat approaching the Republican coast.

In June 1937 the SS *City of Barcelona* left Marseilles with stores and about 300 volunteers on board. Within a mile of the shore, approaching Barcelona, she was hit by a torpedo. At least three men from Britain on their way to join the Battalion were drowned. The Australian Committee for Spanish Relief said that ten Australians also drowned, but there is no record of their names or the full number lost. Harry Dobson, an unemployed Rhondda miner, was picked up by a boat.

A number of volunteers tried to enter Spain in less routine ways. Bob Doyle, with a sea-faring background from Dublin, tried to jump ship at Valencia, only to be caught and ordered back to the Non-Intervention Control Officer. Landing in Marseilles, he made his way back to London, got in touch with 'Robbie' and finally arrived over the Pyrenees. Laurie Lee, the writer, made his own way over the mountains; having no papers he was arrested and put into prison until Bill Rust (then *Daily Worker* correspondent in Barcelona) established his *bona fides*.

The flow of volunteers was uneven. Some weeks only half a dozen would get through to Albacete, though in January 1937 Peter Kerrigan, then British Commissar at Albacete, was overjoyed when fifty arrived in one week. It became increasingly difficult to find volunteers of the necessary calibre. Though after every battle, despite reports of losses, there was a new surge of enthusiasm.

Difficulties arose for the International Brigades in Spain itself. The Prime Minister, Largo Caballero, in January 1937 tried to stop recruitment to them, saying they were an instrument for a Communist take over and later tried to close their Brigades' Albacete Base. Indalecio Prieto, Defence Minister, was also hostile to the Brigades, regarding them merely as a Foreign Legion with no special significance in the Republican Army.

The cost of transport for the volunteers and for the maintenance of their dependants was very heavy and imposed restraints on their numbers. The British Communist Party met the charges from its own funds at first, then Pollitt appealed for funds. Later still the Dependants' Aid Committee assumed responsibility for the families and for the wounded.

Eventually, as the Republican Army became more consolidated, organized and experienced, there was no longer a pressing need for the International Brigades, and recruiting from Britain ended in August/September 1938.

Chapter 4

'We Cannot Stand Aside': The First Few

When John Cornford arrived in Spain with Richard Bennett on 8 August 1936 he said he expected to be 'staying a few days, firing a few shots and then coming home'. He was impatient to get to the front and three days later joined a group of POUM militia facing Huesca, a town in northern Aragon, held by the fascists. He had a rifle but there was little aggressive action. He was the only Englishman in a group speaking mainly Catalan. He was critical of the inactivity and saw the need for much greater help. In mid-September he left for Britain, intending to bring back more volunteers, returning to Spain in October travelling with six others.

Another group of young anti-Fascist intellectuals had also travelled to Spain 'to see history in the making'. Richard Kisch, Tony Willis, Paul Boyle and Lee Aylward, a young Canadian woman, made their own way from London to Barcelona and linked up with a Spanish militia group there.

Nat Cohen and Sam Masters had already arrived on their bicycles and with the others, took part in the attempt to capture Mallorca from the fascists. Not surprisingly the attempt was unsuccessful, since all Barcelona knew it was being prepared, and the militia were largely unorganized. Moreover, the Italian High Command saw the significance of the island as a bombing base and sent in fighter planes to oppose the landing.

The British group were lucky to get away: Kisch alone was wounded. Cohen, who had had considerable experience as a militant worker in the Argentine and in the East End of London, established a high reputation in the fighting. He was elected leader of the group, most of whom were Spanish. The group, a centuria of about 100 men, was given the name of the Tom Mann Centuria, honouring a founder-father of the British trade-union movement and a well-known Communist.

On returning to Barcelona the Spanish militia men went off to their homes on leave, but returned soon after with three hundred men wanting to join the Centuria – a considerable tribute to Cohen's prestige which showed the wide support for the Republic, and recognition that organization was needed in the struggle. Tom Wintringham, then *Daily Worker* correspondent in Barcelona, wrote to Pollitt on 5 September 1936 stressing the value of the Tom Mann Centuria and urging 'more volunteers to make it "British" in fact as well as in name'.

Cohen remained with his group and fought on the Aragon front, until, after a disabling knee wound, he was invalided home in April 1937. Masters, after a spell with the German Thaelmann group near Huesca, and a course at the Albacete Officers' School, joined the British Battalion. He was killed at Brunete in July 1937.

Ovenden and Addley went to Madrid at the end of August 1936 and made contact with a group of militia planning to stop a fascist column advancing on the city. Fifty to sixty men set off in three lorries and one car, with very limited arms. After a skirmish with fascists near Getafe aerodrome, fifteen miles from Madrid, the group realized the need for organization. All voted to join the Army. Ovenden and Addley went to Valencia where they followed a group of people going to the docks and saw a large body of volunteers coming off a boat. Among them were four men marching behind a placard labelled 'British'. Ovenden and Addley joined them, and in the chaotic conditions of that period were accepted into the group and went to the International Brigade Base in Albacete.

James Albrighton, a 19-year-old student from Salisbury, made his way to Spain and enrolled in the Republican Army on 2 October 1936. He was joined a couple of days later by

David Mackenzie, a student from Edinburgh, Sydney Lloyd Jones from Wales and eight other British volunteers. They went into the M.M. (Muerte es Maestro) Centuria, a Spanish unit with a few internationals from several countries. The unit was involved in bloody but chaotic attempts to halt the fascist drive from Talavera and Toledo towards Madrid, fighting at San Martin de Valdeiglesias, and Navalcarnero. Lloyd Jones and others were killed on 14 October 1936 in action against the Moors and Foreign Legion troops outside Chapineria. After action in Casa del Campo and Boadilla, Albrighton, still in a Spanish unit, went as part of the 14th Brigade to fight on the Córdoba front alongside the Number 1 Company of the British Battalion.

During the first few weeks of the fascist rebellion, volunteers like these from many countries made their way to Spain on their own initiative, to help the Republican Government. However, in September 1936 the Secretariat of the Executive Committee of the Communist International took a decision to organize the recruitment of men with military experience. International groups of Socialists and Anarchists followed suit. Wintringham and Cornford, with first-hand knowledge of the situation, urged Pollitt to send more volunteers from Britain.

Prime Minister Caballero and the majority of his ministers agreed, on 12 October 1936 to the formation of the International Brigades, though the official decree was not published until 22 October and some problems concerning the rights and duties of the volunteers and their place in the Republican Army remained to be resolved. Albacete, in the plains of La Mancha, was selected as a suitable base; its communications offered ready access to the main fronts while it was not in easy bombing range. By 14 October 1936 650 volunteers had arrived, and by the end of October 3,500. Individuals, and small groups of volunteers already fighting in the Spanish militia units, made their way there, as did all subsequent arrivals.

It was thought that fifteen to twenty days was the minimum time needed to organize these individuals into fighting units, but because of the catastrophic position on the Madrid front this time had to be greatly reduced. The order was given on the 25 October 1936 to form the XIth International Brigade. It left for the front on 31 October and went into battle on 9 November. The second brigade to be formed, the XIIth, was organized in a similarly short time, going into action on 12 November.

The difficulties at the Base were immense. There was a grave shortage of arms, equipment and uniforms – all the essentials needed for forming efficient military units. Meanwhile the fascists, relying on the flood of trained soldiers and modern weapons now arriving from fascist Germany and Italy, were advancing on all fronts. The difficulties were compounded by vacillations and indecision in the Government over the measures needed to save the Republic and defeat the rebels – most essentially over the formation of a regular disciplined army led by trustworthy officers and Political Commissars.

There were also problems unknown to any regular army, but inevitable in units recruited in such a fashion. Most of the volunteers were revolutionaries: all were rebels against the societies from which they came. They were not being enrolled in any existing army but had to create their own. Could they be expected to submit at once to the authority of one another or of individuals unknown to them? Discipline became a subject of vigorous discussion; rigid regimentation was unthinkable. Was the whistle signalling a meal parade an infringement of personal liberty? Was strong language when under fire consistent with true anti-fascist behaviour? As we have seen, the early units contained a high proportion of intellectuals. They proved to be less tolerant, at first, than workers from the factory floor, of unexplained delays, of incomprehensible orders from above, and of other such irritations which regular soldiers regard as quite normal.

However, if the very character of the volunteers created problems, it also created the understanding and will necessary to overcome them.

In this situation two groups of British were in Albacete,

each unaware of the other. One group went into the XIth Brigade when it was formed; the other into the XIIth. It was not until some weeks later, though fighting in the same areas, that they knew of each other.

In Albacete each group faced similar problems. At first, no one seemed to want them, nor to know what to do with a few English speakers. In neither group was there any realization of the general problems of the Republic in creating a military machine, in welding the loose conformation of the Popular Front into a united organized force. Questions arose continuously; were the shortages and confusion due to genuine difficulties or to inefficiency or sabotage? Both groups faced up to the difficulties independently. They elected their own military and political leaders, and went into the fields to practise marching and drill, even without weapons. Indeed by their cohesion and discipline they attracted attention, and unattached individuals joined them.

The British group that joined the XIth Brigade consisted of Cornford and the six volunteers with him when he returned from England in October 1936, with a further five who joined them. They were formed into Number 4 Section of the Machine Gun Company of the Commune de Paris Battalion. As military leader they elected Fred Jones who, after being thrown out of his public school (Dulwich) for his 'Bolshie' attitude, had served three years in the Guards. Cornford, despite his political ability and his experience on the Huesca front, urged that Bernard Knox, another Cambridge student, be chosen as the group's political leader in this mainly French Battalion, because of his better knowledge of French.

Most of the group had no military experience, though Joe Hinks had been in China with the Red Army. The British Army had dispensed with the services of New Zealand-born Steve Yates because of 'insubordination', and he had become an electrician in London. After a few days Jock Cunningham, from Coatbridge in Lanarkshire, was a powerful reinforcement, bringing his experience in the Argyll and Sutherland Highlanders and his courage in fighting reaction and sadism in the Aldershot 'glass-house'. Sam Lesser, David

McKenzie, 'Mac' McLaurin, Edward 'Burke', an actor from London called Cooper, and John Sommerfield had all been active in the anti-fascist movement as students.

In November 1936, the XIth Brigade went from Albacete through La Roda to the outskirts of Madrid. To their great joy and pride the British group got rifles, some semblance of uniform and, on the eve of going to the front, machine-guns. They were first issued with the St Etienne, a heavy almost useless weapon, but then received British-made Lewis guns and, later still, old, heavy Maxims.

The fascists were within a few miles of Madrid; the Republican Government left the capital for Valencia. Franco announced his impending triumphal entry into the city. But the arrival of the XIth Brigade reinforced the militia units, and the mass mobilization and resistance of the Madrid people ended his dream. Madrid was never taken by fascist arms.

On 9 November the British group were at the front. With other machine-gunners from their company they occupied the cliff crest over-looking the Casa del Campo, the rolling parkland reaching to the River Manzanares. They were near the building of the Faculty of Philosophy and Letters, part of the still unfinished University City. The fascist forces – 20,000 of their best and best-armed troops, backed by German and Italian tanks, guns and planes – had occupied the suburb of Carabanche to the south of the city, and pushed far across the Casa del Campo. The narrow Manzanares river, with one steep bank, was the only physical obstacle between Franco and the centre of Madrid. The city was heavily bombed and shelled, but the people, the Republican Army units, and the International Brigades fought back fiercely, angrily, regardless of losses.

The XIth Brigade was involved in savage fighting in the Casa del Campo and stopped the fascist drive with very severe losses. The British group, part of the defence in depth, only came under artillery fire. But the four Lewis gunners were detached to support one of the infantry companies of their Battalion, which was forced to retreat while the gunners

Madrid and its environs

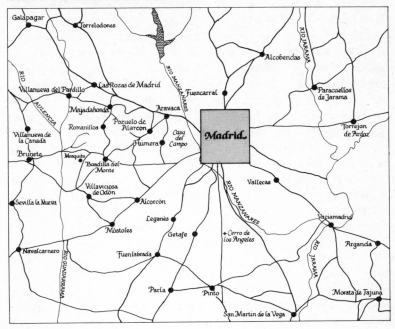

remained behind covering the withdrawal. Three – MacLaurin, Yates and Robert Symes, from London – were killed; Hinks had to fight his way back to safety.

The Commune de Paris Battalion was now moved from the University City area towards Aravaca to mount an attack on the flank of the fascist dagger which pointed at Madrid. It was unsuccessful and after being under heavy fire the Battalion was withdrawn. The British group were marching back at night when a lorry, speeding past without lights, snapped a wire cable across the road. Jones was killed when the cable hit him. He had shown himself to be a capable, cool leader with a stabilising influence on the group. Hinks was elected to take his place.

On 15 November Moors and Foreign Legion troops crossed the Manzanares river, scaled the cliffs, and held a large area of the University City and several streets around for the fascists. The British group, with their Battalion, were sent into the Philosophy and Letters building which had been recaptured from the enemy. The situation was difficult, with the fascists holding other buildings a couple of hundred yards away and with constant sniping and shelling. But there were compensations; only a direct hit from a shell could penetrate the rooms. Despite the shattered windows it was warm and dry, and there were books, in English, to be read in the long hours of waiting. Knox, Sommerfield and Cornford all subsequently described how they had to build barricades of books to block windows and shell holes. Although several of the group were wounded by glass and splinters there were no serious casualties. On 7 December the Battalion was withdrawn for a short rest and to have its heavily depleted ranks filled with new arrivals from the Albacete Base.

The French company commander now insisted that the leader of the British section should be able to understand French, so Cornford reluctantly replaced Hinks. This incident indicated the problems of units drawn from several nationalities, and the need for reorganization on a language basis. However because of the intense military pressure this was not possible until much later.

Checked in their frontal assault on Madrid, the fascists launched a powerful force to cut off the city from the north. This offensive at first made rapid advances. The XIth International Brigade was moved to meet it and, with the XIIth International Brigade, other units and some Soviet tanks drove the enemy out of the small hamlet of Boadilla del Monte.

The British group, now with only one Lewis gun and one heavy Maxim, held forward positions when the fascist counter-attack of tanks, artillery and large numbers of infantry tried to retake Boadilla. The Commune de Paris Battalion took the shock of the attack; it lost two thirds of its men and was forced to retreat. For a time the two British-manned guns were the only barrier between the fascists and the village. Two, of the gun crew on Cunningham's Maxim were killed, but the Lewis and the Maxim kept up fire on the enemy units outflanking them. The British group returned through Boadilla only when ordered to do so.

The entire British group had now been reduced, by death, wounds and illness to five; Cornford, Cunningham, Hinks, Lesser and McKenzie, a medical student from Edinburgh. With a high reputation for courage, discipline and political understanding, they were sent to join the British unit being formed in Albacete where they arrived on 19 December.

The other British group, fighting with the XIIth Brigade, had also been in action near Boadilla. This group had, for the most part, arrived in Spain at Valencia and had formed a group in another barracks in Albacete. Again their efforts at elementary drill and discipline attracted other unattached individuals and the group built up to eighteen, including some Americans and 'Harry the Swiss'. Like the other group they were frustrated and confused in Albacete where military units were being formed under such difficult conditions. They decided to join the Thaelmann Battalion whose core was made up of German and Austrian refugees from fascism. The order to form the XIIth Brigade was given on 1 November, the Thaelmann being one of its three Battalions, moving off to the Madrid front on 9 November.

The Thaelmann Battalion was issued with a semblance of a uniform, including khaki berets and baggy pantaloons, but no boots. Its rifles were either 1914 Lee Enfields, the ammunition for which, as the labels disclosed, had also been packed in Britain in 1914; or P14s which needed different ammunition. Fortunately the volunteers had an opportunity to fire a few rounds on a makeshift range. Several of the group had military experience or training. Bill Scott, a Dublin bricklayer, had been in the Irish revolutionary movement and had fought in the Thaelmann Centuria outside Huesca in September. Addley and Ovenden had been in the First World War, Phil Gillan, a transport worker from Glasgow, though only eighteen, had been in the Territorial Army. Arnold Jeans, a research scientist from Manchester, was elected leader of the group, now number 3 Zug (Section) of Number 1 Kompanie of the Thaelmann Battalion. Jeans was widely experienced, rather older than the others; an excellent linguist, he acted as 'mother', as well as proving a brave, sagacious soldier.

The Thaelmann Battalion went into action alongside Spanish units on 12 November, aiming to take a hill, Cerro de los Angeles (renamed by the local militia Cerro Rojo), where a fascist advance threatened to cut off Madrid from the south. The attack was a shambles. There were no lorries to move men from the railhead, and no artillery support. The objectives were not made clear. It was a testing time for the British group as the realities of war became clear. It was a hot, tiring advance, some men dropping the blanket which they would desperately need at nightfall; there was reluctance to carry extra ammunition. Dave Marshall, a clerk in a London labour exchange, was wounded. Two of the group left the unit. But after this experience the rest settled down as a cohesive, disciplined group.

The Thaelmann Battalion was then sent to Madrid and received a vociferous reception as it marched, behind a band into the suburb of Fuencarral. Here Christopher Thorneycroft, an Oxford student, was made the Battalion armourer. A student of engineering and a pilot, he had tried, without success, to get into the Republican Air Force. However, his ability to repair the assorted, antiquated weapons and even to make new parts was a priceless asset. Despite many enticements to join the British Battalion he stayed with the Thaelmanns through the battles of Jarama, Guadalajara and Brunete. Then he moved to the 35th Division Medical Services where he helped to keep vehicles and equipment functioning.

The British were in almost continuous action on the fringe of University City, fighting for a Civil Guards Barracks and a cement works. Ovenden, Ray Cox (Southampton) and 'Harry the Swiss' were jubilant when they set a fascist tank on fire with a grenade and shot the crew. Life was grim, with heavy, cold rain, sniper fire, and trench digging at night. But after nearly a month in action the Battalion went for seven days' rest, staying in the Duke of Alba's country house, which could comfortably hold the 250 men – all that were left in the Battalion.

On 15 December the XIIth Brigade was sent alongside the XIth to the Boadilla area to stop the enemy's encircling move. The British group passed their fellow countrymen in the XIth unaware of their presence. The Thaelmann Battalion suffered appalling losses and only two of the British group remained in action by 20 December. Jeans, Lorrimer Birch, a brilliant Oxford scientist, Gough, Addley and Messer were killed. Gillan, who had been criticised by his mates for incorrect anti-fascist behaviour (swearing when under heavy fire), was seriously wounded.

Ovenden and Esmond Romilly (nephew of Winston Churchill) were the only two British in the field when the forty survivors of the entire Battalion made a controlled retreat. They were helped by Randall Sollenberger, the medical officer, who found a rifle and joined in, giving covering fire. Sollenberger was an American Doctor studying in London. He had joined the first British Medical Unit, leaving London on 23 August 1936.

Some sort of defensive positions were taken up that night, but the fascists had had enough, their offensive stopped. The remains of the Thaelmann Battalion were withdrawn on Christmas Day.

Romilly, only eighteen years old, had been under great strain. Ovenden took him to Valencia and then on to Barcelona. There had been demands from his family that Romilly should go home, so they went to the British Consul who gave them tickets and passports. They reached Paris on New Year's Day, passing Esmond's older brother Giles on his way out to join the International Brigade. In London Romilly had to go to hospital for recuperation. Ovenden visited the relatives of their comrades who had been killed in Spain, then helped the organization and transport of more volunteers.

After two months of fighting, by the beginning of 1937, the thirty-odd men in the 'First Few' had been reduced by death, wounds and illness to only five fit for active service. However, their sacrifice and their efforts had contributed to checking the fascists and to giving the Republic time to organize and resist.

Chapter 5
The Formation of the British Battalion

The widespread fierce opposition in Spain to the fascist uprising showed itself in the spontaneous formation of militia groups of ordinary Spaniards: 60,000 were in them by the end of August 1936, thwarting the generals' plans for a quick take-over of the country, and keeping many of the main cities and much of the countryside in the hands of the Republican Government.

However, the militia groups were incapable of defeating the fascist military machine once it had received reinforcements from Germany and Italy. Many of the militia were not at the actual front; they owed allegiance to various political parties and there was no centralized leadership or direction. In this confused situation, the political and military experience of some of the foreign volunteers helped to lift morale.

Nevertheless, the real need was to build a unified, disciplined Republican Army. The enemy was advancing rapidly, and unless decisions were made immediately the Republic would be defeated. This demanded a prolonged, difficult and many-sided effort. The parties of the Popular Front differed widely over political issues and held conflicting views on the best way to defeat fascism, and these differences were often compounded by the war itself.

Britons already in Spain saw the urgency of the situation and Cornford had shown the possibilities of recruiting when he returned to Spain with six volunteers in October 1936. On 5 September 1936 Wintringham had written to Pollitt from

Barcelona stressing the value of Nat Cohen and the other British volunteers, saying finally: 'If you have any likely fellows taking a holiday soon in this lovely town send me a selection. People coming out must carry full documents.' He wrote again on 13 September spelling out what was needed.

> We want a respectable number of English comrades, CP, LP or TU, to make a centuria. Send with khaki shorts and shirts with two pockets, then all will be dressed alike and look disciplined. Send 10% of trained men to act as corporals. We want our own group – they will know less than the Germans but discipline and common sense are the two things we need. This war at present looks like going on till February.

In November 1936, after a meeting of the British group in the Thaelmann Battalion, Thorneycroft wrote to Pollitt calling for more volunteers and making suggestions for improved organization of the journey. He said:

> Military experience is not necessary. The work here requires not only enthusiasm but determination and ability to put up with discomfort, and tolerate comrades from other countries with whom misunderstandings due to language often arise.

When the International Brigade Base was set up in Albacete in October 1936, the immediate emphasis was on the creation of infantry units to check the menacing fascist drive on Madrid. After the organization and dispatch into action of the XIth and XIIth Brigades, preparations were made to form the XIIIth, XIVth and XVth Brigades. The Base began to build up the specialist formations and services needed: supplies, transport, records, medical services and, later, military training schools for specialists.

The XVth Brigade was originally planned to be formed from English-speaking volunteers and was formally incorporated into the Republican Army on 31 January 1937. As numbers grew and organization was established, Albacete proved too small and units were sent to villages in the vicinity.

The British were sent to Madrigueras, a small village about

twenty miles away on the rolling plain of vine and wheat fields. The local people, mainly workers on the land, were strongly anti-fascist and supported the Republic. The tower of the large stone church dominated the narrow unpaved streets, with houses and yards opening directly on to them. The only other building of any size was the village hall with a stage and balcony.

The British groups (assorted English, Welsh, Scots, Irish, Cypriots, Australians and others) had their full share of initial difficulties when they were taken to Madrigueras. Very little preparation for their arrival had been made. There was even a brief note of farce when an individual appointed himself commander and threatened anyone who disobeyed him with a revolver.

Early in December 1936, when significant numbers began to arrive from Britain, experienced political leaders were sent out by the Communist Party. David Springhall, a member of the Party's Central Committee and an ex-naval man, became Political Commissar of the British groups. Ralph Fox, journalist, writer and also a member of the Party's Central Committee, became an assistant commissar in the Albacete Base. Peter Kerrigan, leader of the Scottish Communists, prepared to go to Spain as soon as the Scottish Hunger Marches were over. Tom Wintringham, who had been an officer in the First World War, gave up journalism, and on 20 November went to Albacete to become machine-gun instructor for all the groups being organized to make up the XV Brigade. Wilfred McCartney, just out of prison for allegedly spying for the Soviet Union, was sent as a military cadre, as was George Nathan, an ex-army officer who had been noted as a capable military leader.

On 4 January 1937 it was established that there were 450 British in Spain, of whom 145 had already been sent to fight on the Córdoba front. The formation of a British Battalion was assured, and there were hopes, never to be realized, of a second.

It was a complex, daunting task to forge this mass of individuals into a disciplined, organized military unit, within a space of time which had to be measured by the fascist advances on many fronts. The material problems were acute: lack of weapons even for essential training, shortage of uniforms and equipment, insufficient and unusual food. There were also ideological difficulties.

It was not easy for men, straight from the factories and used to the traditions of the British labour movement, to adjust to military organization. There was impatience to get into battle and some resentment of those aspects of training which, like so much military instruction, seemed to be a waste of time. There was only limited understanding of the immense impact of the military rebellion, and of the difficult political situation underlying the organization and direction of the war. In addition, a few volunteers had gone to Spain without fully realizing the harshness of war and did not like what they saw. However, the most significant feature of this period was not the appalling number and immensity of the difficulties, but the speed with which an organized military unit was created which proved able to check much larger and infinitely better-armed regular units of the fascist powers.

The arrival in Madrigueras of the individuals and small groups who had already been fighting had a catalytic effect on the process of consolidation. Springhall, Fox, and a little later Kerrigan, with their varied experiences and talents, provided a stable leading group. Their weekly letters to Pollitt in Britain discussed the problems and how they were tackling them. Always stressing the need for a much greater number of volunteers, they emphasized that, although military experience was most valuable, the essential qualities were proven anti-fascism and experience in the labour movement. Fox wrote that intellectuals and students of the best type 'like Cornford and Knox should come, but not Bloomsbury odds and sods, of whom we have a few'.

Springhall and Kerrigan repeatedly urged greater care in the selection of volunteers, saying that there were about five per cent in Madrigueras who were a nuisance and disruptive, drinking too much and holding up training and organization. They asked for special attempts to find someone with sufficient military experience to command a Battalion or an even larger unit.

As the organization of the XVth Brigade went ahead in December 1936, with Springhall designated for Brigade responsibilities, and Fox and Kerrigan for work in the Base, a request was made for a capable, leading Communist to take over the political responsibility for the Battalion. Eventually, George Aitken, a Scottish engineer with service in the First World War, arrived in time to become Political Commissar of the Battalion before it moved off to its first action at Jarama.

Men continually arrived from Britain, sometimes in small groups, sometimes in sizeable parties of fifty or eighty. This added to the difficulties of organization and military training. It was decided to build a company at a time, No. 1 Company being formed towards the end of December 1936.

The selection of military leaders was also difficult; obviously previous military experience was a useful quality, but it did not automatically qualify a person as a leader in the very different conditions in Spain. The leading group had to assess potential partly on the basis of previous anti-fascist activity and partly on how volunteers developed in the hurly-burly of Madrigueras life. All ranks and appointments were temporary until after action. Though some mistakes were made, the test of battle made the necessary promotions or demotions fairly clear.

Party political organization was set up: Communist Party organization existed on a Battalion and company basis, Labour Party organization existed on a Battalion basis and in some companies. At that time there was a majority of Communist Party members in the Battalion; indeed, on 22 December 1936, of the 23,000 International Brigaders in Spain, sixty per cent were Communists. Party meetings were called but the political commissars at the Base intervened to stop them, since emphasis had to be laid on the united anti-fascist character of the Brigades.

All the other International Battalions had adopted a title, usually the name of a national people's hero. A name for the British Battalion was discussed. Fox wrote to Pollitt: 'Would

Saklatvala have a wide enough appeal to non-Communists at home really to help the growth of the People's Front? If not, what propositions then? I drop the idea of Chartist.'

Shapurji Saklatvala was a leading figure in the Indian nationalist movement and had been one of the early Communist members of parliament in Britain (for North Battersea). The decision to name the British Battalion after him was made in Britain. Springhall urged the sending of some Indian volunteers to heighten the impact of the name, but as far as is known none arrived; nor did the name 'Saklatvala' ever come into official or general use. The Battalion was always known as the British Battalion, and in Spanish (which like most languages does not distinguish between 'English' and 'British') as 'el Batallón Inglés'.

Between the English, Welsh and Scots there were few or no problems; however, many of the Irish volunteers had been in armed struggle against the British Government and tended to be hostile to anything British. Irish volunteers like Bill Scott were among the first groups to come to Spain, and many others working in Britain, Australia and elsewhere, soon make their way there. The first big group, led by Frank Ryan, a Republican leader and journalist, left Dublin in December 1936. On arrival in Albacete, Ryan sent a letter to all Irishmen explaining why the Irish were not all together, but 'at the first available opportunity I will, in co-operation with the officers of the English-speaking Battalion reunite all groups in a distinctive Irish Unit'.

However in Madrigueras a number of Irish agitated to go to the American Lincoln Battalion which was being formed in nearby Villanueva de la Jara and contained a number of Irishmen from the USA. Springhall called a meeting of all the Irish to discuss the question. The main argument advanced by those who wished to leave the Irish Battalion was the wrongs done to the Irish by the British in the past. Powerful arguments against were put by Charlie Donnelly, from Tyrone but living in Glasgow, Peter O'Connor and John and Paddy Power (all from Waterford). They pointed out that distinctions must be made between anti-fascist working-class comrades from Britain and British Imperialism. They argued that British Imperialism and international capitalism were the enemies of both the Irish and the British working class, and that Spain offered a golden opportunity to fight shoulder to shoulder against both. The vote was twenty-six to eleven against remaining in the British Battalion. Springhall reported that those who wished to stay were those with political backgrounds in the IRA or the trade unions. However, all the Irish then in Madrigueras had to go to the Lincoln Battalion, although nearly all the Irish volunteers who arrived later joined the British Battalion and lived with and fought alongside their British comrades without friction.

There was a short period of tension when Nol 1 Company returned from the South to the Battalion and the Commander, Wilfred McCartney, was accused of having been a British army terrorist in Ireland. And again, at the Burns' Night Supper, when the whole Battalion was ready to move off to the front, Ryan demanded that the Irish withdraw. André Marty, French Commander of the Albacete Base was outraged at the timing of this demand and put Ryan under arrest; however Springhall and Kerrigan negotiated his release a few hours later.

These tensions, inevitable against the background of Irish oppression, vanished in action. Two Irishmen, Peter Daly, a labourer in London, from Enniscorthy) and Paddy O'Daire became commanders of the Battalion; many became company and section commanders.

In addition, the Cypriots, with their firmly-held political views and their experiences under British imperialism, made a big impact on the Battalion and won high esteem.

In the early days of the International Brigades there was some national rivalry. Before Brunete, in July 1937, some American voices complained that the British were running the XVth Brigade; after the battle some British accused the Americans of a takeover bid. However the brutal realities of the fighting, the fascist pressure, and above all the growing calibre and therefore influence of the Spanish cadres, drove out these chauvinist attitudes, and it was soon established that leadership was achieved not on the basis of nationality or social background but by ability proven and tried in battle.

Chapter 6
Training, Discipline, Problems

The crucial task now facing the British, and indeed all the International Brigades, as well as the Republican Army, was to create a military force out of a mass of individuals.

It was impossible to create an army with a standardized organization and structure. The pressures of enemy action, the general shortage of cadres and weapons, and the high casualties, meant that there were frequent reorganizations and changes of structure. The composition and strength of divisions, brigades, battalions, and especially companies, were therefore very variable. In the Brunete offensive, for example, the XV Brigade went into action with six battalions. Halfway through the battle, heavy casualties forced the Lincoln and the Washington battalions to amalgamate. In all the battalions the formal companies disintegrated into groups. Training and organization were a constant preoccupation and had to be maintained throughout the war, in and out of action, until the last days of the International Brigades' withdrawal.

The continual arrival of new groups of volunteers, the changing character of the war, and changes in responsibility as a result of casualties, all meant that training remained the concern of all in the Battalion, rank and file as well as leaders. However, the time available for training was invariably limited by the demands of the fighting itself. For the British, as throughout the Republican Army, the difficulties were further intensified by the shortage of experienced instructors and the lack of arms and equipment with which to train.

The International Brigades had certain characteristics which made the task of military consolidation in some ways easier than it was for the Spanish Republican Army. Because a high proportion of Brigaders came from an industrial background, they were more familiar with machinery, more accustomed to the discipline and interdependence of factory life than their Spanish comrades, and therefore more amenable to military organization. In addition, probably a higher proportion had had military experience and were used to handling weapons.

However there were also notable disadvantages. Very few Brigaders had any knowledge of Spanish; the food was strange and difficult to get used to (bacteria which had no effect on most Spanish bodies ran riot through the intestines of the British).

In the early stages of the war the essential thing was to stop an immediate fascist breakthrough. Many of the first fighters picked up rifles and fired them before they had any training. The few ex-regular soldiers often found themselves giving instruction on weapons and tactics in the course of actual fighting. No other alternative was possible, but resulting casualties were heavy.

The initial period of Battalion training in Madrigueras set a pattern which was continued later in the Tarazona Training Camp, and during the few short periods when the Battalion was out of the line. There was plenty of space around Madrigueras for learning the possibilities and limitations of movement through olive groves and vinefields. The disused village theatre, which included a gallery, provided crowded sleeping space, and was used for lectures, weapon-stripping practice, meetings and discussions. The stage itself provided an opportunity for the Battalion's entertainers in the evenings.

The creation of a Battalion was not a simple matter of military training. Though the very great majority of the men were deeply convinced and sincere in their determination to fight fascism, many at first found it difficult to accept military organization and discipline after the free debate and discussion of the labour movement. Those who had had experience in the regular armed forces found it difficult to appreciate the individuality and initiative which are the strength of a people's army. Military and political training had to go on simultaneously and complement one another. McCartney was a competent officer. All agreed that 'he knew his stuff'; but he was more at home dealing with ex-regulars than with the factory militants, even calling them 'Harry's Bolshies'. On the other hand, Springhall and Kerrigan had only limited experience of military affairs, but commanded general respect because of their records at home, and their popular touch. These three leaders worked well together.

In forming the Battalion, and indeed in all the fighting, political leadership was as necessary as military leadership. The character of the war, the need to create a new united army in a divided country – short of nearly everything – gave a political complexion to everything military. As a result, all units of the International Brigades and most units of the Republican Army had political commissars working with and equal in rank to the military commander. They operated at all levels down to companies: sometimes even a section would have a political delegate. Hospitals, training schools, transport units – all the many organizations in the armed forces had political commissars.

The purpose and functions of the political commissars were clearly defined in the *Book of the XVth Brigade*, published in 1938, edited by Frank Ryan with the help of Alonso Elliott, a teacher from Cambridge, and Alex Donaldson, from Coatbridge in Scotland.

> The Commissars are an integral part of the Army. Their role is to inspire their unit with the highest spirit of discipline and loyalty to the Republican cause ... The Commissar teaches the recruits that victory depends on carrying out unquestioningly and unwaveringly whatever order the military command may issue ... The Commissar is an educator in the broadest sense of the word ... A soldier who knows the importance of the military objective and also the reason for it can be trusted to put up a much better fight for it ... The Commissar's work extends to the smallest details that contribute to the material well being and comfort of

> the men ... The Commissar never forgets the interests of the
> soldiers and civilians are the same ... The Commissar co-operates
> closely with the Military Commander at whose side he is
> appointed ... Orders and reports are signed jointly by the
> Commander and Commissar ... At all times the Commissar sets
> a personal example to the volunteers of the rank and file ... 'First
> to advance and last to retreat' is the slogan of the Commissars.

The British units were well served by their commissars, three
out of the eight of whom were killed in action in advanced
positions. In resolving specific problems as they arose, they
had to be sensitive to complaints but to weigh them against
objective conditions in Spain. They also had to work to
increase the understanding of the war and to maintain and
develop contact with the labour movement in Britain (an
important factor in changing the attitude of the British
Government).

The commissars at Battalion level were sent out by the
Communist Party leadership in Britain, in consultation with
leading political figures already in Spain – Springhall,
Kerrigan, Paynter, and the Communist officials John Mahon
and Bill Rust. At Company level the political commissars
were often elected, or took on the job by concensus of their
comrades. All the Battalion commissars had had wide
political experience in Britain, and all had volunteered to go to
Spain as ordinary fighters. Several had been full-time workers
for the Communist Party in responsible positions. Dave
Springhall was London District Secretary and member of the
party's political bureau; George Aitken was the full-time
Communist organizer in the North East; Bert Williams was
organizer in the Midlands and a member of the Central
Committee; Wally Tapsell had been leader of the Young
Communist League and was the circulation manager of the
Daily Worker; and Bob Cooney was a leading Scottish
Communist.

Three Commissars had not been full-time Communist
Party workers: Jack Roberts was a Communist councillor in
Caerphilly, South Wales, with a long record of leadership
among the miners; Tom Oldershaw had been an active

militant among the Battersea workers in London, while Eric Whalley had been a leader of the unemployed in Nottinghamshire. Springhall, Tapsell, Williams and Cooney had studied at the Lenin School in Moscow.

In Madrigueras there was a general atmosphere of enthusiasm and an understanding that time was short before the Battalion might be called into action. Practice in stripping and assembling the few available weapons went on at all hours. Discussion, impromptu and organized, was continuous, on military tactics, the political situation in Spain, and on the organization of the Army. Spanish language lessons were also given.

In this sedate and even somewhat austere atmosphere, discipline and morale were generally high, with the exception of a small group – Kerrigan put it at five per cent – of hard drinkers – who were openly criticized by Kerrigan and Fox, who also urged greater care in the selection of volunteers. In addition McCartney arranged shorter opening hours for the village cafés and set up a Battalion guard-house for defaulters. A very few of these, whom Springhall labelled 'disruptive nuisances', failed to adapt to the life and spirit of the International Brigades; the great majority, in action and in the disciplined, collective atmosphere of the Battalion, turned into reliable fighters.

One of the greatest difficulties in preparing for action arose from the scarcity of weapons and ammunition available for training. Wintringham, using his First World War experience, undertook machine-gun training for the three Battalions being formed in villages near Madrigueras, the Lincolns from the USA, the Franco-Belge, and the British. This was no easy job in view of the wide variety of weapons in use, many of them obsolete: Maxims, Colts, St Etiennes, Chauchots, Lewis and others.

Professor J.B.S. Haldane visited the Battalion and lectured on poison gas drill and grenade-throwing. Training was given in distance-judging, the preparation of range-cards, and basic mapping was put on an efficient basis when Edward Bee, a qualified surveyor from Stafford, joined the Battalion.

MADRIGUERAS.

COMMANDANT VIDAL,   20. 1. 37
COMMANDANT AT THE BASE
ALBACETE.

I enclose Battalion orders for the 20th.

You will observe that Comrade Vidal's theme was repeated, it was moreover
elaborated by the use of rattles, and finally by a developed attack on a
further objective.
The use of written reports from group commanders was insisted upon, and
attached are specimens of those made by group, and section commanders of
such communications.
The use of cover, and the general tactics of the comrades was better than
that which Comrade Vidal observed.
Comrade Vidal will be pleased to know that much attention was paid by the
comrades of the 16th Battalion to his remarks, and that yesterday evenings
many meetings and discussions took place, where Comrade Vidal's criticisms
and suggestions were earnestly debated, sometimes very excitedly, even
heatedly.
I have observed through watching the comrades from a good distance through
field glasses that the flat tops of the cartridge cases on the equipment
reflect the sun very brightly.
The food continues to be excellent and the Battalion is gaining weight.
Billets are cleaner, and the latrines are improving.
Discipline is still backward, too much drinking, and too much arguing,
when orders are given by group and section commanders.
The lack of discipline expresses itself in erratic military performance,
one day the battalion does its work well, indeed sometimes very well, and
the commander begins to flatter himself that great progress is being made,
but the next day the battalion behaves badly, is slack and indifferent,
even conveys the impression of incompetence.

This I believe however to be a feature of all civil wars.

I regret that Commandant Vidal missed Comrade Wintringham and myself
this afternoon.

                    SALUD.

ENCLOSURES   Commandant.

                                Commandant at Madrigueras.

Battalion orders, Madrigueras, January 1937

On occasion Soviet advisers were attached to help in
Battalion training. They were capable, well-trained men but
young, and their only live experience of battle had been gained
in Spain. Their knowledge of the Soviet weapons – rifles,
heavy and light machine guns, anti-tank guns – was of great
value. Often they were withdrawn when the Batallion went
into action, but in the few battles where they remained there
was never any doubt that the British officers were in
command.

The confidence of the Battalion rose dramatically at the end

ENGLISH SPEAKING BATTALION
INTERNATIONAL BRIGADE

MADRIGUERAS   20.1.37
BATTALION ORDERS

8 a.m. parade

SECTION 4/ Special Instructions with Comrade Dickinson

"   5.   Fatigue Duty with Comrade Freedman

"   6.   Guard Duty.

No. 3 Coy.   Tactical Operation, Rep est Manouvre of Commandat Vidal,
             Machine gun rattles will be place by Commander Fry.

Machine Gun Company, Route March.

2 p.m. Parade

Machine Gun Coy.   Machine gun drill

No. 2. and No. 3. Coys   Route March to Tarragona

Company Officers may issue late passes until 11 p.m.
10 Only of these passes may be issued by each Company Commander.
These passes must be returned to the Company Commanders who will
destroy them.

Company Commanders will report every evening at 8 p.m. to H.Q.

                            Commandant

                            Commandant at Madrigueras.

---

of January 1937 when Soviet rifles were issued to every man,
and the prospect of immediate action became clear. The rifles
were of the Remington type, not as heavy or durable as the
British Lee Enfields, but considered reliable by 'old sweats'
with service experience. They tended to fire high if the long,
awkward, triangular-section bayonet was not fixed. Moreover,
there was no scabbard for the bayonet, which had to be turned
upside down and fixed to the rifle boss. As a result many
bayonets were soon lost. However, after the new rifles were
cleaned, and everyone had fired a few rounds and got the feel
of the new weapon, morale was excellent. By the time the
Battalion moved off to the Madrid front, its members were
trained and organized in a way few had thought possible.

The stage of training and some of the problems emerge from

Battalion Orders and the report to Vidal, a Frenchman who was Military Commandant of the Albacete Base, made by McCartney on 20 January 1937.

Madrigueras remained the British collecting and training base until the training for all the English-speaking units was concentrated in Tarazona de la Mancha, a process which was completed by the end of July 1937. The length of training depended on the exigencies of the military situation. Eventually it became possible to maintain a cadre of men, including those still recovering from wounds or those who had shown ability in action, to direct the training. In addition, as we have seen, the supply of Soviet material made weapon-training simpler.

With the growing recognition that the war would be long, and that disciplined, well-trained men were needed to match the better-armed, regular fascist units, the training of specialists began. Machine-gunners, riflemen and observers were trained as reserves for the Battalion. When the XVth Brigade was given Soviet 37mm anti-tank guns in May 1937, they were manned by the British who were given brief specialist training by Soviet advisers.

At Pozorrubio, near Albacete, a school was set up for training officers and NCOs. Wintringham, recovering from wounds, and Arthur Olerenshaw, a musician from London, an ex-Regular soldier and among the early volunteers to see action in Spain, were instructors there for a period. The students were selected from those who had shown ability in action and, in a few cases, from the new groups of volunteers. The school tried to provide basic military training, and was also used to prepare a cadre of capable leaders to be kept in reserve. 'Desertion to the front' was quite common among the British in Tarazona and Pozorrubio because, while accepting the need for training, many wanted to get back to their friends at the front and to fight.

During its existence the British Battalion faced many defeats and heavy losses; yet as Wild and Cooney were able to report after the disastrous Aragon retreat in March 1938, 'the Battalion carried out every order it received'. Discipline rested on political convictions, reinforced by the work of the political commissars. Orders were obeyed – not without some grumbling and beefing – not out of fear of the consequences of disobedience but from a realization, after the first few weeks, that without orders there would be chaos and certain defeat. Promotion was rapid and invariably meant extra work, extra worry and less sleep.

Eleven men in all commanded the Battalion in actual battle: Wilfred McCartney (writer, who had to return before any fighting), Tom Wintringham (journalist), Jock Cunningham (labourer), Fred Copeman (ex-navy), Joe Hinks (army reservist), Peter Daly (labourer), Paddy O'Daire (labourer), Harold Fry (shoe repairer), Bill Alexander (industrial chemist), Sam Wild (labourer), and George Fletcher (newspaper canvasser). All except Wintringham had the opportunity of showing their abilities in action before being given leadership. All of them had been involved in working-class, anti-fascist activities at home, and had been influenced by Communist ideas and activity, although only Wintringham had held responsible positions in the Communist Party itself. In Spain their beliefs were reinforced by struggle and experience. The majority had been manual workers, having left school at fourteen – the usual lot of most in those days, no matter how intelligent or able. Only McCartney, Wintringham and Alexander had been to university; all had experienced the difficulties and frustration of finding work in a period of heavy unemployment. Their anti-fascism was anchored in hatred of the class and social system in Britain.

One of the biggest political problems facing the British concerned leave and repatriation. In the early months, until February 1937, men were able to return to Britain. Some did, and of those a number returned to fight again. But then followed a period of uncertainty, confusion and great difficulty. The early volunteers had not been told of any time limit to their commitment, and some, after a period, wanted to go home – a wish intensified by the grim realities of the fighting, the high casualty rate, and the shortage of food.

Some British army reservists argued tht they must return home to keep within their engagement. The Spanish Government and the International Brigades faced a problem: the Spanish conscripts could not leave the army and go home; the German, Italian and many other anti-fascists would face execution or imprisonment if they returned to their countries. For a period, therefore, all requests for repatriation were refused, even of those wounded or unfit for further fighting.

In September 1937 the Spanish Government incorporated the International Brigades into the Republican Army, and all volunteers were told clearly, before they left their respective countries, that they were in the army until the defeat of fascism. This at least clarified the position.

After Jarama in February 1937 a few men left the front or refused to return after recovering from wounds. After the Brunete offensive the following July, the impact of the harsh physical conditions and the heavy casualties, sharpened by open differences among the British leaders, brought a lowering of morale, and more men left the front. Some were accommodated and did useful jobs in the rear, in hospitals, supply depots and elsewhere, but others remained inactive at the Albacete Base.

Pollitt and Gallacher made representations at top level to the Republican Government requesting a clear position, asking for repatriation at least for the disabled and other special cases, but without success. The difficulties were compounded by some British military and political leaders who made unauthorized promises of repatriation, or work in the rear, after six months' service, or after one wound.

The Base authorities collected the shaken volunteers around Albacete, and the British, French and some other nationalities were sent to Camp Lucas, some thirty miles away deep in the countryside.

The authorities could not decide whether the purpose was punishment or rehabilitation, and as a result of the inactivity morale became lower still. Will Paynter, British Base Commissar, went to speak several times at Camp Lucas and received a very rough reception. Arthur Horner, the widely-

British Battalion banner-bearer

Members of the Tom Mann Centuria in Barcelona, September 1936. *Left to right* Sid Avner, Nat Cohen, Ramona (who later married Cohen), Tom Wintringham, George Tioli, Jack Barry, Dave Marshall

Training with a Soviet-made Maxim heavy machine-gun

Members of No. 1 (Major Attlee) Company. Glyn 'Taffy' Evans, Company Commander (*right, holding banner*)

Members of the British Anti-Tank Battery, 1937. *Left to right* Miles Tomalin, Bill Alexander, Jeff Mildwater

Left to right Ewart Milne, Wogan Philipps, Issy Kupchick (a Canadian killed at Brunete), Stephen Spender, George Green and unknown, with Spanish Medical Aid lorry, Barcelona, 1937

The food wagon arrives at Teruel, January 1938. Battalion Quartermaster 'Hookey' Walker at back of truck in peaked cap

Mobile bathing and delousing unit, Aragon, 1937

Company wall-newspaper in Aragon

Anti-Tank Battery, August 1937. *Standing, third, fourth, sixth and eighth from left* Jim Brewer, Hugh Slater (Battery Commander), Alan Gilchrist, Bill Alexander (Political Commissar); *kneeling, second from left* Miles Tomalin (*with recorder*), Tom Jones (*bottom right*)

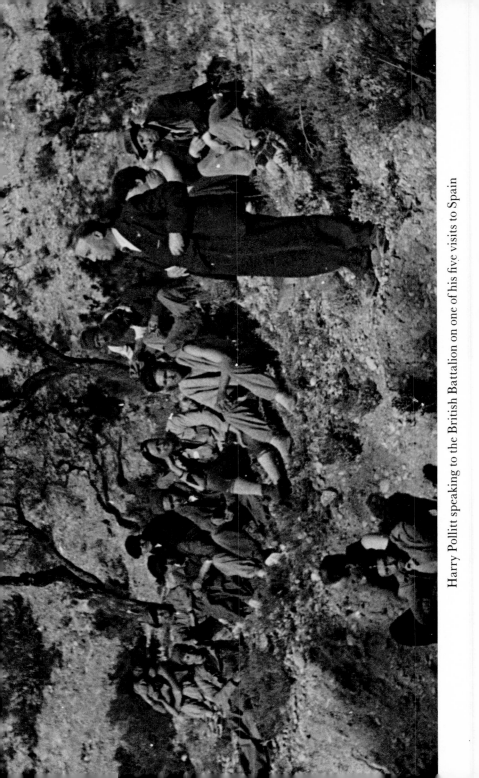

Harry Pollitt speaking to the British Battalion on one of his five visits to Spain

experienced and respected leader of the South Wales miners, also made little impression. Then John Angus, a student from London, classified as 'inutil por el frente' after being wounded at Brunete, went to Paynter after leaving hospital and asked for something to do. He was put in charge of the sixty-odd British at Camp Lucas in late September 1937. At twenty-three he was much younger than most men in his charge, but he immediately took the important decision of making rehabilitation the Camp's main aim. Accordingly he improved conditions, introduced a training-programme, gave no pep talks and – most important – moved the group back from Camp Lucas to the area of the main Tarazona Training Base. Gradually groups of two and three asked to return to the Battalion and to the front, and – led by Angus – everyone boarded the train and rejoined the Battalion in action when the fascist breakthrough took place in March 1938.

Others who left the front without papers were picked up by military and police patrols and put in prison. When the Base Political Commissar heard of their whereabouts, he managed to arrange their release. Despite stories circulating at the time and since, there is no record of any British volunteers being shot in Republican jails.

Yet others who left the front made their way to Barcelona, Valencia or Alicante, and some left Spain altogether. In all 298 made their way back to Britain. Some boarded British ships as stowaways, sometimes with the help of crew members. The British Consular officials, seeing an opportunity to discredit the Republic, used every chance to assist deserters. Viscount Churchill, in charge of the Medical Aid depot in Valencia, boasts in his autobiography (*All My Sins Remembered*, 1964) of how he organized desertions. (In fact, his 'secret' activity was known to the Republican authorities.)

On their return to Britain some of these men went to the press to justify their action with horror stories about casualties, the chaos, and 'Communist repression'. Others, who had panicked, or who were emotionally and physically exhausted, or mentally unsuitable for modern warfare, came to regret their action and played an honourable part in the British labour movement and in the International Brigade Association.

There was only one serious incident of desertion – the only one. In the mountains north of Teruel, during the cold winter of 1938, two men were caught on their way to enemy lines. One was carrying a map giving the Battalion positions with precise machine-gun locations – information which in fascist hands could have led to heavy casualties and defeat. There was very bitter feeling in the ranks against them. They were taken to the rear, court-martialled and sentenced to death. It has been said the sentence was commuted to service in a labour battalion and they were killed later in an artillery barrage while digging fortifications. It has also been said that the sentence was carried out. This was the only episode of treachery in the British record in Spain.

The problem of building and maintaining a military organization from scratch in the course of fighting a heavy war showed itself in unexpected ways. The difficulties of obtaining death certificates and the personal possessions of those killed in action often caused distress. Families wanted definite news; official confirmation was needed for pension and insurance claims. Those closest wanted mementoes of their loved ones.

The shaky organization of records and addresses was compounded by the slow, bureaucratic methods in the Republican Ministry of National Defence. Death certificates were written in French, translated by the Spanish Consular authorities, and then sent either to the family direct or to Robson in London. Three months' delay was customary even when there was no doubt about a casualty. Despite pressure from the Dependants' Aid Office, the base commissars, and from political leaders, the system did not improve.

Certificates for some of those killed at Jarama were not issued until seven months after. Fred White, a miner from Ogmore, South Wales, was killed at Brunete on 6 July 1937 but his death certificate did not reach London until 14 March 1939. Some mistakes, perhaps inevitable in the confused fighting, caused suffering but then great joy when the 'mistake' turned up alive. Jack Coward was a seaman from Liverpool whose family received a death certificate on 17 March 1939 stating that he had been killed on 3 May 1938; he came home alive in 1939. Tom Jones, a Wrexham miner, was reported on 8 March 1939 as having 'died' in hospital on 9 August 1938. He was to return home much later from Franco's jail.

Families wrote most moving letters to the Dependants' Aid Office and to Harry Pollitt when they heard of the death of their volunteer, often asking for details and requesting any personal possessions. The difficulties in complying with such requests naturally caused much distress. Personal effects were supposed to be sent, labelled and listed, to a depot in the Base. Mahon, Kerrigan and Rust were able to track down and send on a few parcels. After the last battles on the Ebro, Kerrigan managed to collect some of the personal effects belonging to twenty volunteers who had been killed; he took them back to Britain himself. However, after their first battle, few volunteers had any personal possessions except a few photos, their latest letters from home, a pencil and perhaps a knife. If it was possible to reach a body, the company or Battalion officer or a close friend would often write to the family, short-circuiting the system, and send on personal belongings.

This account of all the difficulties facing the British, some inevitable, some unforeseen, may seem black and depressing but, as the record shows, the overwhelming majority of the British volunteers stood up remarkably well to the almost continuous physical and mental strains in battle and in Franco's jails. This was partly a product of personal conviction, but partly also because membership of a unit with a single clear purpose gave support and strength to everyone in it.

Chapter 7

The British No. 1 Company Needed for Action

In mid December 1936 a critical situation developed in the south of Spain. The fascist General Queipo de Llano directed a general offensive from Córdoba and Granada, which had been in fascist hands since the July revolt, aimed at the important communications centre of Andújar. The local militia fought fiercely, but for ten days the fascists made important advances and the main road, towards Madrid, was open. The Government reacted by sending units to hold the front, among them the XIVth International Brigade.

This Brigade, of mainly French-speaking units, was being formed around Albacete and needed strengthening. Springhall and Kerrigan were told by Marty that No. 1 Company, the best trained and organized of the English-speaking Battalion, was needed. They were distressed, since the detachment of the best company would delay the formation and consolidation of a complete English-speaking Battalion. However, faced with the urgency of the situation, they had to agree, but on the understanding that the company would return to the Battalion at the earliest opportunity and that no more groups would be detached.

The XIVth Brigade was commanded by 'General Walter', (Karol Swierczewski) a Pole, later to become the Commander of the 35th Division of which the British were to form part. No. 1 Company became part of the French (12th) Battalion (La Marseillaise) commanded by Delasalle.

Nathan, the No. 1 Company Commander, was in high

No. 1 Company attack on Lopera

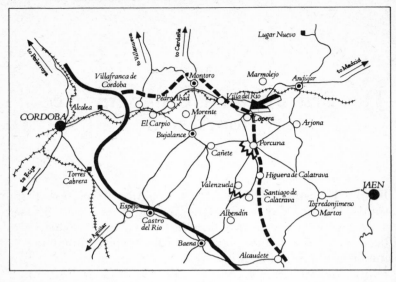

━━━ Fascist line at start of offensive

■ ■ ■ Fascist line when offensive halted

Scale: 1cm to 8km

spirits at the prospect of action; he was already becoming a legendary figure with a stick, a pipe and polished boots – passed on by Ryan because they pinched. The Company Political Commissar was Lou Elliott, a farm worker from Queensland, Australia. In addition, Ralph Fox, who had been working in Albacete against his wishes as an assistant Base Commissar, secured his own release and went with the company, since his experience and knowledge of French were needed.

No. 1 Company was 145 strong and included Jock Cunningham, Joe Hinks, John Cornford (still bandaged), Sam Lesser and Jock Clark, who all already had battle experience, having fought with the Franco-Belge Battalion in the defence of Madrid a month previously. It also included a group of Irish, many of whom had had some military experience with the IRA, as well as Mike Economides from Cyprus and a group of Dutchmen.

However, despite this experienced core, some of the Company had had only five days' intensive training and had never fired a rifle. Nevertheless, spirits were high when their train left Albacete on Christmas Eve 1936, and were not dampened by their Christmas Day dinner of cold Spanish corned-beef on arrival at Andújar. Although their uniforms and equipment were good, their weapons were poor. The machine-guns were Chauchats, which – partly because of their age and partly because of the lack of training and experience of the gunners – usually jammed after a few rounds. At midnight before the Christmas Eve departure, Nathan presented a rifle to each man, shaking hands while number and name were registered. The rifles were Austrian Steyrs of 1900 vintage which, lacking the special clips for rounds to charge the magazine, could only be fired a round at a time.

From the railhead the Company moved immediately to the front in lorries, but strafing from enemy planes forced it to scatter. Nathan Segal, from London's East End, was killed. Patrols were sent forward to Villa del Rio, an important village on the road and railway from Córdoba to Andújar. But the fascists were already there and opened heavy machine-gun fire.

The whole XIVth Brigade was then moved south across the main road with the aim of taking Lopera, about ten kilometres away. The village had been empty on Christmas Day but was now occupied by the fascists in strength. On 28 December No. 1 Company led the advance, coming under heavy fire from artillery, machine-guns, and strafing aircraft.

Nathan led the Company superbly, well backed up by the three section commanders – Conway, Cunningham and Hinks. They moved forward, section by section, well spread out in almost text-book style. However, by the time they reached the last crest, on the very outskirts of Lopera village, they had sustained heavy losses. Fox was killed when making a personal reconnaissance ahead of the most advanced troops. Cornford was killed (the day after his twenty-first birthday) trying to reach Fox's body. In the Irish (Connolly) Section alone there were eight dead and many wounded. The Company would still have tried to go forward but its flanks were open and, in the dusk, Nathan ordered a retreat from the crest. It was orderly and controlled. That night efforts were made to reorganize, feed and re-equip the Company.

The other units of the Marseillaise Battalion had suffered even more severely and were in a chaotic and disorganized state compared with the high morale of the British.

The next day the fascists attacked in great strength. Again No. 1 Company stood its ground but the flanks crumbled and it was nearly encircled; any hope of taking Lopera had gone.

Marty arrived from Albacete with Kerrigan, for whom Ronald Burgess was acting as interpreter, and conducted an inquiry into the chaos and the poor behaviour of the other companies of the Marseillaise. The commander, Delasalle, was arrested on Brigade orders and charged with cowardice and contact with French intelligence services. He was court martialled and eventually shot on 2 January 1937.

Because of Fox's heroic behaviour and the stubborn fight of No. 1 Company, the Marseillaise Battalion was renamed 'Ralph Fox'. Nathan was appointed its commander and Cunningham took over the command of No. 1 Company. Meanwhile the Republic had brought in more reinforcements and the fascist offensive was halted. The front became quiet, Queipo de Llano began to prepare for his offensive against Malaga.

However the special role of No. 1 Company and the XIV Brigade was not yet over. A big fascist force was reported massing for yet another attempt to take Madrid, by an offensive towards the Madrid-Corunna road. On 3 January 1937, led by Nazi tanks, the fascists broke the Republican lines, occupied Las Rozas and Majadahonda and cut the main road in several places. The three Battalions of the XIth International Brigade were thrown into the lines to hold this fascist offensive. The XIVth Brigade was ordered to disengage from the now quiet Andújar front, and to mount a counter-attack to retake the lost villages and clear the road.

The Marseillaise (Ralph Fox) Battalion, now commanded

by Nathan, travelled with No. 1 Company by rail and truck to the Madrid front. A few hours' break in Madrid itself provided a welcome release from the strain and fatigue of fighting and travelling since Christmas Eve. But by the 10 January No. 1 Company was at the front again.

It was a difficult and trying time. The Battalion was tired, its strength much reduced by casualties; it was also short of food, ammunition and equipment. The weather was persistently foggy. The Battalion moved to drive the fascists from the Las Rozas-Majadahonda road, with No. 1 Company in the van.

A significant advance was made with tank support but thickening fog and fierce German tank attacks brought progress to a standstill. The Company suffered more losses, one shell alone killing three men: James Hyndman from Glasgow, Jimmy Kermode from Milngavie in Dunbartonshire, and G. Palmer from London. By 15 January the weather had deteriorated, with deep snow making fighting nearly impossible, and the XIVth Brigade, with the British No. 1 Company, came out of the line.

The way back to the British Battalion was through Madrid, where two days leave pleased everyone. Charlie Hutchinson, then still only eighteen, remembers that the joy of sleeping indoors on a bed in a Madrid hotel was not lessened by the sound of shells hitting the walls.

Back in Albacete the 67 survivors of the 145-strong No. 1 Company which had set out on Christmas Eve received a hero's welcome, with a band and a guard of honour. Marty, addressing the parade, said that No. 1 Company was the best in the Marseillaise Battalion and the whole XIVth Brigade. It had set an example in courage, endurance, heroism and unity of purpose – which all in the International Brigades should emulate.

The Company marched back into Madrigueras led by Conway, since Cunningham had been wounded at Las Rozas. The remainder of the British Battalion, now increased in numbers, gave it a rapturous welcome, and many friendships were re-established. A delegation of London trade unionists

was there and pledged they would go back and win new
support for the Republic, and especially work to end the TUC
support for 'Non-Intervention'.

Everyone felt proud of the achievements and the record of
No. 1 Company whose return greatly enhanced general
morale. All felt the heavy losses, but new arrivals from Britain
came to fill the gaps in the ranks. The Company's experience
of intense action, passed on in many discussions, provided an
invaluable boost to the training and consolidation of the
British Battalion.

Chapter 8

'There's A Valley in Spain Called Jarama'

In the first days of February 1937, the British Battalion and others in the Republican Army were considered ready for action and there was talk of a Government offensive. Springhall was appointed Assistant Commissar of the XVth Brigade, of which the British Battalion was a part. Kerrigan, to his chagrin, was ordered to remain at the base in Albacete. McCartney – on 'ticket of leave' after serving his prison sentence — was due to return to Britain for one of the periodic appearances he had to make to the legal authorities. Urgent messages were sent to King Street demanding a capable and experienced man to take Springhall's place as Battalion Commissar, and urging McCartney's early return to command the Battalion. George Aitken arrived in time to take Springhall's place in the Battalion.

However, before McCartney left, an unfortunate accident occurred when Springhall and Kerrigan were giving him a farewell supper in Albacete. McCartney agreed to exchange his big Mauser revolver for Kerrigan's small .22 Belgian gun. Kerrigan, attempting to explain the mechanism of his revolver, let off a round, wounding McCartney in the arm. It was not a serious wound but McCartney did not return to Spain. Kerrigan was deeply upset, offering his resignation, which was not accepted. Accidents with weapons were not uncommon among so many untrained men.

Wintringham gave up command of No. 2 Machine-Gun Company and took command of the Battalion on 6 February,

The British Battalion in the Battle of Jarama

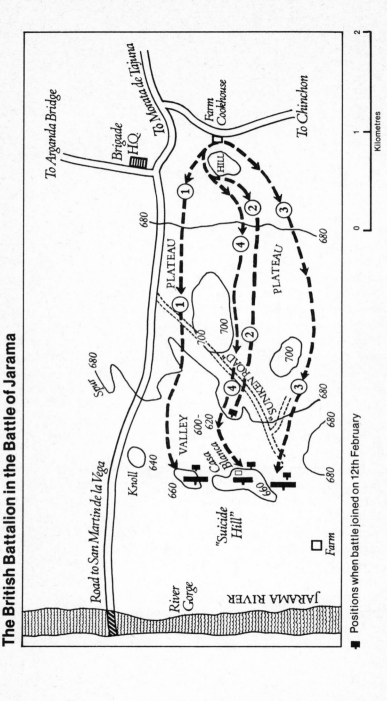

To Arganda Bridge

Road to San Martin de la Vega

River Gorge

Brigade H.Q.

To Morata de Tajuna

Farm Cookhouse

To Chinchon

HILL

680

PLATEAU

PLATEAU

700

700

700

SUNKEN ROAD

Spur 680

Knoll 640

VALLEY

660

600-620

Casa Blanca

"Suicide Hill"

660

680

680

680

Farm

JARAMA RIVER

Kilometres

0   1   2

■ Positions when battle joined on 12th February

the day it was ordered to move off to the front. There were last minute problems: new rifles, steel helmets and equipment were to be issued, checked and cleared. The Lewis guns, the pride of the squad of ex-Service men led by Fred Copeman, a Londoner who had been discharged from the Royal Navy for his part in the 1931 Invergordon Mutiny, were taken away. The Machine-Gun Company, now commanded by Harold Fry from Edinburgh (he had been an army sergeant and worked subsequently as a shoe-mender), got eight heavy water-cooled, First World War Maxims.

As the Battalion moved off from Madrigueras on 7 February, a count was made of the British volunteers in Spain. In the Battalion there were 500; in the Brigade guard sixty; recent arrivals left behind in Madrigueras totalled seventy-five. Twenty-five were left at the Base and in hospital; twenty were in the Cavalry; and there were forty Irish with the Lincolns. Thirty men from the earliest arrivals had already gone home. The total, of some 750 British in Spain (including the Irish), was probably never exceeded.

February 1937 began disastrously for the Republic. The fascists, led by mechanized Italian units, took Malaga in the South on 8 February almost without resistance. On 6 February, having failed to take Madrid by frontal assault, the fascists began a major offensive to encircle it from the south. By cutting the main Valencia road they could stop most food and supplies. In the previous November the Government had left the capital for Valencia, so this road provided the essential link between Madrid and the rest of Republican Spain.

The fascists mustered an attacking force of five Brigades, each of about 8,000 men with supporting arms, from the Army of Africa: Moorish cavalry with reserves and, in addition, regular German army machine-gunners, tanks and artillery. They achieved considerable initial successes, bringing the Valencia road under fire and penetrating deep into Republican lines.

The Government reacted, though belatedly, by bringing the front under the unified command of the Madrid sector. It concentrated many of its best troops there – the Brigades commanded by Líster and by Campesino who had already shown their high quality in battle, and also the XIth, XIIth and XIVth International Brigades. The XVth International Brigade was hurriedly formed and brought up from the Base.

The XVth Brigade was made up of three Battalions: the British, the Dimitrov (volunteers from the Balkans), and the Franco-Belge (also called the Sixth of February). The Brigade Commander was Hungarian, Lt-Col. Gal, with Nathan as Chief-of-Staff. V. Copic, a Yugoslav, was Brigade Commissar until the third day of action when, after Gal had been promoted, he became Commander and Jean Bartel, a Frenchman, became Commissar, with Springhall as his assistant.

When the convoy of trucks carrying the British left Madrigueras, it was given a rousing send-off. The villagers – men, women and children – lined the street and shouted encouragement. There were even a few tears. From Albacete the journey was by rail to Villarrubia de Santiago and then on by truck to Chinchón where the sound of artillery fire gave an ominous warning of the fascist advance. The Brigaders were given a warm welcome and the villagers rounded up every egg to supplement the evening meal.

By 11 February the fascists had crossed the Jarama river, using the bridge on the small dirt road that ran from San Martín de la Vega to Morata de Tajuña. They had taken some of the commanding heights on the last ridge before the Tajuña Valley, and their way was open to the Valencia road. In the early morning of 12 February the British moved forward by truck from Chinchón to an area by a large farmhouse where the Madrid-Chinchón road crossed the smaller San Martín-Morata road. The San Martín road climbed for about a mile to a plateau, covered with olive trees, and then descended through broken hills and ridges to the Jarama river. The farmhouse and buildings around it became and remained cookhouse and rear headquarters throughout the long stay on the Jarama front.

The Battalion stopped at the farmhouse for bread and coffee, filled water-bottles, and checked their weapons. Gal then gave orders for the XVth Brigade to move up the hill towards San Martín with the Franco-Belges on the road and to its right, the British on the left of the road, and the Dimitrovs in reserve. No one knew what troops were on the left flank of the British. Cavalry were supposed to move up, but it was discovered much later that there were no troops: the British left flank was open. There were no maps, not even at Battalion level. No one knew the exact position of the enemy.

The three rifle companies moved forward in open order, scrambling up the rocky escarpment onto and across the plateau, across a dry valley and onto the next ridge of hills where they could see the broken terrain leading down to the Jarama river itself. They had advanced more than two miles, but as they moved down the slopes they came under heavy rifle and machine-gun fire. The fascists were much further forward than had been realized and the advanced British groups withdrew a little to the crest of what justly became known as 'Suicide Hill', where they engaged the enemy. The Franco-Belges, advancing on the right, had come under heavy pressure and had withdrawn, leaving a detached knoll by the San Martín road unoccupied. This was especially grim for the British, since the Moors who occupied it could enfilade the riflemen on Suicide Hill and give cover to any advance towards the plateau.

However, the three British rifle companies were fighting grimly, taking toll of the enemy, firing at every target often until their rifles were too hot to hold. Despite the shock of being plunged at once into heavy action, morale was high, jokes were made, and the treachery of 'Non-Intervention' was cursed.

No. 2 Machine-Gun Company, commanded by Fry, manhandled its heavy Maxims, mounted on iron-wheeled carriages, up the rocky slopes to the plateau, only to find their belts filled with the wrong ammunition. The Battalion armourer, returning from Morata with belts filled with the correct ammunition, had overturned the lorry.

Wintringham withdrew the useless Maxims to the rear under guard, and placed the Company, with rifles, on the

forward edge of the plateau to keep down the enfilading fire
from the Moors on the knoll.

The three rifle companies came under continuous heavy
fire, with the German heavy machine-guns hosing their
positions, inflicting heavy casualties. No. 1 Company, on the
right, was on a bare hill with a slight saddle between it and
Nos 3 and 4 Companies on 'Suicide Hill'. They faced heavy
frontal and enfilading fire from their right and near rear from
the knoll and from the high ground where the Franco-Belge
Battalion had been pushed back. Conway, experienced fighter
from the Madrid and Córdoba front, had taken over
command of No. 1 Company a few days before when
Cunningham went down with a fever. He and the Company
Commissar, Ralph Campeau, from London, were fatally
wounded. Campeau, wounded in the front line, was being
carried to the rear on a stretcher when a burst of machine-gun
fire killed him. Bill Briskey, a leader of the London's Busmen's
Rank and File movement, No. 3 Company Commander, was
killed, and Ken Stalker (a Scot but also from London), who
took over, was killed soon after.

Section commanders were wounded and killed. Though
someone always took on responsibility and command, the loss
of so many of the best leaders was very serious. All was not
well either in No. 4 Company who were in the centre on
'Suicide Hill'. Bert Overton, from Stockton, had been chosen
as Company Commander in Madrigueras because of his
Officer Training Corps experience; but in the middle of the
afternoon his nerve broke and he left the Company without
orders. Returning to Fry on the plateau behind, he remained
there for some time until Fry persuaded him to return to No. 4
Company.

The British casualties were mounting continuously, and the
Moors and the Foreign Legion were infiltrating ever closer,
using the broken ground. The order was given to the remnants
of the three rifle companies to retire to the plateau using a belt
of olive trees on the left as a screen.

They made an orderly withdrawal, bringing all the
wounded with them, while Sam Wild, a labourer from

Manchester who had served in the navy, and a small group covered the retreat across the dry valley.

Seeing the ridge was empty, the fascist troops rushed the top in large numbers and then moved down into the valley, thinking that the impetus of their charge would take them onto the plateau. However Fry, aided by Copeman, had now got his machine-gun belts filled and his guns well placed, and had so far held fire. As the Moorish soldiers screamed forwards, all eight guns opened up at short range with devastating effect, and the charge turned into a rout.

For seven hours, despite heavy losses, the British had held off a powerful attack by very much larger and better-equipped forces. Their fierce resistance had prevented the enemy from discovering that the front was completely open on the left, without Republican troops at all.

The remnants of the British companies made their way back, often without cohesion or a clear idea of where they were going. Wintringham had established his HQ on a track through the olive groves, a hundred yards back from the plateau crest. It was called the 'Sunken Road' because 150 yards of it was two or three feet below the level of the olive groves and gave some cover, besides being a useful landmark. Here it was possible to begin collecting and reorganizing what was left of the Battalion after the day's action. Two rifle company commanders were dead (Kit Conway – veteran of No. 1 Company at Lopera – and Bill Briskey), and the nerves of another (Overton) were shattered. Out of the 400 men in the rifle companies, only 125 were left. Altogether less than half the Battalion remained. Among those killed were Christopher Caudwell (St John Sprigg), the outstanding Marxist intellectual and Communist who had insisted on going to Spain, Clem Beckett, the world-famous speedway driver from Manchester, and Clifford Lawther, a miner from Durham. M. Davidovitch, from London, after leading the very busy stretcher-bearers, often working under heavy fire, was killed while carrying away yet another wounded comrade.

Food and drink, the first since early morning, ammunition and a few picks and shovels were brought up from the rear by

Josh Francis, from Reading, the Battalion Quartermaster. Sleep was brief, deep but troubled. Everyone knew that the attack would begin again at dawn.

Wintringham prepared his depleted forces. He left the No. 2 Machine-Gun Company in its forward position, the only place where it had a field of fire. To protect it against infiltration through the broken, dead ground on its immediate right, Overton's Company was placed on the same front only a hundred yards away. André Diamint, an Anglicized Egyptian, took over command of No. 1 Company facing the open left flank.

Stand-to was at 3 a.m., the cookhouse and the Quartermaster's staff arriving just before with hot food and drink. Then, as darkness lifted, Fry saw that another fascist unit had moved up in the night and was resting unsuspectingly in close formation in the valley between his guns and 'Suicide Hill'. All Fry's Maxims now opened up with a terrific barrage at short range, and the whole enemy force broke and ran back, leaving the valley littered with bodies.

It took some hours before the fascists could prepare another attack. But on the Battalion's right the Franco-Belges, now reinforced by the Dimitrovs, had been pushed further back with heavy losses, leaving the British flank even more exposed and enfiladed. The Battalion was surrounded on three sides, open to heavy fire from rifles, machine-guns and artillery, and to infiltration.

Then without orders Overton withdrew his company to the 'Sunken Road', leaving Fry's No. 2 Machine-Gun Company without support or flank protection.

There are two versions of subsequent events. One repeated in several accounts is that given by Bill Meredith, from Glasgow, Commissar of the Machine-Gun Company. He was a hundred yards behind his company positions, in the olive groves, returning from Battalion Headquarters, when he saw a party of fascists approaching the position singing the *Internationale* and giving the anti-fascist salute. The British, thinking it was a mass desertion, did not fire but raised their fists in welcome. The fascists then took thirty prisoners, shooting Ted Dickinson, from London, second-in command of the Company out of hand. The others were marched to the rear, two others being shot on the way to San Martín.

According to the other story, told by George Leeson, a railway clerk from London, and Don Renton, an unemployed worker from Edinburgh, who were taken prisoner, the Foreign Legion, who had relieved the Moors after their heavy losses, had infiltrated through the broken, dead ground and appeared right on top of the machine-gun positions. This had been made possible by Overton's withdrawal of his company. 'Yank' Levy, a rather excitable Canadian, then shouted, 'They are ours.' His mistake was not unreasonable, because of the similarity of the Foreign Legion and Republican uniforms, and the confused position. Then, in the harsh realization of their capture, the British machine-gunners sang the *Internationale*.

A study of the ground shows this account to be very probable.

When Overton saw the dreadful result of his unauthorized withdrawal he tried to make amends by leading the forty men left in his company in a bayonet charge on the captured position. Only six returned from the attack. Later that night Overton panicked again, was wounded, and left the front.

Meanwhile, Wintringham had been wounded and was taken off to the rear and to hospital. Aitken, the Battalion Political Commissar, took over command. Then Cunningham reappeared, having 'escaped' from hospital, and brought new heart and confidence. That night with only about 160 men left of the Battalion's original 500, all dead-tired, hungry and thirsty, a defensive position was organized along the 'Sunken Road'.

The next day, 14 February, the third in this unequal struggle, a fresh fascist Brigade attacked. Tanks and infantry penetrated the Battalion positions and were able to enfilade the road. Without anti-tank weapons the few could not withstand the intense fire and heavy casualties. The line broke at last and the few small groups that remained trickled back down the slope to the Chinchón road and the Battalion cookhouse.

The fascist offensive, checked for three days, was again on the verge of success. Nothing stood between it and the valley with the vital road link to Valencia.

Cunningham and Ryan then began to collect the small groups along the road. There was some hot soup. Gal, Brigade Commander, arrived and told them of the vital gap in the front. The exhausted and shattered group, now about 140 strong, said they would go back to plug it. Then, in formation, they marched up the San Martín road itself, towards the positions they had left. Others from broken units, Spanish, French and others fell in behind, swelling the numbers. Ryan, experienced in leading banned demonstrations in Ireland, started singing. All joined in, marching together to the ridge where they had been routed. The fascists, apparently surprised and alarmed at this body of men singing and marching to their positions, fell back in the growing dusk from the ridge to their earlier positions. That night the Republican line was strengthened; new units moved in on the left and right. The British had filled the gap: the Madrid-Valencia road was not cut.

Though there was to be more bitter fighting and minor changes of position in this front, the positions taken up by the British Brigaders and their allies in this great recovery remained unchanged and intact until the very last days of the war. Even then these positions did not fall by assault.

In the three days of bloody struggle, from 12 to 14 February 1937, the fighting units had stood up to devastating odds and unprecedented strain. The Battalion services had also proved themselves. The stretcher-bearers and medical orderlies, nearly all without experience, could proudly claim that no wounded comrade had been left behind. Carrying the wounded down escarpments called on every scrap of strength and endurance. When no more stretchers were available, the wounded were carried on blankets or shoulders to the First Aid Post. The Battalion Medical Officer, Colin Bradsworth, a doctor from Birmingham, worked almost continuously, day and night, until he himself was wounded. He dressed the light wounds and did everything possible to ease the condition of the serious cases before evacuation.

A number of British wounded were fortunate: they were taken to a temporary hospital set up in Villarejo de Salvanes, ten miles from Morata. Here two doctors, Alex Tudor-Hart, from London, and Reggie Saxton, from Reading, helped by others from the medical services, using a commandeered hotel bar as a theatre, operated continuously as the wounded flooded in from the whole Jarama front.

The Battalion cookhouse and Quartermaster's staff did well, getting supplies of food, water and ammunition to the front, often under fire, often unsure of the exact positions and in danger of wandering into the arms of the enemy. There were no insulated containers so the food was cold. Because of the casualties there were ample rations, though there were always those unable to contact the truck.

Ernest Mahoney, manager of a left-wing bookshop in Marchmont Street, London, the Battalion postmaster, got to the front lines with letters and papers on the second day of the battle. All too many were not there to collect their mail.

Though the Battalion was later involved in even more bloody encounters, Jarama was its first major trial. The facts show that it came through with a record of individual grit, courage and determination which set standards for all its future fighting.

On 15 February Gal was promoted to command a Division, and the XVth Brigade, in which the British remained throughout the war, was taken over by Lt-Col. Čopíc, a Yugoslav who had fought in the First World War and had then been deeply involved in the revolutionary, anti-fascist struggles in the Balkans.

Nathan, after differences with Gal, left the XVth Brigade and went to the XIVth subsequently returning as Chief-of-Staff of the XVth Brigade for the Brunete offensive. Springhall was wounded on 27 February, helping the Lincoln Battalion in a costly but abortive attack. Soon after, he and Kerrigan were recalled to Britain. Bill Paynter, a leader of the South

Wales Miners and of the unemployed, was asked, and agreed, to go to Spain and take over as Base Commissar at Albacete. Aitken was promoted to become Political Commissar of the whole XVth Brigade. Bert Williams, a Welsh ex-miner and Communist leader in the Midlands, replaced Aitken as Political Commissar of the Battalion. Copeman returned to the Battalion from hospital and was made second-in-command to Cunningham.

The American Abraham Lincoln Battalion (sometimes mistakenly referred to as the Lincoln Brigade) was hurried from its training base, reaching the front on 16 February. In its first action on 23 February, its No. 1 Company was commanded by Inver Marlow, known in Spain as John Scott, a Londoner, working as correspondent for the *New York Daily Worker*, who went to Spain with the Americans and remained with them. He was killed going over the top in his first attack.

Troops commanded by Enrique Líster moved to fill the gap to the left of the Brigade. Other Spanish units reinforced and stiffened the whole sector. The British strength was made up by eighty-five reinforcements from Madrigueras, some of whom had been left behind when the Battalion moved to the front, others being recent arrivals from Britain. As less seriously wounded men recovered, they made their way back from hospital to build up the Battalion's strength. The XVth Brigade was further strengthened by the inclusion of a Battalion of Spanish volunteers.

The intense fascist drive to break through on the Jarama sector dwindled and petered out after the great recovery on 14 February over the Madrid-Valencia road. But the fighting did not end. There were patrols, probing attacks and attempts to improve the position of the lines by both Republicans and fascists. However, as both sides dug in and fortified their positions, major changes became more difficult.

On 27 February 1937 the XVth Brigade was ordered to attack towards the fascist lines. It was a disastrous move since air and artillery support did not materialize. The British were only able to move a few yards forward from their trenches before being pinned down by a curtain of machine-gun fire. The Lincolns, in their first major action, advanced several hundred yards. They paid a terrible price, losing 127 dead and more than 200 wounded, before the casualties, darkness and pouring rain compelled them to retreat. Springhall and George Wattis, an ex-army man from Stockport, went up to the Lincolns from Brigade Staff and went over the top with them. Springhall was lucky: a bullet passed through his jaw-bone without doing any major damage. The only thing which can be said for this tragic attack is that the fascist High Command knew henceforth that this key sector was still held by brave, determined troops.

Life in the trenches was grim and monotonous, especially when March and April brought heavy, cold rains which flooded the trenches and dugouts, soaked clothes and blankets, and muddied the weapons. There were guard duties, stand-to, sniping and mortaring. There was still danger.

In early June the British-manned Anti-Tank Battery of the XVth Brigade moved into the sector. The capability of its 37mm guns was shown when, using very high velocity shells, it knocked out troublesome enemy machine-gun nests.

Efforts were made to improve conditions. The path to the cookhouse was improved. Hot food became more frequent. Clean clothes were made available, and opportunities for washing were provided in the dead ground behind the lines. Political and cultural activities were organized. Company and Battalion newspapers displayed on the trench sides gave news and gossip; newspapers and mail began to arrive fairly regularly. Meetings and discussions were held. On 12 May the Irish in the Brigade, together with representatives of all the other nationalities, met to commemorate James Connolly's death. On sunny days football was played in the olive groves behind the lines.

These extracts from the Battalion diary, probably written by Aitken, give a picture of a week's life there: its dangers, its tensions, and the resilience of men in adapting to their circumstances.

Sunday. Slept in. First time for breakfast cigarettes and chocolates – English. Angus brought and distributed American fags. Comrades reading contentedly.

Monday. Lectured Diamint, our new Quartermaster, on the importance of his job. Reprimand two drunks. Wrote home. Telegram received from prominent labour leaders.

Tuesday. Everybody in unusually good spirits today and turned out smartly. Had a visit from the Editor of *New Masses* and four other Americans. Cde Copeman and 6 others rejoin from hospital.

Wednesday. Raining. Met Japanese acquaintance. Visit of Spender the poet. Anthony Yates brought in along with another cde who could not be identified as he had been laying out there too long. Front very quiet. Mild morning, very little shooting. Shells dropping close to our lines. Select 4 men for the Tank Corps – to be transferred later. Five of the enemy surrendered. Reported that the enemy was weak but preparing to attack. Our men are all ready and anxious.

Thursday. Two cdes come over from fascist lines. More ready to come over. Collections for Spanish Red Aid. Consignment of cigarettes, books, lighters etc.

Friday. Wet night. English tea. Aeroplanes soaring over. Selling cigarettes. Spanish boy of 15 in the trenches. He said he was 17. Very cold and wintry. Cde Tommy Gibbons handed in 1,210 pesetas collected from No. 1 Coy on behalf of Socorro Rojo International [International Red Aid].

There was general grumbling and concern at the long seventy-three days in the line. Protests were made to Brigade headquarters, and Pollitt and Gallacher even took up the question with the most influential military and political people in Madrid, pressing for their Brigade's relief. There may have been two factors in the decision to keep the British and the Brigade so long in the line. The Government was reluctant to move one of its best Brigades when a fascist push of a few hundred yards would have meant disaster for Madrid and while the main Republican forces were still being built up in the rear.

In addition this was a period of debate and differences inside the Government about the role of the International Brigades – whether to treat them as a Foreign Legion or bring them up to strength with Spanish troops as part of the army. Despite general complaints and grumblings, the Brigades accepted their responsibilities and their long vigil.

In early March the British had four days out of the line, but only in Morata, three miles from the front. Showers, delousing, and some wine and sleep worked wonders. Aitken called a Battalion meeting where everyone poured out their problems, criticisms and their opinions of conduct in the great battle. This clearing of the air was useful, and spirits rose higher when Pollitt arrived unexpectedly. After a short meeting in the church, all marched round the village singing the *Internationale*, with Pollitt carried shoulder high.

There was always a close bond between Pollitt and the British volunteers. Everyone knew of his efforts to force the British Government and the labour movement to end the deceit of 'Non-Intervention' which gave Franco the help he needed. He was sensitive to the moods of the men, offering no demagogic speeches but a frank, sometimes brutal explanation of the situation and the heavy responsibilities facing the Brigaders. On all his visits a brown leather bag was packed with letters from home; every query, message or problem raised with him was noted and scrupulously followed up on his return to Britain.

Several writers have tried to portray Pollitt as a 'bogeyman' of the period, not even bothering to check details of his appearance and style, and painting absurd pictures of the man. A more serious and often repeated accusation is that Pollitt was not interested in the well-being of the British volunteers, especially sending intellectuals to their deaths in Spain, saying 'Go and get killed – the movement needs a few martyrs'. However no one has ever produced a scrap of evidence for such a statement and attitude, and the reality was the exact opposite – Pollitt's active concern for the life and well-being of every volunteer.

Besides helping the Battalion to get all possible arms, food and extras, he argued, whenever he spoke to the volunteers, against 'I'm-as-brave-as-anyone' exhibitionism, urged digging in, and agitated for the repatriation of the wounded and those with long service. He said that intellectuals could not be discriminated against and should be allowed to volunteer for fighting; but when shown the unique qualities of Christopher Caudwell, Pollitt wired Albacete for his immediate return, though the message arrived too late. He also personally tried, without success, to convince David Guest that he could make a better contribution to socialism as a mathematician than as a soldier.

In this period in the Jarama trenches, the Battalion was also visited by William Gallacher, Communist MP for West Fife, Ted Bramley, who had replaced Springhall as London District Secretary of the Communist Party, and H.N. Brailsford, the socialist journalist and writer who was a firm supporter of the Republic. Haldane came out again, using his stay to study the effects of bombing, and joining in with his revolver in the trenches one night when there was a brisk exchange of fire.

The British responded to their long stay at the front and their very brief periods of leave with characteristic good-humoured cynicism, while continuing to do their job. This spirit was summed up in a song by Alex McDade, an ex-Army man from Glasgow, later killed at Brunete. The song, sung to the tune of 'Red River Valley', became popular throughout the XVth Brigade and was sung in several versions, a less ironic one becoming popular at support meetings in Britain and the United States.

> There's a valley in Spain called Jarama,
>   That's a place that we all know so well,
> For 'tis there that we wasted our manhood,
>   And most of our old age as well.

From this valley they tell us we're leaving,
But don't hasten to bid us adieu,
For e'en though we make our departure,
We'll be back in an hour or two.

Oh we're proud of the British Battalion,
And the marathon record it's made,
Please do us this little favour,
And take this last word to Brigade.

You will never be happy with strangers,
They would not understand you as we,
So remember the Jarama Valley
And the old men who wait patiently.

In April there was another brief respite from the trenches, in Alcalá de Henares, with a welcome rest, clean up, and relaxation. Here a Battalion meeting was held to discuss the behaviour of Overton in the crucial days of battle. Williams, Battalion Commissar, was in the chair and Aitken outlined Overton's behaviour at the front (Overton himself was not present). It was not a 'court martial'; all were allowed to speak. Feelings ran high, with many fierce denunciations of his behaviour, which had led to many losses and threatened the whole outcome of the battle. At Brigade HQ later, Overton was court-martialled and charged with desertion in the face of the enemy and with promoting himself from Sergeant to Captain, and drawing Captain's pay in hospital. Sentenced to service in a labour battalion, he went up with the Brigade to the Brunete front a week later and was killed by a shell while carrying munitions to a forward position.

Early in May 1937 news reached the front of the fighting in the streets of Barcelona between supporters of the POUM, aided by some Anarchists, on the one hand, and Government forces on the other. The POUM, who had always been hostile to unity, talked of 'beginning the struggle for working-class power'.

The news of the fighting was greeted with incredulity, consternation and then extreme anger by the International

Brigaders. No supporters of the Popular Front Government could conceive of raising the slogan of 'socialist revolution' when that Government was fighting for its life against international fascism, the power of whose war-machine was a harsh reality a couple of hundred yards across no-man's-land. The anger in the Brigade against those who fought the Republic in the rear was sharpened by reports of weapons, even tanks, being kept from the front and hidden for treacherous purposes.

It was known that the British group sent out by the Independent Labour Party had left the Aragon front and was in Barcelona, so Walter Tapsell was sent there from Albacete to try to extricate it from its link with POUM.

The ILP group was originally about forty strong. Some were supporters of the ILP, but others were on their way to join the International Brigades and had found themselves in this group by chance.

The group had been with a POUM regiment on the Huesca front, where its numbers dwindled to some twenty. There was discontent among them, and eight of the group, including Eric Blair (George Orwell), indicated that they wanted to join the International Brigades. They arrived on leave in Barcelona on 26 April. It appears that none of the group took an actual part in the uprising, but they did provide an armed guard for the POUM headquarters and were shocked and bewildered by the events. Four of the group, a Welsh miner, a docker, a lorry driver and a labourer, walked out of the POUM hotel, and later joined and fought with a Spanish Republican Battalion. Tapsell discussed with John McNair, an ILP member and the leading political figure, how the whole group could join the British Battalion. McNair expressed fears of resentment about the group's involvement with POUM and that it might be sent into dangerous positions. A further meeting was arranged but McNair did not turn up. Shortly afterwards the remnants of the ILP group returned to Britain.

Finally on 17 June the British Battalion's long ordeal at the Jarama front ended, and newly formed Spanish units took over the front. The XVth Brigade was withdrawn to the area of the Tajuña valley, about thirty miles from Madrid, but with good road links which could have taken it quickly back to the front. The Brigade Headquarters was in a flour-mill on the river at Ambite. The Anti-Tank Battery was a mile away, also quartered in a small mill, on a river island – a soothing environment after the rigours of the front.

The British Battalion was in Mondéjar, a small, dusty village on the plateau above the river, with cafés around the square and the inevitable dominating church. Some wine was still available, and occasionally delicacies like an egg or an omelette. Weapons were cleaned, clothes washed, and new clothes were issued. Sleep was under cover, in schools, barns, and anywhere else that could be found. Nearly everyone went, in small groups, for a couple of days leave in Madrid where, despite intermittent shelling, there was entertainment, beds with sheets, and variety of food. However all was not rest. Everyone knew that more action could not be far away; consolidation, organization and training went on.

Chapter 9
The British Help to Stop a Gap

In the middle of March 1937 British volunteers went into action again to deal with an emergency on the Southern Front. The fascists made a push to the north west of Córdoba and advanced some thirty miles towards Pozoblanco. Their aim was to open up the route to the important mercury mines at Almadén. They also hoped an advance in the South would draw attention away from their recent dramatic defeat at Guadalajara earlier that month, when units of Mussolini's regular army, trying to encircle Madrid from the east, had been smashed by Republican forces which included Italians in the Garibaldi International Brigade, and Soviet-built fighter planes.

In the South the fascist advance had been checked near Pozoblanco by a Republican counter-attack; however, the position was uncertain and the front very fluid. In Albacete an International Battalion, the XXth, was hastily assembled. The 86th Mixed Brigade was formed from the XXth and two Spanish Battalions – Pablo Iglesias and Carabineros.

About sixty British – a combination of recent arrivals from Britain and some wounded volunteers who considered themselves fit – were formed into a section of No. 2 Anglo-American Company. The others in the Company were a United States Section and a Spanish-American Section (Cubans, Mexicans and Puerto Ricans). The remainder of the XXth Battalion was made up of Germans, Austrians, French, Poles and Czechs together with a few Finns and Swedes. The

Fighting on Pozoblanco sector

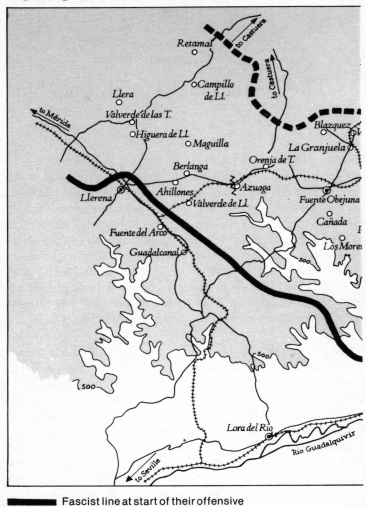

████████ Fascist line at start of their offensive
■ ■ ■ ■ Fascist line when offensive halted

5. The Fighting on the Pozoblanco Sector, March 1937

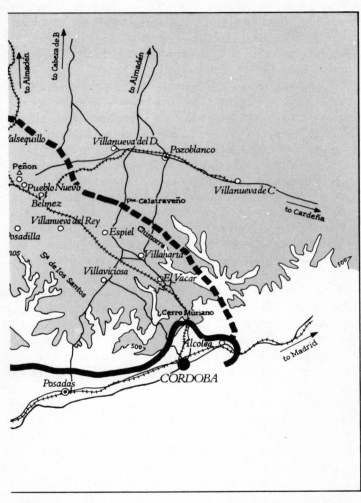

Height above 500 metres   Scale: 1 cm to 10 kms.

medley of languages created difficulties: Peter Daly, a labourer from Enniscorthy in Eire, who had been a sergeant in the British Army, had served in the IRA, and been wounded on the fourth day of Jarama, commanded the Spanish-American Section and said he needed three interpreters to give and receive orders. However, the Battalion was well clothed, and equipped with Soviet rifles.

No. 2 Company was first commanded by Bob Traill, a Londoner and a university-educated linguist who had been working in Moscow. It is not known if he had any military training or experience. He was subsequently appointed to the Command of the XXth Battalion, and later to Brigade Staff, where he went very reluctantly, protesting that he did not wish to be 'thought yellow' by leaving a rifle company. When the Company went into action it was commanded by Roland Dart, with John Gates as Commissar (both Americans). The XXth Battalion was commanded by Morandi, an admired and trusted Italian who had been Chief of Brigade Staff when No. 1 Company had fought at Lopera, and who was nicknamed 'The Fox'.

The Battalion left Albacete on 20 March without any official send-off. When it arrived at Pozoblanco, the town was empty, having been heavily bombed. The Battalion's train moved cautiously forward for some miles, but there was no contact with the enemy. The Battalion detrained and the British section was sent forward on patrol, again making no contact with the enemy.

The Battalion then returned to Pozoblanco and there heard that the Republican forces were attacking on the Almadén front. Morandi and Traill devised the plan of advancing by train along the single track railway towards Peñarroya. Morandi was on the footplate of a pilot engine, which unfortunately emitted great plumes of black smoke. A hundred years behind followed the train with the entire Battalion, rifles and machine-guns at the ready.

Emerging from a cutting a few miles short of Peñarroya the train came under artillery fire. Both train and pilot engine quickly reversed to the safety of the cutting and the Battalion deployed at the foot of an enemy held height which came to be called 'El Terrible'.

The Anglo-American Company was then moved off to the 3,000 feet high Sierra de Chimorra, where Moorish troops held the dominating heights. Life was grim, with torrential rain nearly every day. The terrain was so rocky that it was impossible to dig safe fox-holes. There was incessant sniping from the Moors four or five hundred yards away and there were night attacks. On 18 April, a day of mist and rain, there was a heavy two-hour-long barrage of artillery and mortar fire, which caused casualties in the shallow slit-trenches.

Daly and O'Daire had been promoted to the rank of lieutenant for their capable military leadership and combative spirit. They and the other experienced fighters from Lopera – Joe Monks from Dublin, and Frank Edwards from Waterford – knew there would be an assault when the barrage stopped. When it came everyone was ready. Resistance was fierce, and the action included some hand-to-hand fighting. Bert Neville, the now fifty-four-year old London taxi-driver, distinguished himself alongside the others. Nevertheless, the Company was finally forced out of its positions, with O'Daire steadying the retreat, and formed a new line at a lower level. O'Daire reconnoitred in the dusk and, realizing that the new positions would be untenable in the daylight, organized a counter-attack that night. Helped by a mist, and by Spanish reinforcements, the remnants of No. 2 Company retook its former position, capturing arms and ammunition.

No. 2 Company was then moved to a different sector, north of the Pozoblanco-Peñarroya road and railway, near the village of Blázquez. Here the situation was not at all to its liking as there was an unofficial armistice, which in the circumstances benefited the fascists. There was no fighting and three men from a Spanish Republican Battalion met three from the fascist force in no-man's land, talked and exchanged newspapers.

No. 2 Company attempted to advance towards Fuente Obéjuna, a strategically useful road and rail intersection. O'Daire led a fighting patrol forward but the fascists were alerted, the promised support and reinforcements did not materialize, and the attack was called off.

Meanwhile the English speakers in the XXth Battalion had sent a letter, signed by the thirty odd left out of the original ninety-two, to the Albacete Base asking to rejoin their own national Battalions.

Paynter, then British Base Commissar, finally obtained agreement for their return. He had to make two trips to the front before Morandi, who had been promoted to command the 86th Brigade, received a replacement of German volunteers. Only then did Morandi agree to the release of the English speakers who travelled back with Paynter.

The Anglo-Saxons were given a rousing send-off by the rest of the Battalion. They were equipped with new clean clothes, and many tributes were made to their high morale and fighting qualities.

In Albacete the group were sent on a short leave. Daly and O'Daire went on longer leave to the coast; Monks and Edwards were sent home to Ireland. Traill subsequently became second-in-command of the newly-formed second American Battalion, the Washington, and was killed that July leading it in the assault on Villanueva de la Cañada, near Brunete.

The Anglo-American group had shown not only outstanding fighting abilities but how men of differing languages and nationalities but with common ideals could cooperate.

Chapter 10

The Furnace of Brunete

After the May events in Barcelona in 1937, Largo Caballero resigned his positions as Prime Minister and War Minister. Juan Negrín, another Socialist, became Prime Minister, and Indalecio Prieto took over the War Ministry. Renewed efforts were made to speed up the organization in the war industries. In June the leaders of the Socialist and Communist Internationals met near Geneva and discussed the need for united actions to help Spain. All this led to improved morale and confidence throughout the Republic.

After a mere two weeks' rest and reorganization, the whole XVth Brigade was, with a minimum of warning, moved from its quarters in the Tajuña valley. It travelled at night by truck, by-passing Madrid, to be hidden in the woods near Torrelodones on the Madrid-El Escorial road. The convoy passed many other groups of men, artillery and tanks, all on the move in the same direction with reasonable arms and equipment. The 'old sweats' contrasted this large-scale mobilization with the situation when they seemed to be the only troops moving to Chinchón to stop the fascist drive at Jarama the previous February. Everyone could see that the Government had, in the respite, been able to organize, train and equip many new units. The realization that it was now able to mount an offensive encouraged everyone.

The XVth Brigade was still commanded by Čopíc; but Aitken had been promoted to become Brigade Political Commissar. Nathan had returned from the XIVth Brigade to become Chief of Operations. There were now six Battalions. The British, the Lincolns, and the newly-arrived Washington Battalion of Americans, who had had some weeks' training, formed one regiment of the Brigade, which was commanded by Cunningham, recently promoted Major. The Franco-Belge, the Dimitrovs and the XXIVth Spanish Battalion formed the second regiment. Besides the usual supporting services, the Brigade now had its own British Anti-Tank Battery with Malcolm Dunbar, a veteran of Jarama, in command and Hugh Slater as Political Commissar.

The Brigade was at its highest in numbers. A number of British held jobs on the Brigade Staff. Jim Ruskin was Brigade interpreter, as unflappable when translating in several languages as he was under fire. His family were White Russian, and Jim had worked as a communications technician in Spain, France and the Argentine. He was invaluable in the 'Tower of Babel' at the headquarters until it was realized that his technical expertise was even more valuable in Brigade Transmissions. George Wattis, who had seen sixteen years Regular Army service, was responsible for ammunition and supplies of all kinds, a job which demanded considerable scrounging and improvisation since there were shortages of everything. Bee was responsible for mapping, also an important responsibility, since in the Brunete action he had to draw up original maps as there were none at Battalion level.

Steps were taken to strengthen the leadership militarily and politically. Copeman and Williams became respectively British Battalion Commander and Commissar. George Brown (leader of the Manchester Communists and a member of the Party's Central Committee), who had been working in the office of the International Brigade in Madrid, achieved his wish to join the Battalion, becoming a Company Commissar. Walter Tapsell, a tough, experienced political organizer, who had been working at the Base and in Barcelona, also joined, at first in the ranks. Charles Goodfellow, a miner from Bellshill, held in high regard for his coolness under fire at Jarama, was appointed second-in-command of the Battalion. In addition, as veterans from Córdoba and Jarama recovered from their wounds, the companies were reinforced by tried and experienced men, like Masters, veteran of the Thaelmanns in Aragon.

The Government offensive had two aims: to draw some of Franco's forces from the North, where the brave but badly-led and ill-equipped Asturian forces faced defeat by the very powerful fascist forces encircling them; and to cut off the deep fascist salient, which reached into the Madrid suburbs and even the city itself, and thus relieve the threat to the capital. The main force was to strike south from the slopes of the Sierra Guadarrama, north-west of Madrid, to meet another advance to be launched from Villaverde, a southern suburb of the city. The plan was bold and imaginative. However, in hindsight, and considering the level of training and the reserves available to the Government, it was clearly over-ambitious.

The attack northwards from Villaverde made no headway at all, leaving the whole weight of the offensive to the forces from the north-west which included the International Brigades.

The attack began before dawn on 6 July and achieved initial surprise. The British Battalion and the Anti-Tank Battery were in reserve at first, and watched from the hills as the advancing columns of men, tanks and cavalry moved across the plain below. It seemed a flat, brown terrain with the rivers Aulencia and Guadarrama marked by brilliant green willows along their banks, and the villages on the plain, Villanueva de la Cañada and Brunete, standing out clearly in the bright morning sun. But things soon began to go wrong and mistakes were made.

A Spanish unit supported by tanks failed to take the key village of Villanueva. The XVth Brigade, which was to have by-passed it and marched quickly to take the heights beyond, overlooking Romanillos, was ordered to take it instead. The troops moving down from the hills across the plain quickly realized the vicious character of the terrain – dry sandy soil cut into ravines and deep gulleys, with no cover except the willows fringing the streams. The fields were covered with dry

The Brunete Offensive

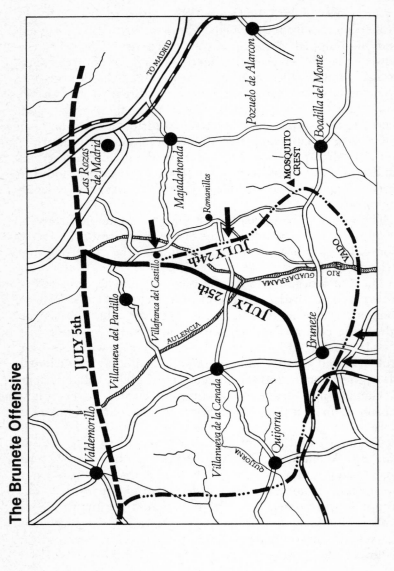

Scale: 1cm to 1km

➤ Direction of Main Fascist Counter-Attacks

TO MADRID

Pozuelo de Alarcon

Boadilla del Monte

Las Rozas de Madrid

Majadahonda

Romanillos

▲ MOSQUITO CREST

VADO

JULY 5th

Villanueva del Pardillo

Villafranca del Castillo

JULY 24th

RIO GUADARRAMA

JULY 25th

AULENCIA

Brunete

Valdemorillo

Villanueva de la Cañada

QUIJORNA

Quijorna

grass and stubble easily set alight by bombs and shells. The heat was exhausting, with temperatures over 100°F for more than twelve hours every day. The Brigaders were not prepared for this, and in the first few miles, blankets, gas-masks (they were not carried after this battle) and even tins of food were dropped to reduce exhaustion. Water-bottles were drained in the first couple of hours. A price was paid in extreme thirst and hunger for this lack of training and control before they even came under fire.

The fascists had made a strong defence round Villanueva with pill-boxes, and machine-gun posts in buildings and in the square stone church-tower. The fighting was confused. With the six Battalions of the XVth Brigade were elements of the Spanish Brigade which had failed to take the village. Casualties began to mount as the Battalions edged forward. The Brigade did not use the Anti-Tank Battery guns, which could have easily demolished the enemy machine-guns. The British were ordered to encircle Villanueva, cut the Brunete road, and then advance towards the church. At dusk, using the ditches and broken ground on both sides of the road, they had got within a hundred yards of the first houses of the village but with the gun in the church-tower still enfilading them.

Suddenly, in the failing light, a group of women and children appeared on the road from the village and began to move towards the forward groups of the Battalion. For a few moments it seemed they were fleeing the fighting in the village. Then it was realized they had been forced to form a screen behind which a group of fascist soldiers were advancing with hand grenades and light machine-guns. Brown, Pat Murphy, a seaman from Cardiff, and the others in the forward positions were briefly deceived, but when the fascists opened fire and threw grenades there was fierce and confused fighting, in the course of which the fascists were almost wiped out, although at the inevitable cost of some of the women and children who were killed. There were several British casualties including Brown, the Company Commissar, who was wounded and then shot dead by a fascist officer. With the rout of this desperate sortie, the two Battalions of a Spanish Brigade, the Dimitrovs, the Lincolns and the British of the XVth Brigade made a general assault on the village in near darkness and mopped up the last groups of fascists.

That night the Brigade slept in and around Villanueva. The kitchen truck came up with food and drink, and ammunition. There was water, and the fascist quartermaster's stores contained all sorts of unaccustomed luxuries – even cheese and real coffee.

The Battalion had to be checked and reorganized since fifty men had been killed or wounded during the day. One Company Commander, Bill Meredith, from Bellingham, a member of the Northumberland Labour Party, and two Company Commissars – Brown and Bob Elliott, a councillor from Blyth – had been killed. The Battalion Secretary, Danny Gibbons from London – one of three brothers fighting in the Brigades – had been wounded. It was well into the morning before the Battalion began to advance towards its original objective – the heights beyond the Guadarrama River commanding the villages of Romanillos and Boadilla del Monte.

That morning Frank Graham, a student from Sunderland who had had to drop his studies through lack of funds, and who had been a scout and runner at Jarama, was acting as observer and scout for Cunningham at Brigade. He caught and mounted a white horse running loose near Villanueva, and rode well forward to the top of the ridge, called Mosquito, which was later to prove to be of crucial tactical importance. The area was unoccupied; there were no enemy troops there at all. However the Brigade Command did not react and rush up forces to take these key heights. Indeed the failure of the Republican Command effectively to exploit the successes and advances of the first day played a big part in the final defeat of the whole offensive.

Elsewhere the attack had gone well. The Brigades of the all-Spanish 11th Division, led by Enrique Lister, had taken Brunete and pushed well beyond it. However, in other sectors the same mistake had been made as at Villanueva: the advance had stopped at fascist strong-points and had not swept forward.

On the second day, which was even hotter than the first, the British moved up towards the Guadarrama river. There was no shade from the sun, or cover from enemy fire. The terrain became even more broken – the soft sandy soil had been eroded into steep gulleys in the winter rains. After a few skirmishes with small pockets of fascists, the Battalion pushed beyond the river, which then still had water in it.

That second day the Republicans tasted the fascist reaction to their offensive. As the British moved out, Villanueva was shelled by fascist artillery which had moved up in the night. On the first day the Republican Air Force dominated the skies but, by the second, German and Italian fighters and bombers had been brought down from the North.

From the third day onwards the fascist planes increasingly dominated the battlefield and the supply routes. The fascist High Command saw the very real threat to its whole position facing Madrid and rushed men and artillery from near and far to the theatened positions. Because of the disruption caused by the delay in capturing Villanueva de la Cañada, General Gal's Division, comprising the XIVth and XVth International Brigades, failed to carry through the original plan, and at the end of the second day the omens for Republican success were darkening.

That night the XVth Brigade made preparations to move forward to take the crucial Mosquito Ridge. All the Battalions had suffered severe losses and their remnants were spread over nearly two miles of front. The British were on the right in contact with Líster's Spanish troops who had moved forward from Brunete. The Washingtons, who had sustained heavy losses, were on the British left flank. Preparations for a further advance were made in extremely difficult circumstances; the broken ground made organization and contact very uncertain. Because of the fascist domination of the air and the open terrain, supplies could be moved only by night. Food and ammunition came up in restricted quantity, though water, of very dubious quality, could still be obtained from the

Guadarrama river. The fact that the evacuation of the wounded had to be left until after nightfall added to the emotional strain.

As part of the whole advance of the XVth Brigade, the British moved forward over broken ground where a series of dry ravines marked where a small water-course, the Vado, would flow to the Guadarrama after the winter rain. They came under rifle fire but still pushed on.

However, it became frighteningly obvious that Mosquito Ridge was now held in strength, from positions well dug in. The only positive feature about the Brunete terrain was that the soft sandy soil made digging-in fairly easy, in contrast to the rocks of Córdoba and parts of Jarama.

Besides troops, the fascists had moved artillery units of all calibres to the front. Holding the heights, they had good observation and brought every movement under accurate and deadly fire. The XVth Brigade had some artillery support and a few tanks, whose role was very limited because of the problems of supply and maintenance in forward positions.

In its advance towards the crest the Battalion came under a two-hour-long artillery barrage, pinning it down, claiming more casualties, and allowing more time for fascists reinforcement.

When Goodfellow, the Battalion Second-in-Command, was killed, Wild took his place until he was wounded two days later. Several secondary ridges were taken but only small groups got within a hundred yards of the crest. Pinned down by heavy machine-gun and rifle fire they were not strong enough to make a final assault. Mosquito Ridge was too firmly held.

In the following two days repeated attempts were made by the British, and along the front by the other Battalions, to take Mosquito Ridge. But the dwindling numbers of active fighters could not penetrate the hail of steel coming down from it.

It was a soldiers' battle since the broken ground, the loss of leading personnel, and enemy domination of air and communications made organized planning nearly impossible. Groups of men fought with incredible bravery in appalling conditions. The three guns of the British Anti-Tank Battery had been spaced out over a wide front to give support to various units. They proved extremely effective as the gun crews gained in experience. They knocked out several enemy tanks and their high velocity explosive shells were very effective against infantry who invariably advanced in groups. At one point, their main ammunition dump was threatened by a grass fire started by a shell. The crews rushed to put out the fire, and John Black, a miner and member of the Labour Party from Dover, the Battery Second-in-Command, was killed in the continuing barrage. However the ammunition was saved.

Conditions continued to deteriorate sharply. The effects of the intense heat grew, and the rivers dried up almost overnight; at first there were a few stagnant pools but they too dried up. Men scraped the dry river-bed and drank the liquid which seeped out. One man found a small pool; in it was a boot with a foot in it; he still drank his fill. The cookhouses had to be hidden in the ravines of the valley and every movement drew shells or aerial attack. Later they were taken back to the hills. Food could be brought only after dark by man or by mule and was always in inadequate quantities. Physical strength drained away with lack of food, water and sleep. However, Tapsell was able to report: 'We had very little sickness – only absolute and complete physical exhaustion.'

The fascists built up total air superiority. Flights of Italian bombers seemed perpetually aloft – only very rarely could Republican fighters engage them in battle. The black Italian Capronis and German Condor Legion Junkers and Heinkels roamed the front and all the rear areas, bombing and strafing any sign of movement – even a solitary truck on a dirt road. The fascist air attack claimed casualties all the time and inhibited the movement of troops and essential supplies. For the first time aircraft became the dominant factor in land fighting.

The medical services had learnt that early treatment and speedy evacuation saved lives and prevented complications. However, such evacuation was now hazardous and very difficult to organize. Casualties had to be carried by stretcher or by mule, often under fire, from the forward positions to the advanced dressing-station which had been established well forward – in Villanueva the first night, and then in a dugout in a gulley in the Guadarrama river bed. There Dr Sollenberger and a team of orderlies gave immediate attention. However, the post was often under artillery fire and suffered air attacks, and the evacuation of the seriously wounded to the main operating hospital in El Escorial came under heavy bombing. In one day, four ambulances taking wounded from the Brigade front were destroyed by bombing or strafing, and the medical services suffered many losses in personnel: Dr Sollenberger and two other brigade doctors were killed; stretcher-bearers and first-aid men suffered heavy casualties. All these factors drained the fighting effectiveness of the British and the whole of the XVth Brigade.

By 11 July, the sixth day of the offensive, the fascists had taken the initiative and counter-attacked all round the salient. They had concentrated many of their best troops, Moors, Foreign Legion and Navarrese, German tanks and many pieces of artillery of all calibres. After heavy bombardment their infantry moved forward, always in groups.

British Battalion machine-gunners and riflemen stopped the attack on the British sector of the front, though a few advanced groups had to withdraw. In this attack on the whole Brigade front, the Anti-Tank Battery carried out an invaluable role, pinning down advancing infantry groups and sending them scurrying back to their original positions.

On the night of 11 July the British, the Lincolns and the Washingtons were moved from the front line into reserve. But they were only a mile behind the front in the Guadarrama valley area itself, and were still harassed by shelling and bombing. However, life was not quite so grim: there was more food, some shade in the willows along the banks, and an occasional pool of water where deep grime could be washed off and sweat-hardened clothes rinsed. But even such meagre relaxation was dangerous. A naked man is a clear target and feels indescribably defenceless if there is overhead strafing.

Both American Battalions had sustained heavy losses; the

Washingtons had been heavily bombed in the open. They were therefore now formed into one Battalion, at first known as the Lincoln-Washington but soon simply as the Lincoln Battalion, from then on the only American Battalion in the International Brigades.

The Spanish units of the Republican Army who had taken over the Brigade positions were new and untried, and were commanded by inexperienced officers. They gave ground, and on the second night in reserve the British Battalions went into forward positions again.

The situation in the Battalion was serious. The numbers had been reduced to under 150, less than half its original strength. It had lost many experienced and capable leaders. Brigade sent Copeman away to rest in Mondéjar to recover from the strain. Williams' heart condition worsened and he had to leave the front. Hinks, veteran of the first group in Spain, became Commander, and Tapsell Battalion Commissar. There were difficulties in Brigade Headquarters. Čopíc had been wounded and Klaus, a German anti-fascist ex-First World War officer, took over. Cunningham was showing the effects of extreme strain and exhaustion. Bee, whose maps had helped considerably to maintain contact and cohesion among the Brigade, was wounded. The Lincolns were withdrawn from the Brigade front to plug a gap near Villanueva del Pardillo. All that remained of the XVth Brigade – small groups not substantial enough to be called battalions – were even more extended.

On 18 July the fascists mounted heavy counter-offensives in three vital sectors, aiming to pinch off the Republican gains. More than 300 of their planes were in the air at a time, and fascist sources say that more than 300 guns were firing at the key village of Brunete alone, blasting a way forward for six divisions of infantry. Líster's defending Spanish Brigades fought back with remarkable tenacity. They were forced out, but then fought their way back into the village.

The fate of Brunete was the key to the position of the British, who had been sent to the southern end of the Brigade front. Despite their ferocious resistance, the Lísters were forced out of Brunete again and had to fall back. This left the British in the most advanced positions in this sector. The Battalion's flanks were open, since some Spanish units had broken and retreated. Moreover the fascists had mustered even greater concentrations on the commanding ridge of Mosquito.

The British, then fewer than 100 men, had broken into two groups. Hinks was on the right, nearest Brunete, leading one group with machine-guns. By maintaining effective fire and conducting a controlled withdrawal, he was able to steady the fallback of the surrounding Spanish groups – they had ceased to be units – and to make organized retreat. Many soldiers from broken or disorganized units, seeing a nucleus of cohesion and order, joined this group.

Tapsell took command of the other remaining British group, on the slopes of the Vado, but, with no units on its flank and under heavy attack, it was forced to withdraw. In fact orders for the British withdrawal had been sent much earlier, when Brunete, at last, had fallen and the fascist advance threatened to cut off all troops beyond the Guadarrama river. However the orders never got through. Again, seeing the Tapsell group's orderly, fighting withdrawal, small groups of Spanish troops and International Brigaders, with two machine-guns, linked up with it. They fell back from crest to crest, fighting off repeated efforts by strong formations of Moorish troops to outflank them. The two British groups finally joined up behind the Guadarrama river, but now their numbers had been reduced by casualties to only forty-two men.

In these heavy counter-attacks against the Brigade positions, the Anti-Tank Battery had been in almost continuous action. Dunbar received a bullet-wound in the neck, and Slater took over command. Bill Alexander, an industrial chemist from Hampshire, became Political Commissar. The Anti-Tank Battery's guns were placed very far forward, on occasion in front of the infantry. Their high-velocity shells stopped and turned back troops and caused casualties in the attacking groups; and their fire had a steadying effect on the morale of their own troops fighting near them. Since the enemy could observe the Anti-Tank Battery's every movement, and since it came under constant bombing and shelling, the guns could not be hauled by lorries but had to be manhandled by their crews. There was only one way to discover if a track was under immediate fire; a volunteer would be sent to walk slowly along it. If he passed without attracting fire, the gun could be dragged after him.

The British withdrawal had been helped considerably by the ferocity of the Listers fighting around Brunete. After Lister's troops had finally been forced back, a new line was formed across the Guadarrama river. The handful of British, literally staggering with exhaustion, hunger and thirst, took up defensive positions, still under the direction of Hinks and Tapsell, ready to fight on. However, the fascist offensive had largely spent itself. Fresh Republican units arrived, and on 25 July the XVth Brigade was ordered to withdraw from the line and go back to rest. Forty-two men – all that was left of the British Battalion – staggered in the early hours of the morning through the dusty ruins of Villanueva de la Cañada, where 300 had gone into battle nineteen days before.

Nathan, now a major, had gone ahead to organize the movement and the reception of the remains of the Brigade. The kitchens were in the wooded hills near Torreledones, not far from where the Brigade moved into the attack. The area was bombed and Nathan was hit. He was taken to hospital but died there soon afterwards. His body was brought back to the Brigade area and was buried with full military honours. Aitken paid tribute to his calm courage and military ability which had won him such renown and respect throughout the International Brigades. While in Madrigueras in January 1937, Nathan had asked, through Springhall and Kerrigan, to join the British Communist Party; although his application was not accepted, he was told the door was not closed.

That day the British lay down in cool tree-sheltered surroundings near where they had rested before the offensive.

Some slept like the dead; but for many past mental and physical strains and the memories of dead friends inhibited sleep. However, on the evening of the next day, 28 July, a message arrived ordering the Brigade back to the front. Quijorna was reported to have fallen, threatening the whole front with disaster. It was a very difficult moment. Klaus called a meeting of the Commanders and Commissars of all the Battalions. At first Tapsell said the forty-two men were too exhausted and were no longer a fighting unit. Aitken, breaking all military protocol, went off and described the state of the Brigade to Jurado, the Army Corps Commander. Cunningham, standing on a rock, exhorted the men to return. He was followed by Steve Nelson, Political Commissar of the Lincolns. After discussion the men began to form up. There were thirty-seven British – the other five were too sick even to stand. The Franco-Belge, Dimitrov, Spanish and Lincoln men fell in; they had all suffered severely, though not to the same extent as the British. The Anti-Tanks, though depleted in numbers and having had a gun taken by another Brigade during the withdrawal, were prepared to go, and the Brigade services were ready to move up. However, at the very last moment another message arrived cancelling the move to the front because the situation had been stabilized and the danger of encirclement overcome.

Then came a night of sleep – troubled and disturbed by nightmares of the hell all had been through; but real sleep, away from danger.

The fighting on the front died down. Then the XVth Brigade was withdrawn to its old quarters, the British Battalion to Mondéjar, the Anti-Tanks to the mill on the Tajuña river, with Brigade Headquarters a few miles downstream in Ambite.

The strain of the casualties and conditions in the Brunete offensive brought to a head all the differences among the British Battalion leaders. Although some of their disagreements were argued in private, some violent arguments took place among the whole Battalion, sharpening the general difficulties and doubts during the battles.

Even at Jarama there had been differences and difficulties in the leading group, and when Harry Pollitt was at Morata in March 1937 he had brought Aitken, Cunningham, Copeman and Williams together to discuss the situation. It was agreed that Cunningham should call the others together every week to hammer out the differences and then write a report to Pollitt. There was an improvement but Brunete fomented all the differences. Cunningham had exploded with rage when charged by Brigade Command with weakness in his control of the three battalions in his regiment. Copeman and Williams had been removed from the British Battalion. Tapsell, in a state of distress, had publicly questioned the courage and ability of the Spanish units, and had been arrested and sent to Valencia by Cunningham as a result.

Then Cunningham, Copeman, Williams and Tapsell all returned to London. Aitken followed shortly after, having applied for leave.

In London the disturbing situation was discussed at length by a number of Communist leaders including Pollitt, Springhall and Palme Dutt, together with the leaders returned from Spain, who made all kinds of statements and accusations. It was said that Copeman had been removed by XVth Brigade Command because of his irrational behaviour, that Williams had been ineffective as Commissar, that Tapsell had become demoralized under the strain and undermined the unity of the army, that Cunningham had become over-ambitious yet had been incapable of doing his work on Brigade Staff, and that Aitken had not resisted orders which sent the British into impossible positions where they had been decimated.

The differences were too deep to be overcome: it was clear that the leaders could not all go back and work together. Finally Pollitt took the initiative and it was decided that Tapsell and Copeman alone should return to Spain while the others remained in Britain.

Meanwhile in Spain, Bill Paynter, Frank Ryan and Bill

Rowe, a leading Communist appointed Assistant Commissar at the Albacete Base, were working to restore the British Battalion in numbers, morale and fighting ability, and finding a new leadership to do this. There could be no breathing-space in the fight against fascism.

Chapter 11

Contact with Home

Only a tiny handful of British volunteers were of military disposition. Some of those who had previously served in the regular forces had enlisted because the food and pay provided an escape from unemployment and hardship. Overwhelmingly the volunteers were peaceloving individuals compelled by the situation and their beliefs to take up arms. As C. Day Lewis's poem 'The Volunteer' put it: 'We came because our open eyes/Could see no other way.' It was this outlook that made everyone look for and treasure all contact with ordinary civilian life, whether in Spain or back home in Britain.

Miles Tomalin, a writer and poet from London fighting with the Anti-Tank Battery, wrote in the middle of the Brunete battle:

He gives but he has all to gain,
He watches not for Spain alone.
Beyond him stand the homes of Spain,
Behind him stands his own.

This verse was used in a New Year's greeting card for members of the XVth Brigade to send home.

Most contact with the Spanish people was in the poor, inland villages where life was generally hard and grim. Though the customs and the homes were different, the British felt in tune with the fortitude and warmth of the people, so like those in their own mining valley or mill town.

Despite language difficulties, friendships were built up in every village. Clothes were washed and repaired – though soap and thread had to be provided. But most treasured of all were the invitations to sit on a chair, share a bottle of wine, and exchange family photographs and – as far as possible – stories of life in Britain and in Spain. The girls were beautiful and exciting. Hopes ran high but age-old customs still prevailed and romances were few. However, two or three volunteers did get married and brought their wives back to Britain. These contacts with ordinary Spanish people, when volunteers were not at the front or in training, did much to relieve the stress of action and to deepen understanding of the Spanish struggle.

There were other, more formal, organized contacts with the Spanish people. When they were not in action the International Brigades drew less than their official ration allotment, and the balance was sent to children's homes. In addition, volunteers – though often hungry themselves – would spontaneously hand over bread to children. The People's Front Committees in Madrigueras, Mondéjar, Marsa and all the villages where the British stayed for any length of time, arranged meetings and fiestas where speeches, music and songs in both languages built up friendship and unity.

Especially memorable were the occasions when the local leader of the People's Front invited a delegation to sample the contents of the village wine cellar. As more and more Spanish soldiers came into the British units, friendships with their families developed and so did interest in family and village news. Despite language difficulties and the overriding demands of the fighting and of being often on the move, the British valued every civilian contact and were never made to feel like foreigners or outsiders.

The Republican Government was keenly aware that it needed world public opinion and support to offset the fascist support for Franco. It therefore encouraged visitors and delegations of all kinds to come to Spain to see the conditions in the Government areas and the evidence of German and Italian intervention. The position in Britain was especially important, since Chamberlain was the instigator of the policy of 'Non-Intervention', which was only clearly denounced by the TUC leaders in the National Council of Labour on 27 July 1937.

The British volunteers had, by coming to Spain, shown how much they believed in the importance of the military struggle; but they all also recognized the importance of political activity at home which could, by ending 'Non-Intervention', effectively swing the military balance against fascism. None knew better than they just what 'Non-Intervention' was achieving. So political understanding reinforced emotions, making for the closest contact with home.

The first labour movement delegation was from the London Trades Council in December 1936. The delegates visited Madrid and were in Madrigueras when No. 1 Company returned from action in Córdoba. On their return to Britain they spoke at many meetings, setting a pattern for other delegations, calling for solidarity and the end of 'Non-Intervention'.

Many other trade union delegations came to Spain, with the miners especially prominent. Arthur Horner, President of the South Wales Miners, was sent officially by his Executive Committee to express solidarity with the Spanish people and to inquire about the Welsh miners in the Battalion. He came again with Jim Bowman (later to become chairman of the National Coal Board) and Will Lawther (later the President of the Miners' Federation of Great Britain), whose brother, Cliff, had been killed in action at Jarama. These visits and the subsequent campaigns in the coalfields brought a flow of recruits to the Brigades, food and other collections from the mining villages, and £70,000 from British miners to help the children of the Asturian miners. Above all, the miners led the fight to get the TUC into action on behalf of Republican Spain.

The visit in December 1937 of three Labour MPs – Clement

Attlee (leader of the Parliamentary Party), Ellen Wilkinson and Philip Noel-Baker, was seen as especially significant in the hope that it would stiffen Labour's fight against 'Non-Intervention'. The MPs met Government Ministers in Madrid and were shown material evidence of large-scale German and Italian help to Franco. They condemned 'Non-Intervention' as a farce and promised to exert maximum pressure to change the policy. This was fervently welcomed because throughout their time in Spain the British volunteers felt ashamed and angry that their Government was the architect of 'Non-Intervention', and that sections of the labour movement were lukewarm in their support of, or were even hostile to, the Republic. The delegation was moved and impressed by its visit to the International Brigades, praising the spirit of the volunteers and giving the clenched-fist salute. On its return, Tory MPs tried to censure members of the delegation in Parliament for their conduct and for their association with the British Battalion.

A group of seven MPs from all parties, including Tories, visited the Republic in November 1936 and on their return wrote a very effective pamphlet describing Spain's needs. A group of students, including future Tory Prime Minister Edward Heath, met members of the Battalion and of the Medical Services. When Pandit Nehru and Krishna Menon met the British near Marsa, they received an especially warm welcome because of their anti-imperialist records.

Professor J.B.S. Haldane wrote after his third visit at Christmas 1937:

> Within the last year the British Battalion has changed from a group of extremely brave but untrained men into a unit which would be a credit to any professional army. But at what a cost!

Haldane's writings on the effects of the fascist bombing of civilian centres were not only searing exposures of fascism, but were to influence British air raid precautions when the Second World War began.

Many journalists and writers came to Spain and wrote

articles and poems in support of the people's struggle. Most visited hospitals and some met the British units. Bill Forrest of the *News Chronicle* and Sefton Delmer of the *Daily Express* were always welcome and could be trusted to attempt to break through the web of lies and slanders in most of the British press. Ivor Montagu, Sidney Cole, Alan Lawson and other film-makers shot film and took photographs, often from dangerously exposed positions. They filmed captured weapons, proving the large-scale intervention of Hitler and Mussolini, the bombing of cities and the grim realities of the war – material which had a profound effect on British public opinion.

However, the most emotional welcome was given – not only among the English-speaking volunteers – to Paul Robeson, the black American singer, when he arrived in December 1937 with his wife Essie, and Charlotte Haldane of the Dependants' Aid Committee. He visited many hospitals but, to his own regret, was not allowed to go to the Teruel front. He sang, in his own words, 'with all my heart', the songs the volunteers wanted and needed.

During his visit he learnt many International Brigade songs which he went on to sing in concerts in Britain and all over the world.

Harry Pollitt visited the British volunteers five times. His visits had the profoundest impact on the volunteers, and a very substantial influence on the labour movement in Britain. Every time he returned, his speeches and pamphlets, and his articles in the *Daily Worker* greatly encouraged all aspects of the Aid for Spain movement.

A number of volunteers from the fighting units and the medical services were sent back to Britain to explain the position and to ask for more aid, renewed supplies, food, money and additional volunteers. Most important of all, they sought to step up the pressure on the Government and on the labour leaders to end the sham of 'Non-Intervention'. They spoke at countless meetings large and small, talked to influential local figures, and visited factories and work-places.

This activity, ignored by the national popular press, did

much to counter the slanders against the Republic, and laid a basis among ordinary people for sympathy with, and activity on behalf of, the Republic. Medical personnel in Spain all had passports and were able to travel freely, often returning to Britain for short visits, speaking at meetings, winning more money and support, and then returning with ambulances full of much needed equipment. Max Cohen, wounded by shrapnel in his ambulance at Brunete, went home for treatment, spoke at many meetings, including one with Attlee, then returned to Spain. Nurse Mary Slater, sent home for a rest period, used the opportunity to address meetings around Lancashire before returning to Spain. These two were typical of many. After Brunete, Arthur Nicoll of the Anti-Tank Battery went home to Dundee for medical treatment. The anti-fascist movement in the city rose to a new level as a result, and one hundred men went to Spain from Dundee, sixteen of whom were subsequently killed in action. Nicoll himself returned to become Commander of the Anti-Tank Battery, bringing his younger brother with him.

In March 1938 a delegation of returning wounded Brigaders went to the Labour Party and to TUC headquarters to urge an end to 'Non-Intervention' and increased support for the Republic. This work continued and extended as more Brigaders were invalided home. The more the British people learned of the real character of fascism, the greater was their support for the Republic and their opposition to Chamberlain's appeasement policy.

Whenever things were quiet – sometimes during a lull in battle itself – nearly everyone wrote home. Pencils, paper and envelopes remained available in many village shops. Writing was difficult for some, as most had left school at fourteen: however, letters were written, not only to wives, parents and families, but to trade-union branches, political friends and work-mates. The Republic knew that many of its soldiers found letter writing difficult, so post cards were printed with a propaganda drawing and slogan, with room for a brief message.

In Britain, letters from Spain attracted general interest. In the tightly-knit communities of the coalfields they were passed round and read out at trade-union branch meetings. Some local papers even made a regular feature of letters from local men. Aware of this interest the political commissars encouraged letter writing, and in their turn supporters in Britain were urged to keep in touch with volunteers whom they knew. After the Aragon retreat in March 1938, when the British press carried lurid stories that the Battalion had been liquidated, Wild and Cooney wrote letters to the national press giving the facts and urging immediate help to the Republic. Every man was strongly urged to write to his local paper and organizations, and many did so.

There were continuing problems about sending and receiving letters and parcels. In the early days there was considerable disorganization as the Republic had to create not only a military postal service but also a system of censorship for incoming and outgoing mail in many languages. Even more difficult was the delivery of letters to men on the move, in hospital, or in convalescent home or training camp. There was often distress when letters to or from Britain were delayed or did not arrive.

The Brigade postman for much of the time was Ernie Mahoney, whom for medical reasons it was decided not to send into the Jarama battle as Company Commissar. There could have been no better choice for such a difficult job, so important for morale. Mahoney managed to find his way to the front on the second day of the Jarama fighting. He got to the Brunete front every day, even though his small van was often shelled or strafed and on one occasion set on fire by a bomb. The distribution of mail in times of heavy casualties, when names were called out but not answered, could be very distressing; everyone thought of the wives and children at home whose men would never read their letters.

Many letters from home enclosed a packet of Woodbines or a bar of chocolate, easing if only for a day the deep craving for tobacco and sweet things. There were difficulties when larger supplies of comforts were sent to all the volunteers. Springhall was at his most scathing when a promised large consignment of cigarettes turned out to be only boiled sweets. In addition, a lorry-load of tea, which would have been ambrosia, went by mistake to Madrid.

In June 1938 a decision was made at the Base that all cigarettes from outside Spain should be pooled and divided equally among the International Brigades. This suggestion created uproar and was soon abandoned. The Spaniards wanted something stronger than Woodbines or Goldflakes; French cigarettes and Lucky Strikes, though better than nothing, 'smelt' and could not bring real satisfaction to the tobacco-hungry British.

A much-appreciated gesture was the dispatch from Britain of Christmas parcels in December 1937 to all the British in Spain. A small surplus was given to the Americans, who were very generous in passing on some of the more ample comforts they received. Each parcel contained cigarettes, toothpaste, razor-blades, chocolate, sweets, a small Christmas-pudding and a Christmas card.

Mahon, then British Base Commissar, did a great job, overcoming bureaucracy to get the parcels off a boat in Valencia and then, with Frank Ayres, driving round delivering them to all the units with British volunteers – the Battalion, the hospitals and the service units. They failed to deliver personally only to four volunteers in the Republican Navy, whose parcels they had to leave at the guardhouse of the Cartagena naval base.

However, the most important contact between the volunteers and home was the Dependants' Aid Committee. When recruiting began in earnest it was obvious that some financial help must be given to the wives and families left behind, otherwise a severe limitation would be placed on recruitment. Weekly allowances were therefore paid to those dependants who were in need. At first this was carried out by the Communist Party, out of collections at meetings and donations from supporters. It is probable that in the first few months donations also came from larger parties outside Britain. The grants were a shilling or two above the Unemployment Assistance Board rates – inadequate, but all that was available – and were paid out by local officials of the Communist Party. It was an extra responsibility, but it meant contact with the families. Elderly parents and dependants, unmarried wives, adopted children – all were accepted as needing a grant. Because of the local character of the 'administration' there were only a few complaints of attempted false claims or shortcomings. However, this system entailed a heavy financial strain. Would-be volunteers were questioned as much on the size of their family as on the strength of their anti-fascism.

In June 1937 responsibility for looking after the families was taken over by the Dependants' Aid Committee. This was very broadly sponsored, with seven MPs from Labour, Liberal and Tory parties, trade-union and Co-operative leaders, J.B. Priestley, D.N. Pritt, KC, and other well-known figures. Charlotte Haldane, the Secretary, had very close ties with the Battalion; her husband J.B.S. Haldane was a regular supporter and visitor to Spain, and her son Ronald Burgess was one of the youngest volunteers.

The first floor of 1 Litchfield Street, near Cambridge Circus in London, was taken over as an office and soon became a busy centre with many voluntary workers handling and directing the appeals. Brigaders back from Spain on leave, organizers of propaganda tours, and those invalided out made the office their base. In addition, Robson did most of the interviewing of volunteers in a room above the office. Such multi-purpose usage helped to maintain close liaison and contact but gave rise to difficulties. In the House of Commons, Tory MPs attacked the Committee, saying that it breached both the 'Non-Intervention Agreement' and the Foreign Enlistment Act.

When the Dependants' Aid Committee was established in July 1937, £700 a week was needed to meet grants and commitments; by 20 September the same year no less than 1,100 wives and children were being helped. To raise this sum regularly required a continuous propaganda campaign and organization. Besides appeals at public meetings, regular collections were taken at numerous pits and factories.

Odhams Press, print shop of the Labour *Daily Herald*, raised a total of £1,500. By the end of November 1937, Dependants' Aid had raised £43,358, a very considerable sum in those days, comparable to perhaps ten times that figure today. Of this, £7,420 came from trade-union committees, with the miners in the lead. Walter Citrine, General Secretary of the TUC, in his hostility to doing anything to help the Republic, studied the union donations to check that they were not infringing their own rules. Another feature of the fund was the regular donations, small and large, from individuals in every corner of Britain.

The Dependants' Aid Committee and local groups set out to help families in other ways, apart from and in addition to financial assistance. Social events, outings and picnics for the children, even a fortnight's holiday (a rare event in those days), helped families to bear the absence or indeed the loss of husband and father.

In all its activities the Dependants' Aid Committee stressed its political aims – to help the defeat of fascism and the victory of the Spanish people. The volunteers in Spain went into battle with greater confidence in the knowledge that, as far as possible, their families in Britain were being cared for. Such – at the front – was the important effect of the Committee's existence.

Chapter 12
Into Aragon

Juan Negrín, who had become prime minister after Largo Caballero's resignation in May 1937, took energetic steps to complete the organization of the army on a regular basis throughout the Republican zone. A single army command was set up with overall control.

There had been discussions and differences of opinion on the role and the organization of the International Brigades. There were two points of view: that they should continue in their partly independent position, and that they should be incorporated into the Spanish Army and given the status of shock units. Negrín accepted the latter plan, overcoming the hostility of the Minister of War, Prieto, towards the Brigades. Although the Official Decree was not published until 23 September 1937, the changes began after Brunete in July and had a considerable effect on the reorganization of the XVth Brigade and on the British volunteers.

A major innovation was the incorporation of Spanish Republican soldiers into every International Brigade. In each Brigade there was to be a complete Spanish Battalion. In each of the International Battalions there was to be one wholly Spanish company. Then, in each of the International companies there was to be at least one section of Spanish soldiers.

As was well known, the Brigades had been involved in nearly all the bloodiest fighting; however the first drafts of Spaniards to join them were all volunteers from other units of the Republican Army. This demonstrated not only the courage and conviction of the Spanish volunteers themselves, but also the affection and respect which the Internationals had already gained among most of the Spanish people and the Republican Army.

Many writers on the International Brigades ignore the presence and role of the Spanish soldiers in them, and indeed the part played in the war by the whole Republican Army. This book is a history only of the British volunteers and does not even attempt to describe the part of our Spanish comrades. But it must be continually remembered that after August 1937 the Spanish brothers-in-arms who fought shoulder to shoulder with the British in every battle usually formed the majority of the Battalion effectives. Without their courage, high morale and combative qualities, the British Battalion would have been able to achieve little. A more accurate title for the Battalion would have been the 'Spanish-British Battalion'.

The XVth Brigade was now incorporated into a different Division, the 35th, commanded by General Walter, a Pole who had seen service with the Soviet Red Army. He was a hard but efficient commander and soon won much more respect and confidence among the British than Gal, who had been Divisional Commander at Brunete. Walter had commanded the Brigade in which No. 1 Company had distinguished itself on the Córdoba front (see Chapter 7), and he continued to hold a good opinion of the British.

Back in its old quarters in the Tajúna valley, the XVth Brigade had a very brief, two-week respite. There was some relaxation, but the time was mainly spent in reorganizing, and in repairing weapons after the devastating strain and casualties of Brunete.

Peter Daly became British Battalion Commander. The survivor of two bullet wounds – while leading a section at Jarama, and while commanding the British-American company of the 20th Battalion on the Córdoba front – he was an experienced, trusted leader. Paddy O'Daire was appointed second-in-command. Wounded in January 1937 when fighting with No. 1 Company at Lopera, he had returned to action with the British-American Company in the XXth Battalion, being promoted to lieutenant in the field for bravery and military expertise. Ryan, now working in the Albacete Base where he kept a watchful eye on the wellbeing of all the Irish volunteers, was proud that two of his fellow-countrymen were ready to tackle such important, but difficult, responsibilities.

The new Political Commissar was Jack Roberts, a Communist Councillor in Caerphilly who had played an active part in rebuilding the Miners' Union after the General Strike. On his way to Spain he had been arrested and spent two weeks in a French gaol, but he had arrived in time for the battle of Brunete where he had been responsible for political work in a section of the British Battalion. With this limited experience of war, he now had to face the most complex and daunting problem of how to raise the fighting morale of the Battalion.

The first problem was to fill the ranks since, of the handful of survivors from Brunete, a high proportion needed hospital treatment. However, new recruits arrived from Madrigueras, and men who had been wounded at Jarama or Brunete came back from hospital or convalescent camps. Moreover many who had given way under the strain of Brunete recovered and rejoined the ranks. The two weeks' rest, the fine weather and the cool Tajuña Valley did wonders for nerves and bodies. The men of the Anti-Tank Battery almost lived in the river flowing round their mill at Ambite. A visit from Arthur Horner, sent by the South Wales Miners' Federation to visit the many miners in the Battalion, boosted political confidence as he told of the growing opposition in the trade unions to the policy of 'Non-Intervention'.

On the 18 August 1937, when the Battalion received its next marching orders, it numbered just over 400 men, of whom just under 200 were British. The XVth Brigade was now made up of the British, the Dimitrovs, the 24th Spanish Battalion and the Lincolns. One Briton, George Wattis, commanded the Spanish Company of the Lincolns. Čopíc was still Brigade

Commander, but Aitken's place as Commissar was taken by
Steve Nelson, with another American, Robert Merriman,
Chief of Staff. The British were well represented on the Staff.
Dunbar, recovered from his wound when with the Anti-Tanks
at Brunete, had received well-deserved promotion and became
Chief-of-Operations. Bee was still responsible for mapping.
Wintringham, after recovering from his wound at Jarama, had
had a spell as an instructor at the NCO's school at Pozorrubio
and now returned and was attached to Brigade Staff.

The Republican High Command was preparing an
offensive on the Aragon front. By attacking there it would
bring action to a dormant front, and also relieve pressure on
the Northern Front which faced heavy fascist attacks. The aim
was to take the important city and communications centre of
Zaragoza.

The Battalion went by truck and slept the night in the
bullring at Valencia, where its numbers increased as men who
had been in hospital or rest-camp near by 'deserted to the
front' and joined their friends. Many received fresh uniforms
(not always new), better boots and equipment, and – most
cheering of all – light Russian machine-guns, Diktorovs.
These had a Maxim lock with an air-cooled barrel on a tripod
mounting. They were effective weapons, much easier to
handle than the heavy Maxim gun with its steel shield and
cast-iron wheeled carriage. Next morning the whole Brigade
moved off in box-cars along the coast railway and then inland
to Caspe and Azaila. In the jolting goods' trucks it was a slow
but enjoyable journey during which everyone caught up with
some sleep and enjoyed the luscious fruit, picked when the
train made its frequent halts.

The part of the Aragon front where the XVth Brigade was
deployed was south of the river Ebro, and the Brigade had the
river, deep and fifty yards wide, on its eastern flank. Away
from the narrow river plain the terrain was an arid plateau,
eroded by streams, dried up for most of the year, with
occasional barren, flat-topped hills. It was an area the Brigade
came to know only too well.

The Aragon front had been largely quiet since the Autumn

Map of the Aragon and Ebro areas

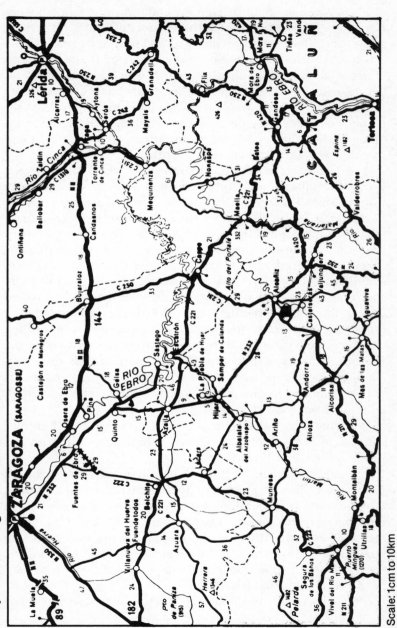

Scale: 1cm to 10km

of 1936, when the mainly Anarchist columns moving out from Barcelona and Catalonia had halted on encountering serious opposition. Because of the political and military situation, the units on the front had not been fully subjected to the processes of organization and unification which, since November 1936, had transformed the armies of the Madrid and Centre fronts into units of a regular army. This was shockingly brought home when the Brigade saw the pitiable, often fouled and dirty shallow trenches, with no attempt, after the many months, to build fortifications in depth.

The 45th Division was north of the river, the 35th – with the British Battalion – was to the south. The plan was that both would drive to take Zaragoza, some thirty miles away. On 24 August the XVth Brigade began its assault on Quinto, a village on the edge of the lush Ebro valley and the dry plateau above it, straddling the main road to Zaragoza. While the other three Battalions were fighting their way into the village, the British Battalion was in reserve, with the old-timers speculating on what dirty job would face them when called into action. After street-fighting through the narrow winding lanes, the last fascist stronghold – the massive stone-walled church dominating Quinto – was overcome. By now the Brigade Command had grasped the potential of the Anti-Tank guns and they were used to the full, blasting strongholds and even accurate enough to shoot explosive shells through windows from some distance.

Wintringham was wounded in the street fighting; subsequently his wound developed complications and he was invalided home in November 1937.

Though the village of Quinto had fallen, a decisive position, Pulburrel Hill, still stood out to the east. It was a natural strong point, its sides falling away at forty-five degrees, except for a narrow neck joining it to the plateau. It was skilfully and heavily fortified with concrete emplacements and revolving gun-turrets. However, the only water supply came from the river 400 feet below and 500 yards away, and the pipe had been cut by a Lincoln patrol.

On the afternoon of the second day the British were ordered

to take Pulburrel Hill. Daly was told by Brigade that it was 'lightly held'. But when the Battalion began to advance across the plateau, it ran into murderous machine-gun fire from the hill and sniping fire from the last fascist positions in the village. Daly was hit in the stomach in the first few yards. He died later in hospital at Benicasím. O'Daire became Commander and Arthur Ollerenshaw Second-in-Command. The Battalion Commissar, Roberts, was also hit. After recovering from his wounds he was for a short time at the Officers' Training School but was subsequently sent home to defend his Council seat. Alec Torrance of Carlisle took Roberts's place, but he too was wounded.

O'Daire realized that Puburrel Hill was strongly held; he could see that the barbed-wire was still intact and that further advance across open ground would be suicidal. So at dusk he withdrew the Battalion until artillery support could be provided.

At dawn the Battalion moved forward, again with artillery support and the Anti-Tank guns. Jeff Mildwater, a London bricklayer, moved his gun and crew 200 yards forward of the infantry, and knocked out several machine-guns. The advance was helped by covering fire from the Lincolns and by a large flight of fascist bombers dropping their load by mistake on Pulburrel Hill itself.

The fascist forces surrendered, worn down by continuous fire and thirst, as the final assault prepared to go in. George Buck of Nelson in Lancashire was the first to reach the central key-point, and tore down the fascist standard – an exploit which helped him to win the Navalpera Medal for exceptional bravery and devotion to duty.

The Brigade Commander, Čopíc, had criticized O'Daire for pulling the Battalion back the previous evening, but O'Daire, a keen student of military affairs, went to him and produced from his pocket British Army Field Service Regulations Part III which showed that he was correct in taking his decision.

With Quinto cleared, the next main obstacle on the road to Zaragoza was the fortified area around Fuentes de Ebro. The plan was that, when this village had been cleared, the whole

XVth Brigade should get on lorries and, protected by tanks and armoured cars, dash straight to Zaragoza, linking up with the other advance on the north bank of the Ebro. However after three days Fuentes had not fallen and the plan was abandoned. The Battalion spent this time reorganizing and preparing for the venture. It is not known if another Battalion Commissar was appointed to take over after Roberts and Torrance had been wounded.

The XVth Brigade was then sent to complete the capture of Belchite, which had only been surrounded in the advance. It was a small town of considerable strategic importance which had a complete perimeter of modern fortifications, barbed-wire, trenches and tank obstacles. The Anti-Tanks, on trucks, got there before the infantry battalions and joined with the Spanish units on the outskirts of the town.

The effective strength of the Battalion, Spanish and British, had been reduced to just over a hundred and morale was low. It had reached the outskirts of Codo, on the way to Belchite, when it was ordered to go to Mediana on the Zaragoza-Belchite road. The fascists had brought in heavy reinforcements of men and guns, and were counter-attacking there, aiming to 'relieve the beleagured Belchite. Because it was feared that the Spanish units in Mediana could not withstand a major attack, some members of the Battalion refused to carry out this order.

O'Daire, who had recently joined the Communist Party of Spain, took the unusual step of calling a meeting of British Communist Party members in the Battalion. Only seven appeared, mainly Welsh miners. After discussion there was full agreement that the advance on Mediana was essential. The group rallied, the order was accepted, and the move began. However, because their trucks came under long-range artillery fire, everyone scrambled out and completed the move on foot. An advancing fascist column turned and retreated, and the Battalion took up positions on the broken hills overlooking Mediana in the valley below.

The yellow soil was soft and the Battalion soon dug in, well protected from shelling and aerial strafing. There were continuous night patrols and skirmishes in the broken ravines and gulleys leading down to the valley. O'Daire and Ollerenshaw were kept continuously busy, raising morale and confidence. They were ably assisted by Hercules Avgherinos, a Cypriot whose experience at Brunete and Jarama, and whose command of languages, made him an invaluable officer.

This active defence was sufficient to prevent the fascists from mounting a direct drive down the road to relieve Belchite. With the town's final surrender to Republican forces on 5 September the pressure on the British lifted and they were moved into reserve positions with the rest of the Brigade.

In the meantime, the British Anti-Tank Battery was fully engaged, with the Lincolns, the Dimitrovs and the 24th Spanish Battalion, in the bombardment and fight for Belchite. In the first two days of the attack, the Anti-Tank Battery's three Soviet-made guns fired 2,700 shells. The No. 1 gun was fired at such a rate that its barrel burst and it had to be withdrawn from action. The effectiveness of the guns depended upon their accuracy, high velocity and the flat trajectory of their small shells which, by penetrating a door or a window, could greatly ease the advance of the infantry fighting its way from house to house.

Jim Sullivan, from Glasgow, positioned his gun on a mound by the Azaila road overlooking the whole town of Belchite. The barrel poked out from a hole in the thick wall of a farm shed. Ammunition and supplies had to be carried across an open threshing-floor under fascist machine-gun fire, but Sullivan's gun dominated the southern side and the rear of the fascist headquarters in the town.

In the final assault the gun commanded by Jim Coomes, a Co-op worker from Hammersmith, played a decisive role. The crew manhandled it down into the street, firing at very short range. In the last encounter the advance was made under fire and sandbags were pulled off a fascist barricade, enabling the gun to be poked through and to be fired at fifty yards' range into the fascist *commandancia*. Coomes was killed by a burst of machine-gun fire, but the action of his gun, with the ferocious street-fighting of the Lincolns, and propaganda from a loudspeaker, brought about the final surrender of the remnants of the fascist troops. Coomes, Frank Proctor and others in the Battery were cited for bravery in this action.

Although the XVth Brigade was in reserve for ten days after the capture of Belchite, there was little rest as it had to be in position and ready for any supporting action at the front. The weather broke; cold torrential rains made activity difficult and living conditions grim. Because the fascists commanded the air, it was unsafe to take quarters in the villages, and the bivouacs in the fields offered only misery and discomfort.

An army decision had been taken to organize the Brigades by language – to ease communication problems. The Dimitrovs therefore now left the XVth Brigade and were replaced by the Mackenzie-Papineau Battalion, soon to be known as the Mac Paps. This was a newly-formed battalion of Canadians, though many Americans helped swell its numbers. Jack Lawson was badly missed in the Anti-Tank Battery cookhouse when he went off to join his fellow countrymen; his experience in the Canadian backwoods helped him to slaughter and then turn the oldest of mules into palatable stew.

From the British Battalion, O'Daire went off to the Senior Officers' School at Pozorrubio for training in the handling of large units – battalion-size and over. He came back to the Battalion only for the Ebro crossing. Ollerenshaw and Avgherinos were given responsible jobs at the Base. Harold Fry, the Machine-Gun Company Commander taken prisoner at Jarama and then exchanged, had insisted on returning to Spain and was appointed British Battalion Commander. The Battalion Commissar, selected by the Communist leadership in Britain, was Eric Whalley, a young worker with an ILP background who had joined the Communist Party and had been one of the leaders of the unemployed in Mansfield.

Mildwater was promoted from Gun Commander to take over the Anti-Tank Battery from Slater who went to Madrid.

On the 11 October 1937 the XVth Brigade was concentrated around Quinto and was briefed for a Republican operation against Fuentes de Ebro, a different version of the plan for the September offensive. The 24th Spanish Battalion was to be carried on tanks through and beyond the fascist lines, while the other three infantry battalions assaulted the fascist positions and consolidated new lines. An advance was then to be made along the road to Zaragoza. This sector had been quiet since the earlier abortive attacks, but the number of fascist troops at the front had been increased and the defences had been improved. Six to eight hundred metres separated the Republican from the enemy trenches.

The idea of tanks carrying infantry into an assault was novel and untried. But everything went wrong. Republican staff-work and organization were not yet capable of mounting such a complicated action. The infantry was late moving into the forward trenches, and in the morning light of 13 October the enemy was fully alerted to the attack and claimed numerous casualties.

The Anti-Tank Battery, in excellent positions on the plateau side of the Quinto-Fuentes road, able to see and knock out enemy machine-gun nests, was forbidden to open fire. The artillery barrage supporting the attack was very limited, and there was an hour's delay before the Republican Air Force made one high-level bombing raid.

After another hour's delay, during which their engines could be clearly heard by the fascists, forty-odd tanks charged over the Brigade trenches with the 24th Spanish Battalion clinging to their sides. The Spanish infantrymen had had almost no preparation and little briefing, and were still carrying blankets and mess-tins. The Soviet-made tanks travelled at high speed and many men were shaken off them.

After the tanks had passed over their trenches the XVth Brigade went over the top and followed them, but they were soon left far behind. The fascist machine-guns, still largely intact, now went into deadly action. The Mac Paps, on the plateau edge, had to advance eight hundred metres across open ground before reaching a gulley in front of the main fascist defences. They lost nearly a quarter of their strength in their first move. The Lincolns, in the centre, advancing across six hundred metres with very little cover, were also pinned down with heavy losses. The British were between the Lincolns and the banks of the Ebro, and also faced an advance of six hundred metres.

The fields, which no one had been able to reconnoitre, were cut deep by water-filled ditches. Fry and Whalley, perhaps eager to establish their leadership like most other commanders, led the Battalion and were killed in the first dozen yards. The whole Battalion was pinned down by heavy machine-gun fire, suffered many casualties and did not reach enemy lines.

In this action the Spaniards in the Battalion set the highest standards. Cipriano, a twenty-six-year-old illiterate peasant from Aragon, emerged as a natural leader, showing the courage and initiative which were to make him Company Commander later.

The tanks sustained heavy damage since the fascists were prepared with petrol bombs and grenades, and the Republican infantrymen could not get near enough to offer protection from such anti-tank weapons.

In this chaos, the Brigade panic order 'Everything forward' reached the Anti-Tank Battery. However, any attempt to manhandle the guns out of cover would have meant disaster; so Mildwater, Alexander and Sullivan ran forward to reconnoitre. Mildwater was hit in the knee on the way back (he was eventually invalided home). The Battery stayed put and provided effective fire from its positions. Otto Estenson, a seaman from Stockton-on-Tees, took over command.

That night, fighting patrols went forward from all the battalions to help recover some of the tanks and crews, while first-aid men collected the wounded. Paynter and Mahon (who had just been appointed Base Commissar) came up to assess the position of the British.

During the next ten days the British Battalion remained in the front line trenches with George Fletcher, an ex-army sergeant and expert machine-gunner from Crewe, in command. Patrols were sent out and there was intermittent firing, but no major action. The fascists, anxious to find out how strongly the line was held, shouted across the trenches and made an attempt at fraternization. Some from both sides began to respond but fire from the Republican trenches brought this to a hasty end.

Once again, the weather broke, bringing torrential rain. To everyone's great relief the Brigade was now pulled out of the trenches, assembled at Quinto, and the move began back to the old quarters at Mondéjar and Ambite. The train journey was made more bearable by Quartermaster 'Hookey' Walker's success in turning out regular hot meals from a field-kitchen on a flat rail-car. 'Hookey', with long experience as a Regular, was renowned throughout the Brigade, not only for getting food and drink up to the Battalion in the most exposed and difficult positions, but also for his ingenuity in 'organizing' supplies to augment the basic rations – often a mule on the hoof, chick-peas and olive oil.

However, the British were to see Aragon yet again.

Chapter 13

The Snows of Teruel

On 23 September 1937 the Republican Defence Ministry published the decree on the status and organization of International Brigades. Some clauses formally regularised what was already practice while other parts could not be fully carried out. The phrase in the decree, 'providing that the necessities of service permit', recognised the increasing pressure of the fascists on the Republic and its Army.

The decree formally recognised the International Brigades as an integral part of the front-line troops of the Spanish Army, subject to the same regulations and with the same organisation as other units. Volunteers for the International Brigades had to undertake to remain in them until the end of the war while requests for leave outside Spain would be decided by the Ministry. Promotions to non-commissioned and officer rank were to be made by the Commands of each Brigade and confirmed by the Base. The role and activity of the International Brigade Base in Albacete was regulated and, in some ways, limited. The Base was responsible for training new volunteers, allocating them to the different International Brigades and then keeping records. The Supply, Medical and Postal Services became the responsibility of the Ministry. This meant a reduction in the number of personnel at the Albacete Base, and it was decreed that all Base personnel must have served at the front for three months.

The decree formalised what every volunteer had painfully learnt from one year's battle experience: organisation, discipline and trained leaders and soldiers were necessary to defeat the regular German and Italian units, the core of Franco's Army. The greater emphasis on the role of officers, which included saluting, caused some discussion, but among the British it did not cause great concern. All those with experience of the fighting had seen that leadership devolved upon those who had proved their quality in battle, and was not imposed from above by any caste or class. The man who yesterday fought at your side as an ordinary soldier and comrade might well be your commanding officer tomorrow: one owed him respect because of his worth as a man, not because of his rank or uniform. And he remained a comrade.

The statement in the decree that volunteers for the Brigades undertook to remain until the end of the war, with the Ministry of Defence deciding on requests for repatriation or leave outside Spain, limited speculation and rumours. After long political argument this approach became more generally accepted.

The decree brought changes in the British personnel at the Albacete Base. When Bill Rowe, a gardener from London, who had been Assistant Base Commissar, developed the symptoms of acute tuberculosis and had to return home, he could not be replaced. When Bill Rust, a member of the Political Bureau of the Communist Party of Great Britain, came to Spain at the end of November, his formal position was that of *Daily Worker* correspondent without a military position or pay from the Government. When Mahon returned to Britain in February 1938 there was no one in the Brigade Base with overall responsibility for the British volunteers, though Rust maintained very close and regular contact.

While the XVth Brigade, after the Aragon fighting, was in reserve in the Tajuña valley, there was some reorganization. The battalions were unchanged but were given numbers. The British with the longest active service, became the 57th, the Lincolns the 58th, the Spanish the 59th, and the Canadian Mac Paps the 60th. The numbers were used in official orders, but the names stayed in general use.

Čopic continued as Brigade Commander, but Dave Doran,

an American, took over as Brigade Political Commissar after Steve Nelson was wounded at Belchite. The British had a strong group in the Brigade Staff. Dunbar, who had been awarded the Navalpera medal for consistent bravery in action, continued as Chief of Operations, Ruskin was in charge of Transmissions, Bee of Mapping. Wattis left the Lincoln Battalion and was responsible for supplies in the Brigade. Mahoney maintained his reputation for getting the Brigade mail moving in the most hazardous or difficult conditions. Bob Cooney (a well-known Communist from Aberdeen) had, after much pressure, been allowed to volunteer to come to Spain and was allocated work in the Brigade Political Commissariat.

After the difficulties and problems of morale in the Aragon, John Mahon, from the Base, took steps to raise the fighting spirit and efficiency. He organised, on 20 November, a conference of all the leading British personnel from the political side. Twenty-seven attended and there was a lively but practical discussion on necessary steps in all the British units – medical, training, as well as fighting. Concern was shown about the best way to maintain a flow of fully-trained recruits so as to keep the British element in the Battalion to some two hundred. A decision was made to keep back a substantial number of recruits in the Tarazona training base to form the basis of a new British company when needed. There was also a discussion on how to make the best use of men unfit for front-line service and awaiting repatriation. At the end of the two-day conference there was an improved feeling of unity and confidence that the problems could be overcome.

Copeman and Tapsell returned from Britain at the very end of October 1937. Pollitt wanted Copeman to be given a position on Brigade Staff, but there was opposition in Brigade. Ryan successfully insisted that O'Daire should be withdrawn from command of the British Battalion and sent for high level officer's training. Copeman then took over command of the Battalion – though he did not see action again. Tapsell filled the vacant position of Battalion Political Commissar. Alexander was moved from the Anti-Tanks to become

Battalion second-in-command. The companies were led by the veteran fighters, Wild, Fletcher and Cipriano.

In the Battalion there was regular training of all kinds, with a young Soviet Red Army instructor attached for a time. Special emphasis was laid on digging in, mobility, and use of ground and cover. Physical health and morale were improved by the provision of regular meals, washing facilities and sufficient sleep, together with concerts, sports and short leaves to Madrid. By the 15 November 1937, with the return of the wounded men from hospital, the British numbers had built up to 150 out of the Battalion strength of 600. This reinforcement of experienced fighters from earlier battles, able to pass on the lessons, also helped to raise spirits and efficiency.

On 6 December Attlee, Ellen Wilkinson and Philip Noel-Baker visited the XVth Brigade and the British Battalion. It was dark when they arrived, late, at the square in Mondéjar where the Battalion was parading to greet them. Attlee appeared a little apprehensive in the light of the flickering torches of oiled rope but welcomed with enthusiasm the proposal that No. 1 Company should be named after him. Arrangements were made for a monthly report of the Battalion and No. 1 Company to be sent to Attlee. He replied warmly after the first report following the Teruel battle:

> I was very pleased to read of the special mention of the Company in General Orders for their fine work in the battle for Teruel, and I am very sorry to hear that heavy losses have been sustained. The Company has most worthily honoured its high reputation. Please give my fraternal greetings to all.

The second and subsequent reports received only formal acknowledgements. Later, in the desperate days of the Aragon breakthrough, Wild and Cooney made an appeal to him for greater efforts for help for Spain.

Late in 1937, having received more men and armaments from Germany and Italy and having completed the conquest of the North, Franco was preparing for what he hoped would be a final offensive. However, the Republic upset these plans by launching its own offensive, capturing the provincial capital, Teruel, on 17 December. This was carried out by Spanish units alone. But General Walter's 35th Division, consisting of the XVth and XIth Brigades, was moved as a reserve to the east of Teruel.

So on 10 December 1937 the Brigade said goodbye for the last time to Mondéjar and Ambite, and went by train to Caspe in the Aragon. Then it marched through Alcañiz to the small stone-built village of Mas de Las Matas. With the news of the capture of Teruel, spirits were high and the Christmas period was one of general enjoyment. Everyone was under a roof; 'Hookey' Walker rustled up extra food, including a very fat pig, wine and nuts. Everyone received an individual parcel from Britain. Pollitt, on his third visit to the Battalion, with J.B.S. Haldane, turned up with a briefcase full of letters, messages and news from Britain. Christmas 1937 was a memorable day.

Two days later Copeman went to hospital for an appendix operation; complications developed and he was invalided home in April 1938. Alexander was appointed Battalion Commander, Wild became Adjutant, and Tom Davidson of Aberdeen took over No. 3 Company.

The fascists had brought up reinforcements and opened heavy attacks all round the Teruel salient, aiming to recapture the city. On New Year's Eve the Brigade was moved by truck nearer to the front. The weather had been cold but now became bitter, the temperature falling on some nights to minus 20 degrees Centigrade with snow everywhere drifting two and three feet deep. To have to live in the open was cruel misery and added new perils to the dangers of war. The twisting narrow roads on the high mountains made travel slow and hazardous, and entailed extreme discomfort for the Battalion, jam-packed in the Soviet-built trucks.

The British were positioned near the small, abandoned, wrecked village of Cuevas Labradas, on the slopes of the 3,500 feet high Sierra Palomera, and came under shrapnel fire from artillery as they moved up. Digging in the frozen soil was extremely difficult and exhausting, but they knew from harsh

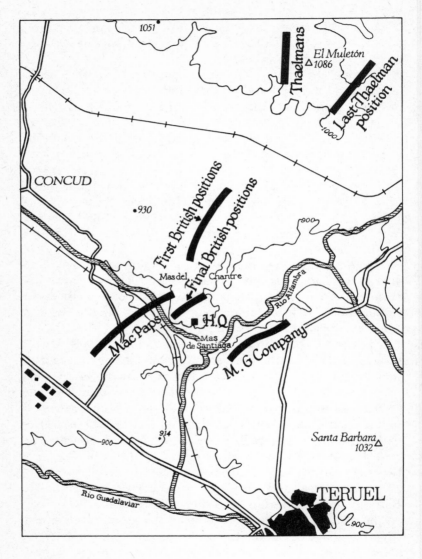

The defence of Teruel, January 1938.   Scale 1 cm to 500 m

experience that the shallow ditches left by the Anarchist units there before them offered no protection from shrapnel shelling or from strafing. So despite the very low temperatures, bitter winds and deep snow, strong defensive positions were built and casualties from long-range rifle and machine-gun fire were low. However, the fascists had mustered a very powerful airforce, which gave them complete control of the air when the weather made flying possible.

It was too dangerous to remain in any building by day, but at night, leaving patrols at the front, the Battalion went back to shelter where it was possible to eat and sleep in the comparative warmth of barns and ruins. Before dawn the British reoccupied their positions in the snow. Several different positions were occupied, and in each defences were dug. From one the Battalion took shelter at night in a railway tunnel. It was safe, but the heat from the bodies and the small fires turned the frozen ground into slush, and the icicles hanging from the roof into drips of misery. The move at dawn into the arctic weapon pits was almost welcome. There were cases of frostbite, but some warm underclothes had been received from Valencia, and the Quartermasters always managed to bring food to the front though it was inevitably cold, sometimes frozen, on arrival.

A useful device for protection of the body was to cut a slit in a blanket which could then be slipped over the head to act as a poncho. It broke the snow-filled winds, but allowed freedom of movement. Machine-gun locks had to be taken out, wrapped in cloth, and carried near the body to prevent them from freezing up. Rifle-bolts often had to be warmed in the hands or trouser-pockets before they could be moved. There was only one benefit from the extreme cold. Everyone was lousy, for washing was impossible, but even the lice were too cold to crawl and bite.

It was in this isolated, exposed and vulnerable situation that the Battalion was shocked and infuriated by the attempted desertion to the fascists of two men, one carrying a map with the layout and positions of the Battalion machine-guns. If this information had reached the enemy it would have made it easy for them to surprise and annihilate the whole Battalion. The demand for the sternest action to be taken against them was strong and unanimous, and they were sent to Brigade for court martial.

Having been checked in their attempts to break out of the flanks of the salient, the fascists built up their forces to 80,000 men, 600 guns, and the biggest air fleet yet seen in action. Now they drove directly at Teruel itself. First the XIth International Brigade was sent in to check the drive. Then on 14 January the XVth Brigade was moved directly to the tip of the fascist spearhead, called by Čopić 'the post of honour', on the outskirts of the town. The Lincolns were actually in the town itself, and the 59th Spanish Battalion held advanced positions on La Muela, a hill in front of the city. The Mac Paps were on the eastern flank of La Muela, straddling the railway-line and the gorge of a stream running north to the fascist HQ in Concud.

The British Battalion was on Santa Bárbara, a hill with precipitous cliffs to the River Alfambra, and commanding an easy approach to Teruel itself. The Machine-Gun Company was placed in strong, covered emplacements built by the fascists as part of their defences of the town. They were on the very edge of the cliff, so that only a direct hit could harm them, and had a wide, commanding field of fire over the Mac Paps and towards the Thaelmanns who were hanging on to El Muletón, key to the flank approaches of Teruel. George Fletcher's gun crews, part British, part Spanish, were in a unique position to use their expertise.

The guns of the Anti-Tank Battery were placed supporting the Battalion. Arthur Nicoll, now in command, had one gun on the cliff top, well-placed and very hard to hit. Estenson, second-in-command, had a gun actually in Teruel itself – well camouflaged in a road behind wrought-iron gates which the gun crew opened to fire and then closed before the position could be spotted by fascist observers. The third gun was on the right towards the Thaelmanns on El Muletón, but too far away to give them really effective support. All three guns fired almost continuously during the three-day-long battle, knocking out machine-guns, or persuading fascist platoons, invariably advancing in a group, to retreat rapidly to safety.

On 17 January the fascists launched a heavy direct assault on the XVth Brigade positions, using big formations of their 80,000 men. Their artillery, able to fire at very short range because the Republic had virtually no artillery or aerial support, systematically set out to shatter opposition before the infantry dared to assault. The Thaelmanns on El Muletón and a battalion of *Marineros* (Spanish marines), who were on two rounded hills between them, and the Mac Paps, took a terrific hammering and sustained heavy losses. However, when fascist infantry and some cavalry moved up to take their positions, the British machine-guns and anti-tank guns on the cliffs of Santa Bárbara went into action and took a heavy toll even at a range of 1,500 yards. The fascist artillery lifted its fire, trying to silence the guns, but had little success because of the uniquely strong positions of the British guns.

The next day the last remnants of the Thaelmanns were driven off their mountain. The fascists now concentrated everything on clearing the Marineros off their positions and rolling up the Mac Paps. Then Teruel would be open before them. Under an intensive barrage the Marineros broke and left their hills, leaving the valley open. Fletcher's guns again hit hard as the fascist units occupied the positions.

The Brigade now ordered the three British rifle companies to move down from Santa Bárbara to the valley below, across the Alfambra River. The river was fast flowing but was only fifteen feet wide and two feet deep, and was therefore no obstacle to infantry movement. The move was to close the gap and protect the open flank of the Mac Paps. Wild led No. 3 Company first down a steep gulley in the cliff face. No. 1 and No. 4 Companies and the Battalion Command followed, but the move, in full view of the enemy, now came under heavy shell-fire as men scrambled down the cliff face. One of the casualties was Francisco Zamorra, a Spanish-speaking Welshman from Abercrave in West Wales, the Battalion interpreter. His forbears were among those brought from Spain many years previously by strike-breaking employers.

The Battalion hastily dug in, forming a five to six hundred yard arc with its back to the Alfambra and the Santa Bárbara cliff. The Mac Paps were on the left, the remnants of the Marineros on the right. The command post was on a fortified hillock across the river, by the deep gulley which ran north to Concud. The night was spent digging, and in checking weapons and ammunition, since everyone knew what the dawn would bring. Next morning the fascist artillery plastered the whole Battalion front, an extra heavy share falling on No. 1 Company. The other two companies were also under rifle and machine-gun fire from the hills which the Marineros had been forced to leave.

Thinking that no one could survive the fire, and using dead ground, two squads of Moorish cavalry charged across the front towards the Mac Paps' command-post. They were virtually wiped out by the Mac Paps with the considerable help of small groups of No. 1 Company riflemen, led by Frank West, a carpenter from Hammersmith, who had hung on in very advanced positions.

Nevertheless, in this situation the three companies were compelled to retreat and again dig in on a narrow arc only one hundred yards around the command post. The machine-guns on the cliffs kept up a nearly continuous and devastating fire, enabling the withdrawal to take place in an orderly way.

The next day the fascists made a concentrated attack on the block-house and the rifle companies in the tight semi-circle around it. But the Battalion stood its ground and the fascists were beaten back. They then abandoned their attempt to retake Teruel by direct assault, and the fighting in that area died down.

Lt.-Col Juan Modesto, Commander of the 5th Army Corps, in an order of the day, commended the British Battalion for its stand. Alexander was promoted in the field to Captain, and Tapsell was commended for his work as Political Commissar.

A few days later Charlotte Haldane, Secretary of the Dependants' Aid Committee, together with Rust, visited the Battalion. On a dark night she came down the cliff, crossed the river, and visited the trenches and block-house. Later that night on Santa Bárbara a board was fixed and a simple tribute paid to the twenty-one British killed in the action. On 3 February the Battalion was relieved and pulled out of the line, having lost in the Teruel actions nearly one third of its strength through death, wounds and sickness.

Preparations now began for the XVth Brigade to move back to the Madrid sector. The British were concentrated away from Teruel, but then the Brigade was on the move again, not to rest in reserve but to go into action. The whole Brigade was concentrated in the area of Segura de los Baños, about forty miles north of Teruel. The fascist drive to retake Teruel by a deep encircling movement had made dangerous progress. A diversionary attack was planned, intended to break through an Anarchist-held dormant sector of the front. Then the plan was to move deep into fascist territory and occupy a key road centre through which supplies and reinforcements poured for the battle at Teruel. The concentration was carried out in effective secrecy, and the Battalion enjoyed the enforced seclusion and rest, hidden in barns and buildings for a couple of days before the attack. Cooney, who had not enjoyed his work in the Brigade Political Commissariat and had hankered to be with the British, now joined the Battalion as a soldier.

The attack began well, with the Lincolns and Mac Paps taking well-fortified positions by surprise. Then barbed-wire and heavy fire slowed their advance, giving time for the fascists to reinforce their positions. The British Battalion was now sent, at night, into the line on the flank of the Lincolns, ready to move forward to Vivel del Río, the objective of the attack. The fascist resistance stiffened, with artillery fire and repeated flights of bombers and strafing planes. But the pilots were very unsure of the position of the lines, so the bombers dropped their loads well in the rear and the Battalion lay still while the fighter-planes were circling.

The No. 1 Company, commanded by 'Taffy' Glyn Evans, a miner from Cefn Cribbwr, South Wales, veteran of Jarama and Brunete, then began to push forward and got within sight of the roads and the village. A fascist flank attack was pushed back by rifle and enfilading fire from the Machine-Gun

Company, and the advance continued. Patrols from the Spanish Battalion actually crossed the road on to the commanding hills beyond, but the forces available were too limited to hold and consolidate the positions. During this advance Alexander was wounded and Wild took command of the Battalion. Alexander was finally invalided home in July after complications had set in.

The operation had been carried out with drive and competence, and the Brigade and the British Battalion were again singled out for commendation by the 5th Army Command. However, it had not succeeded in its aim of drawing pressure away from Teruel. The fascists had crossed the Alfambra river and were close to encircling the city and the Republican troops still in it. On 19 February the Battalion was withdrawn from the positions it had taken and moved to the Celades area, where it had first fought in the snow, ready to hinder the fascist encirclement. However, the Spanish troops of El Campesino fought their way out of the town and the fascist trap.

The Battalion was now rushed to the south of Teruel to meet the threat of a possible push down the Valencia road. But the fascists made no attempt against the strongly fortified positions.

The XVth Brigade was now withdrawn a few more miles from the front, to Puebla de Valverde. Its active role on the Teruel sector was over.

Chapter 14

The Fascist Breakthrough

The Battalion spent a few days in reserve behind the fortified zone outside Teruel, providing an opportunity for Wild and the officers to reorganize and incorporate men returning from hospitals and convalescent homes. When the immediate threat of a fascist attack from Teruel seemed over, the whole Brigade moved further from the front to Lecera. Everyone was eagerly awaiting the move to the promised rest in the rear. Because of the fascist domination of the air the days were spent in the fields – not a hardship, as the snows had given way to spring warmth. Barns and similar buildings were used only at night.

However fascism was preparing a mighty offensive, and not only against democracy in Spain. On 13 March 1938 Hitler's forces marched into Vienna. The British Government entered into servile negotiations with Mussolini with the aim of freeing his hands in the Mediterranean. Franco's military advisers had now decided to open their big offensive across the Aragon plateau and into Catalonia, so as to cut the Republic into two. They therefore concentrated the most powerful forces yet seen in the war, assembling fifteen divisions, as well as many auxiliary units.

Four divisions of Mussolini's army, mostly mechanized, were already in position near Segura de los Baños when the XVth Brigade made its attack there. Four divisions, including Foreign Legion and Moorish units, were already facing Belchite and Azaila. Five divisions were to drive towards

Alcorisa. Besides the Italian tanks and armoured cars, there was a German tank corps with about 150 tanks. The fascist artillery massed 600 guns, with anti-tank guns in addition, and an airforce containing more than 900 planes, drawn from Hitler's Condor Legion, the Italian Air Force, and the rebel air force. All these units were well armed and supplied by Germany and Italy, and had ample transport and petrol, much coming from the USA. In men alone the fascists had a five to one superiority over the Republican forces; in machines and material the disproportion was incomparably greater.

Suddenly, on the morning of 9 March, this massive force of men and machines was unleashed against the Republican lines on a fifty-mile front. Every gun and every plane available was used to smash the front, break the morale of the defenders, and open a speedy way to the Mediterranean. Only the first objective was achieved: the small and poorly-armed Republican units holding the front were forced into full and general retreat.

The XVth Brigade was hurriedly ordered forward at once from the Lecera area and established its HQ in Belchite. Čopic had been sent away for medical rest and leave, and the American Chief of Staff, Robert Merriman, was in command. Belchite looked even more desolate and battered than when the Brigade had captured it a few months before. The XVth Brigade was spread out on a very wide front, the Mac Paps almost detached to cover a possible gap near Azuara, and the Lincolns on commanding hills to the west of Belchite. The British were sent north along the almost straight road towards Mediana and Fuentes de Ebro. On their right flank were the 59th Spanish Battalion, who linked up with the Thaelmanns of the XIIIth Brigade covering Codo.

Tapsell had gone on sick leave and Tom Oldershaw, a building worker from Battersea, London, who had been the Machine-Gun Company Political Commissar at Teruel, took his place. Francis, who had been wounded at Brunete, had returned to command No. 1 Company, only to be killed in the first day of the battle.

Belchite was empty of troops when the Battalion moved

through. But down the road from Mediana small groups of stragglers were moving – the remnants of units who had broken at the front. The British moved forward for about two miles through the sparse olive groves and bare fields. It became very clear that there were no organized Republican units in front of them, and that the enemy was very near and in considerable force. Soon the British came under attack from strafing planes, artillery, machine-gun and rifle fire. The Lincolns, Spanish troops and Thaelmanns on their flanks came under even heavier pressure and were forced to move back. Nothing had been done to build fortifications and there was little in the way of good, natural defensive positions. Faced with possible encirclement by tanks and infantry, the Battalion was forced to move back towards, and then through, Belchite. There were casualties, but the withdrawal was orderly and controlled. On no fewer than five occasions, when there was a ditch, gulley or buildings which offered a position, the Battalion stopped and gave battle. Its resistance delayed the fall of Belchite by one whole day, and the British Battalion was the last Republican unit to retire through the town.

The final withdrawal from Belchite was very hazardous because of shrapnel fire from the fascist artillery and machine-gun fire from advanced units. However, a culvert and the bed of the Aguavivas river provided a way out, with cover. Though the dead had to be left, all the wounded were picked up and evacuated to the rear.

The Anti-Tank Battery, commanded by Nicoll, had its three guns placed well forward of Belchite with good fields of fire. They fired very effectively all day against tanks, vehicles and groups of infantry. When belated orders came to pull out, two of the guns were moved safely – thanks in part to the herculean efforts of Jim Brewer, an unemployed worker from Rhymney Valley, Wales – and were loaded on trucks with two of the gun crew, and sent back. One gun could not be withdrawn, so the breech-block was taken out and thrown into the river. Later one of the two surviving guns and the lorry towing it were set on fire when strafed by a low-flying aircraft. The remainder of the Battery made their way back, in small groups over the hills. Later Nicoll made an unsuccessful attempt to get more guns in Barcelona. The Battery personnel were henceforth incorporated in the British Battalion or the Brigade Machine-Gun Company. The defence of Belchite was the last battle of the British Anti-Tank Battery.

At dusk the Battalion set up defensive positions astride the road to Lecera to block any attempt to break through with tanks or lorried infantry. A few Mac Paps, Lincolns and Spanish troops who had lost their units, turned up and were incorporated into the defence. 'Hookey' Walker managed to find the Battalion with the kitchen truck and everyone had an ample meal, the first for twenty-four hours. Later that night the unit moved back about a mile and took up stronger, more defensible positions. Everyone dug in; little urging was needed.

Late in the afternoon of the next day, 11 March, which passed without action, Wild and Oldershaw decided to find out what was happening in the Brigade. They went back to Lecera, where Brigade headquarters were reported to be, and found the village in fascist hands. They hurried back to the Battalion which was assembled and ordered to march silently, striking eastwards across country.

This move and the many to follow were extremely difficult. Large-scale maps were always in short supply. Because of the suddenness and the scale of the retreat, Wild had nothing except a small-scale commercial map showing only towns and main roads. The sun and the stars at night had to be used to give direction.

Contact was made with some of the Brigade Staff on the outskirts of Vinaceite in the early hours of 12 March. Some rest was possible, but in the early afternoon the troops holding the front retired precipitately and in some panic.

The fascists were trying the techniques, later developed and used with even greater success in France in 1940, of moving tanks and armoured vehicles across the fairly flat, dry, open country and making deep encircling movements. Their planes were used in direct support, attacking ground positions and directing artillery fire. Their infantry, however, were usually reluctant to give battle until all resistance had been battered by planes and guns. The deep penetrations often caused premature, uncontrolled retreats, though the resistance at Belchite, Codo and other places showed that this form of attack could be slowed and blunted by determined groups of men in properly fortified positions.

At 4 p.m. on 12 March the Battalion was ordered to move once again across country and to take up positions on the road from Hijar to Alcañiz. The Army Corps was trying to bring the front under some control and ordered that all that was left of the XVth and XIth International Brigades should move to defend Alcañiz.

This march was hell for the Battalion. The heat was intense, there was no water. Even at Vinaceite boots and feet were in a sorry condition. The moving columns were strafed by low-flying planes for mile after mile, each strafing run breaking the line of march. The remnants of other units were on the move, and it was almost impossible to keep together as an organized unit. Some of the Battalion got left behind or mixed up with other units. Despite this, someone, probably a veteran from the Hunger Marches, had a mouth organ and this gave some help to morale.

Next morning, the 13 March, the Battalion was in position occupying a hill on the Hijar-Alcañiz road. Hijar had been heavily bombed and was in fascist hands. The British stayed in position all that day, digging in frantically that night. But the next morning showed that there were no units on the flanks and the enemy were working to their rear. The British began to move back down the road to Alcañiz but came under fire from positions dominating the road. Though they did not know it, the Italian fascist units were already in Alcañiz. Once again the Battalion had to take to the hills, striking east towards Caspe, soon putting a ridge between themselves and the enemy machine-gunners.

One moving episode cheered everyone and at the same time illustrated further the cruelties of the war. In command of the Spanish company of the Battalion was Cipriano who had been outstanding in action since before Teruel, and had proved himself a brave and competent leader. On the road the Battalion met a group of civilian refugees fleeing to escape the fascist advance. One of these was Cipriano's wife. It was their last meeting. He was killed later.

The British-led group now contained a substantial number of International Brigaders and Spanish troops who had lost their units and needed direction and organization, and Wild and Oldershaw organized continuously to keep the group together.

At first the going was over trackless country, one hill following another. Eventually a track was found leading in the direction of Caspe. Continual vigilance was essential for no one was sure of the depth of fascist penetration. Many had been without sleep for three nights. The shortage of food and water added to exhaustion and debilitation. Some men had lost or dropped their rifles, but two small tanks which had attached themselves to the group carried the heavy and light machine-guns. That night the British group reached Caspe, some twenty miles to the east of Hijar, though the route taken was even longer. The group remained organized, with a military and political leadership, but it could no longer properly be called a Battalion.

The grave, even disastrous, position at the front created an acute crisis in the Republican Government. Prieto, Minister of Defence, was saying publicly that all was over and the Government should capitulate. His defeatist views were already well known and had been expressed in his attitude to the armed forces: he had tried to do away with political commissars and had shown hostility to the International Brigades.

The news of this governmental crisis aroused a strong reaction among the people and the democratic organizations. Demonstrations occurred demanding stern resistance. The two main trade-union bodies, the UGT and the CNT, agreed to work together and then officially joined the Popular Front, so strengthening the anti-fascist struggle. Then Negrín, the Prime Minister, took over the Defence Ministry from Pínieto.

In those critical days the British at the front knew little of this. They knew that, although most units of the army fought bravely and skilfully, some had left the front after being abandoned by their officers; and also that no attempt had been made to build fortifications in depth behind the fronts. Hitler and Mussolini were throwing enormous forces into Spain to further their own expansionist plans. The news of the political crisis and popular support for continued resistance seeped through to the British from an occasional Barcelona newspaper which got to the front. There was no need for discussion: all welcomed the new unity and hoped that it would show itself in greater efforts at the front and in the rear.

Dave Doran, the Brigade Political Commissar, and others of the XVth Brigade Staff had also reached Caspe. All units and stragglers were organized for its defence. It was recognized as an area where a defence line could be built and the calamitous retreat could be checked and even halted, while new units were being rushed from the Madrid and southern fronts.

That night the British-led group slept in the olive groves beyond the town. They received some food, more rifles and ammunition, and again organization was established. There are no reliable figures as to the numbers. Some say there were 150 British and Spanish in the group, some say much fewer. In any case it was but a fraction of the 500 who had marched forward to defend Belchite.

Early next morning, on 16 March, Doran ordered the British to move through the town westwards towards the dominating heights which were already in fascist hands. They came under intense air and artillery attack. Oldershaw was wounded in the advance. He was put, under cover, in an archway; he was not there when a party went to carry him to the rear, and he was never seen again (political commissars were given short shrift by the fascists).

Then the fascist infantry advanced and partly encircled the British group. The Lincoln group on their flank was forced to retreat. There was confused hand-to-hand fighting. Wild, Harry Dobson, a Rhondda miner, Bobby Walker, an ex-Scots Guardsman from Edinburgh, and Joe Norman, an ex-Navy engineer from Manchester, were taken prisoner but escaped by knocking down their captors, who were looting their possessions, with fists, boots and a tin of bully-beef in a sack. Wild, Dobson and Norman got safely back but Walker became isolated, made his way across country, and eventually had to swim the Ebro to reach Republican territory.

All the defending groups were ordered to the fringe of the town itself, where they maintained bitter resistance while the enemy was filtering forward among the buildings. That night the fascists moved tanks and patrols into Caspe itself. Dunbar, who had now managed to find his way back to Brigade from leave, organized bombing patrols with grenades. Wild was able to muster only twelve men, but they did an effective job.

Finally the British were forced to retreat through Caspe under intense and short-range rifle and machine-gun fire. On the 18 March they were ordered to move again across country to Maella. Even more depleted in numbers, in extremes of exhaustion and with almost all ammunition expended, the group waded the Matarraña river, tributary of the Ebro, and arrived at Batea.

The defence of Caspe, by a few hundred exhausted, poorly-armed men of the XVth Brigade, had broken the momentum of the drive by two fascist divisions and had given time for the Listers and the Garibaldis to form a line, weak though it was, blocking the way to the Mediterranean.

The remnants of the XVth Brigade assembled in Batea and Corbera and were reorganized. Men, alone or in small groups, straggled in for days to warm welcomes from their friends who had supposed them killed or captured. All had stories of strain and extreme hardship as they made their way back after being cut off from the Battalion. Without food and water, without maps and with strong enemy patrols everywhere, the movement was hazardous. Often they hid during the day and moved only at night, afraid to go to farms for food and directions in case the fascists were already there. One group got away by attaching themselves to the rear of a fascist Italian column advancing at night and then breaking away.

Most of those captured by the fascists were shot on the spot.

Morgan Harvard, a big-bodied miner from the Swansea Valley, was more fortunate. Badly wounded in the arm and shoulder, he was being carried on an improvised stretcher by three others. Progress became slower and slower, and the bearers were at the end of their physical reserves. After discussion, with Harvard taking the lead, he was left, under shade, with the little food and water available. His friends feared the worst but he was lucky and was later discovered to be in a fascist prison camp.

Some groups were cut off for as long as ten days. The fortunate ones managed to slip through the fascist lines; others were taken prisoner or were shot breaking through the fascist front line.

At Batea there was sleep, rest and food. New arms, rifles, machine-guns, and ammunition were issued. There was rapid reorganization since everyone knew it was but a temporary lull in the fascist offensive.

Four of the five International Brigades were now in the threatened sector. The Government, realizing the critical situation, deciding to close the Albacete Base and all the training and holding camps in the south and to move their personnel north to Catalonia. It appeared almost certain that the fascists would cut the Republic in two. Some parts of the International Brigades' base and services were re-established around Barcelona but on a reduced and limited scale.

The threat to the very existence of the Republic created a ferment in the hospitals and convalescent homes. There were meetings, discussions, and mass volunteering to return to the front. In Benicasím Hospital, all the British who considered themselves fit to fight (not infrequently contrary to the doctors' opinions) volunteered to return to action. Fletcher, who was recovering from wounds, had been promoted Captain for his continuous skilled leadership. He led the determined large party back to the Battalion. Those wounded and unable to walk, and all the medical personnel, were moved by train. The journey north to Catalonia was nerve-racking as the fascists bombed continuously, trying to destroy completely the only rail bridge across the Ebro at Tortosa.

The wounded lay helplessly as the bombs screeched down while the trains inched their way across the already damaged bridge.

The reinforcements, British and Spanish, brought the Battalion strength to 650, the highest ever. Despite the shock and strain of the recent retreats, the veterans, the returned wounded, and the new arrivals from the training camps were soon consolidated in the Battalion organization. Morale rose. Wild was promoted Captain in recognition of his courageous, undaunted leadership, but then he was sent to Barcelona for medical treatment and rest. Fletcher took over command of the Battalion, and Tapsell returned from his sick leave and took over again as Battalion Political Commissar.

While the Battalion and the Brigade were using this brief period for rest, reorganization and consolidation, the fascist forces were still trying to break through a few miles away. But they were checked and in some places driven back by the Listers and other crack troops hurried from the Centre Front. However, on 30 March 1939 the fascists launched a powerful new offensive, south of the Ebro, where they had already made the deep penetration, and also to the north along the line of the River Segre and around Lérida.

The XVth Brigade was alerted and ordered to move westwards nearer to the front line positions held by Republican troops. By the end of that day all four Battalions of the Brigade had suffered heavy casualties and become so disorganized that the Brigade was no longer a unit, but only groups of men led by individuals who took over responsibility and leadership.

Fletcher had been ordered to move west from Gandesa through the small village of Calaceite and take up positions in support of and in reserve to the Listers. The Mac Paps were ordered on their right nearer the road to Batea. Just before dawn on 31 March the British met a column of Italian tanks, armoured cars and infantry.

Fletcher has been criticized after the event, by writers not involved, for lack of vigilance; however, the facts do not show this. The Battalion was moving fast, since it knew the penalty of occupying positions in daylight with fascist domination of the air and long-range artillery. There was an advance group in front of the main body, and groups detailed to watch the flanks. A Spanish officer, stated to be from the Listers, was guiding the column, and Dunbar, Brigade Chief of Operations, and Ryan, of Brigade Staff, were with the Battalion. No one in Brigade or Battalion knew that the Listers had retreated and the front was open. There had been no movement of retreating troops. The British were the first to meet the powerful fascist forces now driving forward on this sector. But within hours all the other Battalions had met that offensive and were overcome.

In the half light the Battalion, one file on each side of the road, was rounding a bend when a column of light tanks came round, running between the two files. Some thought they were Republican, and Tapsell approached a tank and spoke to the Commander. Then hell broke loose. The tanks on the road opened fire, another group came from a wood on one side, and large numbers of Italian infantry charged, shouting and firing. Fletcher shouted: 'Scatter and make for the hills.' It was every man for himself as the tanks moved up and down the road, firing and running over men. The Machine-Gun Company was at the rear of the Battalion and a number with their guns got into position and opened fire. They were able to knock out some tanks and kill a number of Italian infantry, and this gave time and opportunity for some of the Battalion to make their escape, in a number of cases breaking away from their captors.

The machine-gunners held their positions on the hills for over an hour before the threat of encirclement forced the remaining few to retreat. The losses of the Battalion were severe. Out of the 650 men who marched through Calaceite that morning, 150 were killed or wounded, though the full count could not be known till much later when the names of the 140 taken prisoner became available from Burgos jail. Tapsell was last seen trying to fire his revolver at a tank commander, but was not seen alive again.

The groups of men who had escaped the first onslaught

made their own ways to the rear through rough, enemy-occupied country. Many were shot down or made prisoner. Cooney, No. 1 Company Commissar, and a small group, made their way over the hills only to find the enemy already in Calaceite. They had to take to the hills again. Other groups made contact with the remains of the Brigade in the next couple of days. But others wandered for seven or eight days before they finally broke through the fascist lines and got across the Ebro, some by boat others by swimming.

The XVth Brigade command had been broken up in the fascist surge forward. Merriman and Doran had been killed. Copic was cut off, almost alone, and had, like so many of the Brigade, to find his own way to the Ebro. However, Dunbar, who had been wounded in the Calaceite fighting, got out of the field dressing-station and moved back the following day to the Gandesa area.

Marty appeared and a beginning was made to create some cohesion and organized resistance. Dunbar established contact with the eighty-odd British collected at the road junction, where the small road to Batea joined the Calaceite-Gandesa road, and with a sizeable group of Mac Paps who had got away from their battle. Alan Gilchrist, a schoolteacher from London, and Frank Proctor from Liverpool, both of the Anti-Tank Battery, who had driven forward from Mora de Ebro looking for the Brigade and who were unaware of the scale of the collapse, joined the group which made its way, some through Gandesa itself, some through the fields, fighting off another attempt at encirclement. In the early dawn of 2 April Dunbar led them to take up a position about one and a half kilometres to the south-east of the town. Here the road from Gandesa to Tortosa ran through a cutting flanked by a steep-sided ridge, impossible to assault and difficult to outflank. Dunbar saw its potential for a delaying action – enough to stop the fascist advance for a limited time. However, every hour gave time for the Republic to get men and material to safety beyond the Ebro, and time for new troops to form a line to stop the fascists racing to Tortosa and the sea.

The group had one machine-gun and a handful of grenades, but nearly every man had a rifle and ammunition. In a splendid defensive position, and with a feeling that someone knew what to do, morale rose sharply. In the early morning Gilchrist led a small patrol forward to the outskirts of Gandesa and returned without incident, but reinforced with some Spanish soldiers who had found their way there. The group was now about 200 strong – British, Canadian, Spanish, a few Americans and Thaelmanns. A small tank with a Spanish crew appeared from the rear and stationed itself in the cutting where the road ran through the ridge.

The fascists attacked. Their heavy artillery had not yet moved up, low cloud stopped their air activity, and they were over confident. Cavalry patrols were driven back, then an infantry attack was repulsed. One of a group of armoured cars was set alight by machine-gun fire. Throughout the entire day the defending group stood fast while the enemy column was halted below. Because of its position casualties were low despite continuing fire throughout the day. As darkness fell, its delaying task achieved, Dunbar gave the orders for the group's withdrawal. Walter Gregory, a Nottingham shop worker and a veteran fighter since the first day at Jarama, stayed behind for a while, firing furiously and throwing grenades to give the impression that the position was still held. Then he caught up and joined the British group.

The group marched down the road towards Tortosa in high spirits, singing, and with someone playing a mouth-organ. On the road they met Wild in a truck. Hearing of the disastrous retreat, he had abandoned the medical treatment he was having and set out to find the Battalion. On 3 April, after a couple of hours' sleep and some food, the British crossed – near Cherta – in small boats to the northern side of the Ebro.

The day's successful defence at Gandesa gave the Listers more time to move into positions further down the river and to check the fascist advance for several more days. The fascists did not reach the sea until 15 April. But they had then cut

Republican Spain in two.

The following day Chamberlain signed the Anglo-Italian Pact, giving fascist Italy a free hand in the Mediterranean, and effectively allowing Mussolini to keep his regular troops in Spain until victory.

Chapter 15

The Fight Goes On in Franco's Gaols

Those British unfortunate enough to be taken prisoner were severely tested in Franco's gaols and needed every scrap of their courage, and all their conviction. Groups of British were taken prisoner at Jarama, during the big retreat across Aragon in 1938, and in the last battles of the offensive across the Ebro.

Thirty men were taken, including Fry the Commander, when the Machine-Gun Company was surrounded on the second day of the Jarama battle in February 1937. They were disarmed, their pockets were emptied, and they were herded to the dead ground below their position. Then, surrounded by Foreign Legionnaires, they were marched to the rear. Phil Elias of Leeds asked if he could smoke. He lowered his hands to get tobacco from his pockets and was riddled through the guts by a burst of sub-machine-gun fire. John Stevens, a Londoner standing next to him, was killed by the same burst. Ted Dickinson, another Londoner, the Company Second-in-Command, tall, erect, with a military bearing, was wearing riding-boots and breeches. He was singled out as a leader and shot in cold blood. Fry had stripped off his insignia. All the British prisoners were lined against a wall, and a firing-squad was drawn up to shoot, but an officer ran up and stopped the execution. Their hands were tied behind their backs, viciously, with telephone-wire which cut the skin. They were then marched further to the rear by Moors on horseback who lashed out freely with their whips. Though full of fears for the future, the prisoners were amazed and proud to see the masses of fascist tanks, artillery and men who had been stopped by their defence. They were jeered at by Italians; Moors threatened to kill them; but they were taken on trucks, protected by Civil Guards, to the jail in Navalcarnero. During their eight days there they were interrogated by Merry del Val, son of a former Spanish Ambassador in London. Fortunately they were seen and photographed by a *Daily Mail* reporter. When a picture was published in the paper, it gave hope to the families and lessened the danger of summary execution.

After their heads were shaved, and they had been finger-printed, the group was moved on to Talavera where, because the prison was so crowded, they were put in an old factory, sleeping on straw. The place was crammed with local people who had been rounded up and imprisoned for their Republican views. Every evening a covered van, soon dubbed the 'Agony Van', called, and a group of handcuffed Spaniards were led out. They were shot on unconsecrated ground but then buried in big pits in the cemetery.

Groups of British prisoners were taken out every day to work, some on the roads, some to cover the bodies in the cemetery pits. One sergeant in charge of the armed escort, however, would take them back to prison through the working-class streets. Women from the houses would give them small gifts – bread, cigarettes, fruit. These were deeply appreciated, augmenting the starvation rations and raising morale.

After three months the group were taken to Salamanca and tried as a group by a military court. The charge was 'aiding a military rebellion'. The defending officer, who they had never seen before, pleaded for mercy saying they had been misled. By agreement no one spoke in court. Five, apparently chosen at random – George Leeson, Morry Goldberg, Harold Fry, Jimmy Rutherford and C. West from Lymington – were sentenced to death and everyone else to twenty years' imprisonment.

After this farce of a trial, all were returned to the Model

Prison in Salamanca, built to hold 250 but now packed with 5,000 civilians. Each evening as the 'Agony Van' arrived, the five British under sentence of death wondered if their names would be called. The guards added to the tension by opening every cell door before calling out the names of that night's victims. The British names, in fact, were never called.

In May 1937, an exchange was arranged of the British prisoners for fascist officers in Republican hands. They had a bath, the first since capture, were given clean clothes, and were lined up in front of a ciné-camera while shots were taken of them receiving cigarettes, which were taken away when filming was done. Then twenty-three, including Fry, whose rank was still unknown, and Rutherford of the Edinburgh Labour League of Youth, and a member of the Free Fishermen of Newhaven and only nineteen years old were taken to the French frontier. There, under threats of continued detention, one comrade who had been 'appointed' by the group gave a feeble 'Viva Franco', and they passed into France and home.

Fry, Rutherford, Tom Bloomfield, a miner from Kircaldy, Basil Abrahams, a baker from London, and two others insisted on being allowed to return to the Brigade. In six weeks they were back in Spain and were even given their pay, then seven pesetas a day, from the time they were captured.

George Leeson, a clerk from London, and Morry Goldberg from Stepney, a clothing worker, both under sentence of death, were kept behind for no obvious reason, except perhaps anti-Semitism among the fascists. But they were moved in with the Spanish prisoners. Each morning and each night the Falangist officers came in and selected a number of prisoners for execution. The two felt isolated but were sustained by the friendship and active help from the Spanish prisoners whose families were allowed to send in food. Leeson was released in September after questions in the House of Commons and a campaign in which the returned prisoners played a leading part; but Goldberg was not finally released until November 1937.

When the Battalion met the Italian armoured column near

Calaceite on 21 March 1938, many were taken prisoner on the spot. Later that day, and for the next eight to ten days, the fascists captured small groups as they made their way through enemy territory towards the Ebro. Some prisoners were shot on the spot. But the fascists had been dropping leaflets from the air urging the International Brigade to desert, which may have discouraged immediate executions.

After capture the main group were marched back to the rear surrounded by Civil Guards with sub-machine-guns. Fortunately a group of foreign journalists was there and someone called out 'We're British'. An American journalist came over and spoke to the group. After that a general execution would have created difficulties for Franco, who had been attempting to pose as a 'Christian gentleman'. So began a long, brutal, systematic campaign to break the prisoners, physically and morally.

They were herded into a cowshed without food and water. The manure provided a convenient hiding place to get rid of all money, papers and letters. Then they were led out, one by one, for interrogation by English-speaking Italian officers. After a prisoner had been taken out there would be a burst of machine-gun fire so that the remainder thought that death was near. The feeling among the group was low. Many felt they had dishonoured their cause by being captured. Some who had just joined the Battalion were shattered by the sudden violence of war. All were uncertain, having heard of the cruelty and terror experienced by the earlier group of prisoners. Ryan, of Brigade Staff, set an immediate example of courage. He made no attempt to disguise his rank and when asked by his Italian captors if he was a Communist replied, so that all around could hear, 'I am an Irish Republican but if I were a Communist I'd be proud to say so.' Later they were herded as exhibits – filthy, unshaven, and ragged – through the streets of Zaragoza.

Some began to hum revolutionary tunes. It was possibly Ryan who struck up Connolly's 'Rebel Song', taken up with gusto and spirit by nearly all the prisoners. Later, in prison, Ryan said that, as the senior officer present, he would not give the fascist salute, and he never did so during all his captivity. Later he used his standing and his religious beliefs to secure the removal of a vicious priest who vented his sadism in the compulsory masses.

During the second day in the military prison of Zaragoza, the prisoners were interrogated by Merry del Val, who had interrogated the prisoners already taken at Jarama. He recognized Jimmie Rutherford, whose return to Spain had been announced in *Our Fight*, the newssheet of the XVth Brigade. Later Rutherford was taken away and executed.

Within four days of capture the leading Communists began to organize. Danny Gibbons, George Ives and Lionel Jacobs, (a clothing worker), all from London, Joe Norman of Manchester, and Jack Jones, a miner from the Rhondda, had all known one another as Communists in Britain. They had a brief, furtive, meeting and decided to form a committee. They were very aware of the dangers of this step: with the big batch of newcomers to the Battalion, they did not know everyone and were afraid of stool-pigeons. So they told no one of their decision and their organization, but worked as a unit. They agreed on an approach which guided the behaviour of prisoners throughout their captivity: it was to stiffen the morale of the group and to get everyone home alive and strong to continue the antifascist struggle. Soon another group of Communists, unaware of the first, met and adopted very similar objectives and approach. Later the two committees became aware of their parallel work, and a single, but still secret organization was formed.

Most of the prisoners were later taken to the San Pedro Concentration Camp near Burgos. A few were taken to a prison in Bilbao where Tom Picton, a miner from Rhondda Fach, was shot in cold blood. There was no apparent reason for this crime, except that he was a very big strong man, an ex-boxer with a deep contempt for the fascists. San Pedro was a two-hundred-year-old convent crammed to the very last inch with six hundred or so International Brigaders of every nationality, who were kept apart from the several thousand Spanish prisoners. Here the efforts to break and intimidate the men sank to new depths of sadism. They slept on the floor in long rooms, literally shoulder to shoulder, with very little light or ventilation. It was stifling in summer but freezing cold in the depth of winter. There were three taps to provide water for drinking and washing for all the prisoners. These allowed five minutes access a day for each man. The lavatories were open, of the crudest style, and were often blocked. Lice, dysentery, rheumatism and skin diseases affected everyone. The food, mainly beans and a little bread, was barely sufficient to keep men alive, and was often bad, and not properly cooked. Many of the badly wounded had been shot on the spot when captured, but those with minor wounds received no special treatment. Anyone desperate enough to report sick to the Camp doctor received the 'Italian fascist medicine', a large dose of castor-oil.

Three of the fascist jailers were especially brutal. 'Sticky', a small man with a thin stick, lashed out at every man as they moved out to collect their food, especially selecting the biggest prisoners for his attentions. 'Tanky' had been wounded in a tank in action against the International Brigades and worked off his spite with a weighted crop. 'Froggy', with bulbous blue eyes behind spectacles, hated the British in particular. Every day or so a prisoner, by chance or for some imaginary offence, was taken out and beaten unconscious by eight or ten guards and then thrown back on the floor of the dormitory.

Not everyone could stand up to the strain of the treatment and the conditions; at least two had offered to collaborate with the authorities. The secret group of Communists arranged that individuals who were better able to resist the harsh conditions should sleep next to those showing strain, and by discussion and help in all ways, try to raise their confidence and morale. Disputes, bullying, petty pilfering, inevitable in such circumstances, were sorted out among the prisoners and were not reported to the authorities.

The British Communist Committee established contact with the other national groups and soon there was a secret committee and an agreed approach for the whole camp. Paper was obtained on the pretext of learning Spanish. Jimmy

Moon, a laboratory technician from Reading, helped to produce the hand-written *San Pedro Jaily News*, which was circulated among the prisoners. Headed by a sketch of the prisoners enjoying themselves in idyllic surroundings – a reference to a report in the *New York Times* praising prison conditions in Franco's Spain – it contained the little available news from outside, jokes – humorous stories about individual reluctance to wash – and similar material. It helped to raise morale, but production was stopped when a copy in circulation disappeared, no one knew where.

By the end of April 1938 substantial group spirit, with self discipline, had been established. A 'house committee' was formed to look after social life. The May Day concert, preceded by plenty of rehearsals, was such a success that further concerts were prohibited. Draughts and chessmen were made out of soft bread or soap. Classes were organized on any subject in which a prisoner felt competent to instruct. Marxism, British working-class history, economics, electricity, mathematics and other subjects were taught in regular classes. Throughout the day the 'San Pedro University' made an inroad into boredom and raised morale, until the classes had to end, like the newspaper, in face of repression.

The authorities tried everything to undermine the prisoners' spirits and philosophy. Articles by Oswald Mosley and other British fascists had to be read by one prisoner to everyone. There were systematic interrogations, always under the threat of violence, by German, Italian and Spanish intelligence officers. Besides questions about the political and domestic background of the prisoners there was an element of perversion. They were photographed in the nude, asked about their sexual lives, when they first had sexual intercourse, whether they had ever used a prostitute, and similar questions. Mass was compulsory and anyone who did not join in the responses was beaten up on the spot under the direction of the priest. The authorities had used extreme brutality to get the men on the daily parades to raise their arms in the fascist salute and to shout 'Viva Franco'. The Communist committee

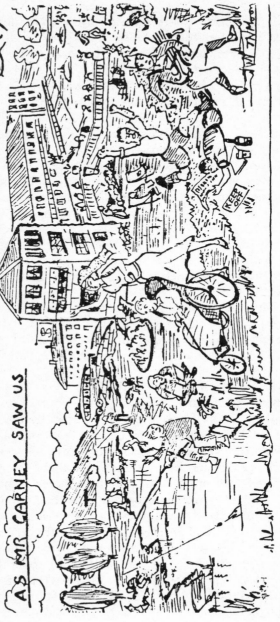

Masthead drawing on *San Pedro Jaily News*

decided to do this rather than face continued crippling beatings, though some shouted 'Viva Blanco', or 'Fuck you'.

Then the fascists arranged a show: a visit of top-ranking officers, and Colonel Martin, the British military representative in Franco Spain. The prisoners were paraded; the officer in charge gave the command; but not an arm went up, not a man shouted. The British felt fine, though the fascist revenge was an all-round vicious beating with rifles, sticks, boots and rubber-hose. Again they were paraded in front of Lady Austen Chamberlain, a relative of Neville Chamberlain, the Prime Minister. Not an arm was raised and she left angrily, shouting abuse.

In September, Walter Gregory, Frank West, George Wheeler, and some others captured in the last days before the withdrawal of the Battalion, were brought to San Pedro. They contributed useful experience, news of the Ebro offensive, and of the outside world.

In mid June one hundred British prisoners were taken from San Pedro to Palencia where they were kept while negotiations were going on for their exchange for Italian regular soldiers captured by the Republic. Life in Palencia was hard but not so grim as in San Pedro. Some letters and money came from home and the hope of a possible release lifted everyone's spirits. But it was not until the end of October 1938 that the group were allowed to clean up and were given some fresh clothes. They were then taken to San Sebastian gaol and kept until confirmation of the release of the Italians. Then at Irun, led by Clive Branson, an artist living in Battersea, they marched, erect and soldierly, over the International Bridge to France. One, tempted by the almost forgotten fresh fruit, broke ranks to take an apple from a stall, but got a thump from his mate. After delousing and some food the party were guarded like criminals across France to Britain.

Left in San Pedro, the remainder of the prisoners were subjected to even greater physical violence. However, in February 1939 another exchange was arranged: one British prisoner for ten Italians. The British were listed alphabetically and there were insufficient Italians to go round, so ten men whose names were last on the list were left behind and kept in prison at San Sebastian for three more months. Things were grim: the prisoners' organization had been broken up, Spanish prisoners were taken out and shot every day (part of the prison wall was chipped away by bullets from the execution squads). Though Red Cross parcels arrived at Christmas, the food was so inadequate that some developed scurvy and all had deep sores covered with jelly-like pus. The defeat of the Republic, the Nazi occupation of Czechoslovakia, and the imminence of world war, brought a prospect of prison for the duration. But pressure in Britain, in which D.N. Pritt, MP, played a leading part, secured their release at the end of April 1939.

A few of the prisoners were in a bad state physically and mentally and could do little on their return. But a large majority recovered quickly from their ordeal and resumed political activity. Remembering their own experiences in Franco's hands, they played a particular part in the campaign to secure the release of all International Brigaders and Republican prisoners.

Jack Coward's experiences were told in his aptly-titled pamphlet, *Escape from the Dead*. After service in the Republican Navy he joined the British Battalion and was commanding No. 4 Company when it was ambushed at Calaceite. He got away to the hills and linked up with a party of guerrillas. Captured, he escaped and again linked up with a group of peasants. They were bombed and Coward became dumb from the shock and his hair turned white. Caught once again he was not identified as an International and was sent to the San Pedro Concentration Camp where 6,000 Spanish civilian prisoners were kept apart from the International Brigade prisoners. At the end of the war some prisoners over forty-five years old – Coward's white hair made him look much older – were given provisional liberty. He made his way to Vigo on the north west coast and, behaving like a drunken British sailor, walked on to the docks and stowed away on a British ship. He hid, covered with coal in the bunkers, until the ship reached Gibraltar. Finally, back in Liverpool, his mates in the Dockers' Union branch welcomed him 'as the best news for many months'.

However two British prisoners still remained in Franco's hands: Frank Ryan and Tom Jones. When the exchange of prisoners began to be negotiated, Ryan was moved from San Pedro to the Burgos Penitentiary. Jones, a miner from Rhos, in North Wales, had been captured, badly wounded, in the very last fighting in September 1938, on the Sierra Pandols with a machine-gun Battalion of the XVth Army Corps. Surviving, despite badly treated wounds, physical violence, and threats of shooting, he was sent to Burgos after being sentenced to death by the Zaragoza Military Tribunal. There were about 600 other International Brigade prisoners there, mainly from Germany, Austria and the Balkans, countries which soon came under Axis control. But the prison was packed with over 5,000 Spanish male prisoners, of whom 600 were shot or garrotted in the next few months. The others faced thirty years' imprisonment. It is possible that German intelligence agents had picked out Ryan and Jones, both known in the nationalist movements in their countries, hoping to use them in Nazi subversive activities.

The death sentence on Jones was eventually commuted to thirty years in prison. Thrown together in these appalling circumstances, the two Celts became very attached. Ryan was in contact with his family and the Irish Ambassador to Franco, and so received money and food parcels. He shared these generously with Jones and the Spanish prisoners, especially the Basques. Ryan and Jones won the respect even of the prison guards by their bearing and courage. They were told of the tremendous amount of mail, addressed to them, which arrived at the prison, letters, petitions and food parcels, though Ryan was only allowed to see letters from his family and the Eire Embassy in Madrid.

However, it was a trying and difficult time for both men. There was violence all round them; they slept on the floor with limited space. Lice, skin disease and tuberculosis spread everywhere. Food was scarce and poor. The political situation and prospects tested their convictions: the defeat of the Republic, the German-Soviet Pact, the victories of the fascist powers: all made the future look very bleak indeed. There was little relief when Ryan was told, after living under a death sentence for seventeen months, that he now faced only thirty years' imprisonment. Both men read and studied everything they could get hold of: both studied Spanish, and later Ryan began to learn German. They gave English lessons to some of the Spanish prisoners.

Jones had managed to get news out to his parents of his continued existence; they had already received his death certificate and obituaries had appeared in the local paper. A campaign developed for their release. Ryan's case attracted international concern; broad, influential committees worked in England, Ireland, Canada and the USA for his release.

Jones was released on 20 March 1940, after a painful, emotional parting with Ryan. Back in Britain he took news to Ryan's family in Dublin and suggestions to his many friends for the campaign for Ryan's release.

The international campaign had an impact on the Irish Government: its ambassador in Spain visited Ryan frequently in Burgos. An Irish priest often travelled from Madrid to meet him. The Franco authorities knew that their treatment of Ryan was being closely watched. Later, in July 1940, Ryan was taken to Germany. Details of the transfer and the reasons for it are uncertain. But when Jones last saw Ryan he was nearly stone deaf, very thin, and suffering from rheumatism and chest pains – the results of his harsh imprisonment. He died and was buried in Dresden in June 1944. There is no scrap of evidence that he collaborated in any way with the Nazis. Today his memory is honoured by German anti-fascists. His body was brought home and reinterred, as a staunch anti-fascist, in Dublin on 22 June 1979 at a ceremony widely attended by leading figures from the labour and Nationalist movements.

The International Brigaders of other nationalities, especially those whose countries were occupied by the Nazis, suffered on in Burgos largely forgotten by the wider world. But the volunteers who had reached their homes did not forget them, and campaigned for their safety and release.

Chapter 16

'Across the Ebro': The Last Offensive

When the great retreat of March and April 1938 was over and the fascist armies had reached the Mediterranean, part of the Republican army began to reassemble on the north bank of the River Ebro. To this army, soon to be known as the Army of Catalonia, came the remnants, and they were no more than remnants, of the XVth Brigade.

Men, alone or in small groups, from all the Battalions got across the river: some by boat, some by the bridge at Mora de Ebro before it was blown up on 2 April, some by swimming. They had moved in enemy territory for several days, dodging fascist patrols, often being helped and fed by the peasants. Lewis Clive, a Labour Councillor from Kensington, an Oxford Blue and an Olympic rower, reached the river with a non-swimmer. After helping him across, Clive swam back to fetch his light-machine-gun. Dobson and a small group fought their way through the fascist lines to reach the river; then the swimmers pushed logs with non-swimmers clinging on. Sid Booth, a Manchester railwayman, escaped capture at Calaceite in a group of twenty; without food, in a state of extreme exhaustion, the group dwindled to three. After a dispute about the direction to take, Booth went on alone to safety. Others were shot or taken prisoner in the last dash from the enemy; some drowned in the wide, fast flowing river. Across the river, men waited, hoping for the safe arrival of their friends, but after ten days no more arrived.

It was a difficult time for the army and for the Republic.

The crossing of the Ebro

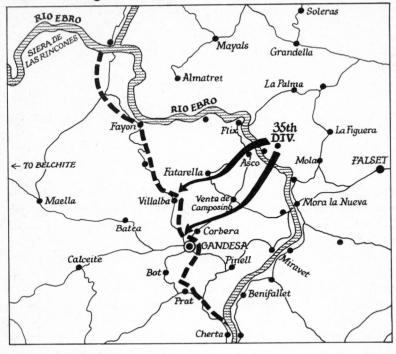

■ ■ ■ ■ ■ Line of maximum penetration   Scale: 1cm to 10km

Everyone was deeply conscious of the long period of retreat during which the fascists had the initiative. Clearly in the memory of everyone was not only the usual immense fascist superiority in men and arms but also their organization, system of communications and command – the advantages of a regular army over the newly-built Republican force.

Would the fascists push ahead across the river and extend their victory? There was some defeatism, some desertion and there were some who drifted from the front. The British Battalion issued a directive deploring 'in a certain number of our comrades a map-conscious ideology. This has to be broken down.' It added that the time of retreats was over. 'We should now be concentrating on making ourselves an efficient fighting unit. This will necessitate hard work and sacrifices on the part of many of us.'

The job of reorganization and the transformation of morale began. The Government crisis was overcome, leaving Negrín in a strong position, supported by big popular demonstrations in Barcelona and other cities. Wider unity developed behind the Government's policy which set out thirteen points for victory and peace and a programme of sound democratic changes.

Marty, Longo and other leaders of the International Brigades began to produce cohesion and organization. Copíc, who had escaped from the fascists outside Gandesa, crossed the river, and began to reorganize the XVth Brigade, establishing collecting points for the scattered Battalions, and obtaining food, clothes, weapons and medical care for those most in need.

An essential need was to raise morale and confidence. A meeting of all the leading Communists in the Brigade was held, a very unusual event. Officers, political commissars, and rank and file got together and agreed on the steps to restore fighting efficiency. Then meetings and discussions were held by the remains of the companies. The need to resist, to fight on and to fortify was stressed.

The British Battalion, though in a sorry state, was in better shape than the others in the XVth Brigade. The group of sixty-odd men who had held back the fascists for the whole day outside Gandesa formed a confident core. By 10 April the Battalion had collected 140 British and some eighty of its Spanish members. Sam Wild was still Commander and Bob Cooney had been appointed Political Commissar to replace Tapsell. When the call was made for volunteers to dig positions along the river, and to establish patrols along its banks, everyone came forward, though many were still in poor physical condition.

With the move to Catalonia and the scaling down of the Brigade Base, a number of experienced and capable volunteers were freed and joined the British and other fighting units. Volunteers were still coming from Britain and included men of very high calibre who had responded to the grave threat to the Republic. These reinforcements helped create new confidence.

Rust, who was now based in Barcelona, visited the British nearly every other day during the critical first few days of consolidation on the banks of the Ebro. He interceded personally with La Pasionaria, Modesto and Lister to get what was possible by way of clothing and arms for the British. Pollitt, having heard of the heavy British losses, flew out to Spain. He spoke to the Battalion on 14 April, then visited the wounded and the medical staff in Brigade hospitals.

Franco's supporters in Britain had filled the newspapers with stories that the British had been annihilated. Some Brigaders, who had made their way home, justified their own desertion by well-embroidered horror stories. These caused great concern among relatives and could have weakened support for the Republic. The visits of some reporters, old friends of the Republic and the Battalion, especially Bill Forrest of the *News Chronicle* and Sefton Delmer of the *Daily Express*, to whom members of the Battalion talked with confidence, knowing that their stories would be true and fair, were able to provide some counterbalancing reports in Britain.

From the Battalion itself came an organized campaign to explain the situation and to appeal for help especially for the ending of the 'Non-Intervention' policies. Wild and Cooney sent a personal letter to leading figures and organizations of the Labour movement. The four Labour councillors in the Battalion – Clement Broadbent of Dewsbury, Lewis Clive of Kensington, Jack L. Jones of Liverpool, and Tom Murray of Edinburgh – wrote to the Secretary of the Labour Party urging 'that our leaders turn a deaf ear to compromise and press ever more vigorously for the Party's declared policy that the British Government's support of 'Non-Intervention' be reversed'. Broadbent and Clive were both killed in the Ebro offensive. Every member of the Battalion was urged to write to his own local organization. Many did so, and it was notable that the great movement in Britain for aid to Spain renewed its efforts, raising increased sums for medical supplies and food. The support for the Dependants' Aid Fund, then stretched to the limit, increased.

It was during this period (summer 1938) that Churchill moved from his previous position of support for Franco, though Chamberlain extended his disastrous policies of appeasing fascism.

The XVth Brigade was reorganized. Čopic handed over command and left Spain. Major Valledor, who took over, was a brave and experienced Spaniard. After the defeat in his native Asturias he had escaped from prison and made his way to rejoin the Army. John Gates, an American, who became Brigade Commissar, had been Commissar of the 20th International Battalion, and so was known and respected by O'Daire and others who had fought on the southern Pozoblanco front. Dunbar, now recovered from his wounds received at Gandesa, became Chief of Staff. Slater, from the Anti-Tanks, after recovering from typhoid, became Chief of Operations. Ruskin was still in charge of Transmissions, but now most of the personnel were Spanish.

After the first few days it became clear that the fascists were not immediately attempting to cross the Ebro. Their drive was towards the south and Valencia, and this was stopped by fierce resistance.

For some days the British Battalion provided patrols for some ten miles of the north bank of the Ebro, to prevent any crossings by small groups of fascists. There was an occasional exchange of rifle fire. Attempts were made at propaganda by shouting across the river. On a couple of occasions a small group crossed the river at night by boat to fetch fruit and food from the deserted fields. But the front was quiet and the Battalion went for more training and rest at Mola, some miles from the river. They were given a specially warm welcome by the local people, and very close relationships were soon established.

Two movements came into being in the Army, both aiming to improve its efficiency and fighting spirit. Members of the British Communist Party had been given membership of the

Spanish Communist Party, and many non-Communists had asked for and been given membership. But in the fighting units no one troubled much if a man had a membership card or not. Separate meetings and discussions were held only in the most exceptional circumstances, as at Quinto or during the Aragon retreat. Now a Communist Party organization was set up at Brigade level, and extending to Battalion and company level. In the Battalion Billy Griffiths, a building worker from the Rhondda, was made responsible. But the organization as such did not have much impact or deep roots. Its role was unclear and ill-defined; there was a tendency to see it as a check and watch-dog on the work of the military and political commanders – almost as a parallel leadership. The leading personel had been designated from the top not by the rank and file.

In the Battalion, Wild and Cooney had general support for their leadership which had been well proven. In the companies, the commanders and commissars, were men who had emerged as natural leaders in action. However the separate organization continued in being; membership cards were issued but kept centrally, and efforts were made to extend recruitment. However it was without great effect. Instead, individual Communists tried, according to their abilities, to influence events by their general behaviour and example.

The second of these movements, the Activist Movement in the Army, was launched from a meeting in Barcelona on 6 July 1938. Under the slogan 'Every soldier an activist – every activist a hero', it recruited individuals to become exemplary soldiers. They aimed to master the use of every weapon, their own and the fascists', to study military tactics and fortification, to raise their own political understanding and then to help everyone in their section, company and Battalion to reach similar standards. John Peet, a journalist, and George Green, a musician, both from London, were the leading members of the movement in the Battalion.

Competitions were organized in weaponry between units and Battalions, and a great deal of individual instruction went on. This was especially useful when the Battalion received very young Spanish conscripts, many of whom could not read or write and who were without military training.

However, in the weeks before the Battalion went into action again, morale rose very high, and training developed rapidly. This, coupled with the British good-humoured reluctance to be publicly labelled a 'good boy', meant that the Activist Movement never really caught on: it simply was not needed, for the spirit was already there.

In mid-May the Republic planned an offensive on the Lérida sector across the River Segre, and the XVth Brigade moved to be in position about thirty miles from the front. The British Battalion had to march there – some fifty miles, during heavy rains. The offensive never achieved a breakthrough and the Battalion moved back to Marsa: this time they were lucky, and travelled by truck, not foot-slogging.

The Brigade settled down around Marsa for the longest period of rest and training it had ever enjoyed in the war. The British were in a steep-sided valley whose bushes provided cover from spying planes and shelter from the hot sun. Groups of friends built brush huts (in Spanish *chavolas*), of varying degrees of elaboration, while No. 1 Company even planned to build an open-air theatre. The Battalion's area was affectionately named Chavola Valley as a result.

There was a vigorous programme of military training and physical fitness. The Battalion strength was built up. There was a big reinforcement of Spanish soldiers. Unlike the first groups who had volunteered to join the International Brigade, these were young conscripts. All had to be trained in the use of weapons – rifle, light-machine-gun, and mortar (these, of Soviet origin, had been added to the Battalion armoury). They also had to be trained in the use of cover, ground and movement.

Intense political discussion took place at all levels, on the threatening international situation and on the Negrín Government's thirteen-point programme. Spanish lessons were organized. However there was also time for recreation: football matches, boxing, fiestas of all kinds – and occasional leave to sample the strong wines of the neighbourhood. Groups went out to visit the wounded still in the various hospitals of Mataró, Vich and Sabadell, taking with them news, a few cigarettes and small gifts.

There were many welcome visitors. Peter Kerrigan, who had now replaced Bill Rust as *Daily Worker* correspondent in Barcelona, came with Pandit Nehru and Krishna Menon, accompanied by leaders of the Republican Government, Alvarez del Vayo and Pablo de Azcarate. The warm reception and instant sympathy with the leaders of the Indian national liberation movement illustrated the strength of internationalist feeling among the British volunteers. In addition, groups from the Battalion went to the rear to meet various delegations of visitors from Britain, mainly trade union leaders and students (including future Tory Prime Minister Edward Heath). All the various meetings were used to impress the visitors with the reasons for ending 'Non-Intervention' and for helping the Republic in face of the growing menace of fascism and international war.

Training became even more intense as it was sensed that the period of rest would not last much longer. The Battalion was now 650 strong, about a third of it British, with a solid core of Spanish, who had been with it for some time, providing an experienced cadre for the younger men drafted in.

Nearly all the fit British personnel in Spain were concentrated in the Battalion. The Anti-Tank Battery, despite frantic efforts, had failed to get more guns, and most of its members went into the Battalion. Nicoll, the last commander, became a section leader in No. 1 Company, while Gilchrist became Commissar of No. 1 Company. The last groups of recruits from Britain were under no illusions as to the hardships and dangers they faced but had insisted on volunteering. Tom Murray came to join his brother George of the Anti-Tanks and his sister Ann of the medical services. Jack L. Jones added to the large group of 'Scousers'. David Guest followed his sister Angela, who was working in the Medical Services. Throughout every company there were many tried and veteran fighters with long experience in Spain. Whenever new leaders were needed there were men ready to step into the breach, if necessary on their own initiative, without orders.

The Battalion was now organized into five companies, with Wild in command. Cooney, now confirmed as Political Commissar, had Morris Miller from Hull as his assistant.

The training took on new, different forms: groups of men were trained to dash across a *barranco* (a dry river-bed), and then to take up positions covering the crossing of the others. Everyone soon grasped the intention: the Republican Army was going to attack across the Ebro. Expectancy and confidence rose high as the veterans recalled the long retreat from Belchite, chased by the fascists. The aim was to show the world that the Republic was still a force to be reckoned with and to divert the fascists from their drive south towards Sagunto and Valencia.

On the nights of 23 and 24 July, the XVth Brigade moved closer to the river banks, part of a general movement of men and material of all kinds, including boats. The Republic prepared to cross on a fifty-mile front from Mequinenza to the sea. The Battalion was sheltered in the dry bush-covered gulleys, and was issued with ammunition, grenades and iron rations.

Early on the morning of 25 July the crossing began. The first boats were guided by local peasants who knew the currents, the terrain and the best landing-points. The Mac Paps were the first of the XVth Brigade to cross, near Asco. Initial resistance was slight and had been overcome when the British landed. Their orders were to drive on westwards inland towards Corbera and Gandesa, by-passing any opposition. They moved forward in open order, but headed by a Republican and a Catalan flag. Within a couple of hours the fascist aviation came into action, having been flown up from the Levante front. However the Battalion pushed on, regardless of the bombing planes, and by afternoon it was only two kilometres from Corbera. Groups of fascist soldiers surrendered and wanted to be taken prisoner. But escorts could not be spared, so the direction was pointed out and many of the prisoners went unescorted happily to the rear. The XIIIth (Dombrowski) Brigade was moving to take Corbera, but its flank was threatened by a force of Moorish troops dug in on the steep hills. The British were ordered to work with the XIIIth Brigade and to take the area. It was no easy task at night since the positions were well fortified and the Moors expert at mountain warfare. The Battalion cleared the hills and the XIIIth Brigade took Corbera. The Battalion had now been on the move, advancing over open country and in action, for twenty-four hours. Though it had overrun some fascist food stores, which were quickly consumed, the strain was beginning to tell.

The next day the Battalion felt the reaction of the fascist high command to the threat to its corridor to the sea. Fascist aircraft, artillery and men were switched from other fronts and thrown into action, subjecting the river crossings and the roads to constant bombardment. The forward movement of the Republican reserve troops, tanks and artillery, very limited in numbers though they were, was severely impeded. No ambulance got across the river till the third day: the wounded had to be evacuated on stretchers or on ordinary lorries and then taken across the river by boat.

The Battalion was then ordered to push the fascists off a height, Hill 481, soon dubbed the 'Pimple', which was holding up the advance and was the key to Gandesa. It was about a mile to the east of the village and almost within sight of the pass where Dunbar's group had held the enemy column for one day in April. It was a rocky hill with some of the higher slopes almost sheer. The fascists had fortified it strongly, as indeed they had all the commanding heights, with bunkers, trenches and barbed-wire. The British came to know, and hate, every stone and fold of the ground.

They first attacked on 27 July and then learnt from bloody experience the full strength of the fascist position. Many machine-guns were in almost impregnable positions, able to fire on advancing men who had very little cover. The first attempt was driven back and then for six successive days the British Battalion attacked but failed to reach the top. On several occasions small groups got within grenade-throwing range, but the fascists had the advantage of height and cover.

Movement was made more difficult and hazardous because the enemy holding nearby heights could fire from the flanks, while the church and buildings of Gandesa itself offered secure positions from which fire, at short range, could be directed at the attackers. Fascist artillery, now on the front in great numbers, was accurately ranged and kept up heavy, at times continuous, fire.

Conditions in the Battalion area were almost beyond description. The heat was intense, the bare rocks were shell-shattered, the debris of war was everywhere, and the stench of blood and bodies nauseating. In some places it was too dangerous to leave the shallow holes they had dug; men had to relieve themselves where they crouched. The boots, of those fortunate to have them, were cut to pieces and the rope-soled *alpargatas* gave no protection from the rock splinters. The men were emaciated and exhausted, from the heat, from inadequate food, lack of water and of sleep. All supplies, ammunition, food and liquid, had to be carried or brought by reluctant mules over the rocks to the forward positions. The collection and removal of the wounded was difficult, slow, painful for the wounded, and physically and emotionally exhausting for those who carried them. Often the collection and evacuation was possible only at night.

The cost of the attacks and the high spirit of the Battalion are exemplified by the fate of the commanders of No. 2 Company, who made the first assault on Hill 481 on 30 July. Lieutenant John Angus, Company Commander, was wounded; then Lieutenant Gregory, second-in-command, was hit in the neck. Then Sergeant Bill Harrington took over till he was wounded. Then Corporal Joe Harkins, a steel-worker from Clydebank, commanded until he was killed. The next day, 31 July, Clive, returning straight from hospital, took command only to be killed while observing, ready to lead the next attack.

On 1 August, Bank Holiday, the Battalion was asked to make a final supreme effort to take Hill 481. Despite the nerve-racking conditions there were jokes about past and future holidays, the taste of beer, and Hampstead Heath. For twelve hours the Battalion attempted to move forward in strength. Some small groups got within two or three yards of the fascist nests, but each time they were driven back by grenades and concentrated short-range fire. Courage of an unusual order was there but the odds were too great – 'The Pimple' was not taken. Among the many casualties was Harry Dobson, an outstanding Rhondda miner, whose first words when leaving Swansea Jail after completing his sentence for anti-fascist activity were, 'How can I get to Spain?'

John Richardson, from Luton, barely eighteen years old, described the attack in a letter from his hospital bed:

> At dawn we went over the top and the world went mad. Machine-guns sent a hail of bullets at us. Snipers shot at us, shells and trench mortars burst all round. But we reached cover at the bottom of the valley where we lay all day unable to move because of snipers. The heat of the sun became unbearable. The ground scorched and our clothes stuck to our backs. We had no water and my mouth and throat were swollen and hard with thirst.
>
> At 10 p.m. we got the order to attack. We reached the very summit without a mishap. A little while later came the signal for real business. We rose with a yell and rushed forward throwing hand-grenades as we ran. But the machine-guns rained death on us, red-hot lead. Hand-grenades burst all round. Time and time again we attacked only to be driven back. The fortifications were too strong. Solid concrete pill-boxes lined the hill-top and we were only flesh and blood.

The Battalion and the XVth Brigade were then moved into reserve positions. It was not a 'rest'. The area was under artillery fire and one of the few Republican batteries fired over their heads. The fascist air force, now brought in great numbers from the Levante front, kept up continuous bombing of all rear areas, concentrating on roads leading to the river crossings. But there was a chance to catch up on sleep; there was shade and cool under the olive trees, and during one night everyone had a chance to bathe in the Ebro, getting rid of caked filth, dried blood, and grime. Some of the Battalion

British prisoners from the Machine-Gun Company captured at Jarama, 13 February 1937, filmed by Movietone News before their release in May. *Front row second from right* Jim Rutherford *(with crossed arms)*, Harold Fry *(behind to Rutherford's right)*, Skempton *(centre with beret)*, 'Yank' Levy *(with hat)*, Tom Bloomfield *(with moustache)*

Members of the British Battalion before the Ebro crossing, July 1938. Note the long bayonets on the Soviet-made rifles

XVth Brigade Chief-of-Staff Malcolm Dunbar (*with Sam Browne*) introducing Major Valledor, new Spanish Commander of the Brigade, July 1938

British Battalion officers on Hill 481, July 1938. *Standing right to left* Sam Wild (*leaning against tree*), Cipriano (*hand on leg*), Paddy O'Daire, Alan Gilchrist, Bob Cooney (*without belt*), Major Valledor (*with map*); *sitting in front* George Fletcher, with Peter Kerrigan (*behind him*)

British nurses in Spain. *Second from left at back* Margaret Powell, Mary Slater (*with arms crossed*), Ann Murray (centre)

Hospital in a cave near the Ebro river, August 1938

A Company meeting in a *barranco*, May 1937

Group of the British Battalion behind the Jarama Front, May 1937. *Standing, left to right* Bill Meredith (*with pipe*), Fred Copeman, Bert Williams, Charlie Goodfellow; *sitting, in front of Goodfellow* Glyn 'Taffy' Evans

Deputation of wounded Brigaders to Transport House, London, where they saw Walter Citrine (TUC General Secretary) and J. S. Middleton (Labour Party Secretary) to demand more support for Republican Spain, 31 March 1938. John Larmour (*second from left*), Harold King (*next to him*), Tom Fanning (*centre*), Ken White (*right*)

were lucky enough to get boots to replace their *alpargatas*. There was a general issue of parcels from Britain containing cigarettes and chocolate. However, the continuous rolling of artillery indicated that it would not be long before the XVth Brigade would be needed again, and after eight days the orders came.

The Battalion services were under great strain throughout the offensive. Supplies of ammunition, equipment and food were always short because of the limitations of the river crossings. The Battalion kitchens had to be well forward, and were thus subject to shelling and bombing. The food could be taken up only at night, when it could be carried to the forward positions. Mules were not always available. But 'Hookey' Walker, as usual, managed to get food and liquid to the Battalion.

The telephonists and linesmen had never-ending work to keep communications open, which, because of the fluid situation, was essential. The shelling and the rocky terrain meant that telephone-lines were always being broken. The break had to be found by following the course of the cable – a hazardous undertaking. Behind the front the greatest pressure was on the medical services. Dr Leonard Crome, from Edinburgh, who was in charge of the XVth Army Corps Medical Services, and all the medical staff, knew that prompt medical attention and operation could save lives and limbs. But conditions made this almost impossible. There was often considerable delay in getting wounded off the battlefield. The Battalion doctors worked well forward, but even when some ambulances managed to cross the river they were too few. The wounded had to be sent back, often on blood-soaked mattresses, in open lorries to the crossing areas. Some were operated on there, sometimes in caves. On occasions the wounded would have to wait in an open field while bombers circled overhead. Then they were taken across the river in boats. Angus stressed his feeling of naked helplessness as the boat crew left him when bombs were falling near. On the Catalonia side larger caves were used for operations, treatment and care until evacuation could be arranged. The hospital train, which backed carefully into a tunnel whenever planes appeared, as they constantly did, took the seriously wounded to Mataró, Barcelona and hospitals in other towns.

The fascists had now concentrated some hundred thousand of their best troops and a massive array of artillery. Here German Regulars tested and used their new 88mm gun which, as the Allies found soon afterwards in the world war, was a viciously effective weapon. The fascists began a drive on the Sierra Pandols. If they had taken the heights they would have observation over, and been able to dominate, Mora de Ebro and the river crossings. The whole of the Republic's front was endangered. The Listers holding the position under great pressure had suffered severe losses and could have been swamped in a massive enemy attack.

The Brigade, and the British, were ordered to relieve them, and made an exhausting march across open country. The mood was grave and apprehensive but everyone had been told of the significance of the move. The villages of Pinell and Prat de Compte had been bombed into ruins. The mountains in this area were rocky and bare: it was clear that digging in would be well-nigh impossible.

At first the main brunt of the fascist attack fell on the other Battalions of the XVth Brigade, though the long-range harassing artillery-fire claimed British casualties every day. Companies of the British were called out to help the Lincolns and Mac Paps when they faced very heavy pressure. The whole Battalion drove the fascists off an outlying knoll of Hill 666, the key to the Pandols sector.

Then on 24 August it took over the Lincolns' positions on the main height. Scarcely was it in position when the fascists launched an attack of unprecedented severity. The artillery sounded like one continuous roll of thunder. The fire was accurate and the rock splinters as deadly as the shrapnel. When the barrage stopped, the enemy infantry – nearly two Battalion strong – attacked. However the British, although much reduced in numbers and half shell-shocked and defeaned by the bombardment, repulsed the assault and did not give an inch. Morris Miller, the Assistant Commissar, was amongst those killed. Wild was wounded again but did not leave the line. That night the Battalion was relieved by a Spanish unit and went to rest. The Battalion was commended by the 15th Army Corps and the 35th Division for their brave and skilful defence of Hill 666.

Again 'rest' was within artillery range and within sound of the front, but there was no longer the close smell of death. Food and liquid, sleep and shade, and the chance of a wash made life more bearable.

Pollitt arrived and spent two days with the Brigade and spoke to the British sheltered under the trees. As always, he brought the briefcase with letters, a few cigarettes and a notebook for messages for home.

A number of men who had been fighting since the early days were sent home on leave. Among them were Paddy O'Daire and Ted Edwards, a clerical worker from Manchester who had been in action since Jarama and as Secretary had kept the Battalion Diary and records. The two surviving Labour councillors, Jack L. Jones and Tom Murray, were also sent home. Wild went off for hospital treatment and again Fletcher took over the command. The reinforcements of Spanish conscripts showed the manpower problem now facing the Army north of the Ebro. They were very young, almost untrained, and a number were prisoners from Franco's army who had accepted the option of joining the Republican forces.

The smell of the international sell-out to fascism grew stronger. The manoeuvres leading to the British Government's capitulation to Hitler and betrayal of democracy at Munich had begun. Franco, wanting to show his power and desperate for results – he had pushed back the Republican front only two kilometres in forty-three days – launched his heaviest offensive yet in the Sierra Caballs.

Massive, almost continuous, flights of fascist bombers reinforced their artillery concentration. There were 200 guns on a mile-long front. Under this weight of steel parts of the Republican front broke and the whole XVth Brigade was rushed by truck, despite the shelling, to reinforce it. The Battalion went into action at Sandesco and recaptured a position the fascists had penetrated. There was only one redeeming feature to this short action: the ground was softer and digging in was easier. When the line was stabilized, the Battalion was again withdrawn to reserve on the Asco-Corbera road.

The conditions, even away from the front, had deteriorated. The debris of war was everywhere. The continuing shelling and bombing were nerve-racking and every day there were casualties. Two British members of Brigade Transmissions were killed by one shell. Battalion Headquarters received a direct hit but fortunately the strong dugout roof limited the damage to shock only. The Battalion was again made up to strength with 132 more Spanish soldiers, but their calibre was poor, and some had been deserters.

Prime Minister Negrín, in a desperate effort to win international support for the withdrawal of all foreign troops in Spain, had expressed his intention of withdrawing the International Brigades. This news, spread by the Barcelona newspapers and the radio, created great discussion and some concern among the International Brigade leaders and volunteers. Inevitably there was some feeling of relief, since many had faced a long period of almost continuous action and had seen numbers dwindling as death, wounds and illness took their toll. On the other hand there was a sense of shame that the Spanish people would be left alone to fight an even more powerful fascism. The British felt especially bitter since the Chamberlain Government was foremost in the appeasement of fascism.

On the 18 September 1938, when Hitler was already in Berchtesgaden awaiting his guest Neville Chamberlain, the fascists opened another major offensive against the whole Caballs-Pandols sector. The Battalion's rest was interrupted one night to move up to the front, but it was able to return when the line held.

On the night of the 21/22 September when the Barcelona newspapers were being printed and nearly everyone knew that the Brigades were being finally withdrawn, the XVth Brigade was called back to the front. It went without hesitation.

The last battle of the British Battalion

To Venta de Campsines

240
260
280
300
220

Farriols

Mas de Parrot

K.452

Lincolns
•281

BRIDGE

DRY BARRANCO

287
•

K.451

•362

To Corbera & Gandesa

FASCIST TANKS
BREAK THROUGH

No.1 Company

M.G. Company

MAC PAPS

Molino de Farriols

FINAL BRITISH POSITIONS

300
320
340
360

Scale: 1cm to 125 metres

Because of the urgency, the Brigade was ferried forward in a few trucks, through heavy shell fire, to the very rear of the threatened sector. The XIIIth (Dombrowski) International Brigade, in the Sierra del Lavall de la Torre, had suffered very heavy losses: its trenches had been pounded flat. Only remnants of its units were holding out when the British Battalion moved into the sector to the south of the Corbera-Venta de Camposines road. All knew that after the next day the 35th Division was to be withdrawn across the Ebro.

The whole situation was confused and all the positions were dominated by higher ground held by the fascists. The Mac Paps were on the left. Contact with the Lincolns on the right was at the Corbera road where a bridge went over a *barranco*. Frank West commanded a party in an advanced position. He did not know who was on the flanks. One detail was ordered to dig and keep guard, while the others snatched some sleep. But fatigue took over and the whole group awoke with the fascists standing over them with machine-guns, and they were taken prisoner.

On the early morning of 23 September the enemy artillery opened a terrific barrage. The British Battalion HQ counted one shell every second landing on its front alone, and 250 enemy bombers and fighters dominating the sky, bombing and strafing the front lines. Only after five hours of this did the enemy dare to advance. The Lincolns, with an open flank, were forced to retreat. Some of their recent Spanish reinforcements surrendered and went over to the enemy. The fascists, at near brigade strength, occupied the heights and then enfiladed the British positions. Five tanks attacked down the road. The small group of thirty-five British holding the area put three out of action but then was forced to retreat. The two remaining tanks, followed by infantry, reached the *barranco* behind No. 1 Company, inflicting very heavy casualties and taking prisoners. The company fought desperately in hand-to-hand combat but was overwhelmed. John Power, who was commanding, managed to fight his way out with a handful of men. Power, one of three brothers from Waterford who had fought in Spain, had been with the

Lincolns but then transferred to the British.

The enemy tanks and masses of infantry were then amongst the Machine-Gun Company. Fletcher brought up his limited reserves but they were not enough. Though the Spaniards who had been with the Battalion for a time all fought with customary courage and skill, many of the new intake retreated or went over to the enemy. Fletcher and Cooney managed to get some of the machine-guns, and small disorganized groups of men, to the rear and consolidated them on a ridge three-hundred yards back. Fletcher was the last man to retire. They were joined by small groups of Lincolns, Mac Paps and Spanish whose units had suffered similarly. The fascist infantry had had enough and made no attempt to extend its advance.

It was suicide to attempt to reach the wounded until after dark. Roderick McFarquhar, a railway-clerk from Inverness, who had been in Spain since autumn 1936 and was in charge of a group of stretcher-bearers, led them forward to the area of fighting with fascist soldiers all around. The moon was rising but they sorted the wounded from the dead, and brought them – some on their shoulders – to safety.

With the fascists holding former British positions, the fate of many was unknown. Jack Nalty from Dublin, who had been with No. 1 Company at Córdoba in December 1936, George Green, and Liam McGregor, also from Dublin, were among the many with long active service who fell in this last battle of the British Battalion. The figures of the Battalion strength show the horror of this day of action. When the Battalion moved up on the night of 22 September its strength was 377, of whom 106 were British. When it withdrew on the night of the 24th it was 173 strong of whom 58 were British. Two hundred men were killed, missing or taken prisoner.

Just after 1 a.m. on 24 September the Campesinos moved in to take over the front, and orders came for the withdrawal of the XVth Brigade across the Ebro. It was a sad and sombre move; everyone was shocked by the brutality of the last battle. Passing through the areas where they had advanced two months before, everybody remembered their dead and missing friends. Feelings of relief to have escaped death and to be moving out of danger were understandable, but the roar of the guns behind them was a reminder that there was no withdrawal for the Spanish Republican Army.

In this, their last battle, the British volunteers had fought as bravely and as skilfully as they had in their first action as a Battalion at Jarama. But it cannot be stressed enough that throughout the war units of the Spanish Republican Army were facing and stopping similar overwhelming forces with equal courage, sacrifice and ability. The losses of the British in the two months across the Ebro were shared by all the units along the perimeter. And the last Republican troops fought on until 16 November when they were finally pounded and blasted back across the river.

This was the last action of the British volunteers in Spain. However, when all the Brigades had been officially withdrawn from the front and most had left Spain, Alonso Elliott remained behind. He had been working under Luigi Longo at the Headquarters of the Political Commissars in Madrid, and then in the Foreign Cadres Commission of the Spanish Communist Party in Barcelona. Together with Marty, Longo and many others he was helping the final repatriations. After the fall of Barcelona on 23 December, the roads north to the French frontier were packed with retreating people – men, women and children, and the remnants of the Army. There were still in northern Catalonia, groups of Brigaders – Germans, Italians and others – who could not return home, as well as some Canadians whose government was blocking their repatriation. Elliott played his part in organizing groups of these men, who fought desperate delaying actions holding back the advancing fascist tanks and infantry, giving just a little more time for those fleeing to reach the frontier. However, they escaped Spanish fascism only to suffer police repression in France.

Chapter 17

The British in Other Roles

The great majority of the British volunteers served in the Battalion as infantry and in the associated services, but some were involved in other practical roles.

When the Spanish army officers began their revolt against the Republic, their naval counterparts also tried to take over their vessels. However, the crews, alerted and politically conscious, stopped them and disposed of the officers. The Republic then had the craft and the crews but lacked experienced leading personnel. An appeal was sent to Britain for trained naval men to volunteer for service in the Republican Navy. Five were chosen from Merseyside. Later more seamen volunteered to join the Spanish Republican navy but it was decided that they could only join the army in the International Brigades.

The selected group travelled to Albacete, arriving in early December 1936. Jack Coward, the leader, insisted at once on discipline and physical fitness; they exercised by running round the bullring. They were then sent to the Republic's main naval base, Cartagena.

Tommy Hadwin, from Hoylake, had seen active service in the navy at Jutland and the Skagerrak in the First World War. He then signed on for five years at sea, and seven on the reserve as a leading torpedo man. He reached Cartagena on 6 December 1936 and within two days was on a coal-burning torpedo-boat. The crew was efficient but there was a shortage of fuel and its effective fighting range was only fifty miles.

Hadwin asked for a transfer to a bigger ship, a destroyer. He put in more time at sea in twelve months than in all his five years in the British Navy, returning to base only for refuelling. His ship bombarded Melilla where the rebels were shipping Moors and other troops across the Straits of Gibraltar in trawlers. It also shelled Ceuta. After the fall of Malaga his ship shelled the coast road, destroying a bridge, slowing the fascist advance and allowing the fleeing civilians more time to escape. They made regular trips taking food to Mahón, on Menorca, the Balearic island still in Republican hands. After a year's service Tommy became ill and after a spell in hospital came home.

Geoff Marshall, after a time as second-in-command of a destroyer, was promoted to its command. But there were difficulties on the ship and at the end of June 1938 he was arrested. Questions were raised as to his reliability – Kerrigan had to intervene to secure his release from prison and his return to Britain.

Jack Coward, who had been a boatswain in the Royal Navy, served in a similar capacity on Republican torpedo-boats. However, after a year he left the navy and joined the British Battalion, achieving his aim of getting to closer grips with the fascists.

Albert Cole, after twelve years' service in the Royal Navy as a leading seaman, was discharged for his prominent role in the 1931 Invergordon Mutiny. At Cartagena he was made second-in-command of a torpedo-boat. German and Italian warships were patrolling off the Mediterranean coast, and his responsibility was to protect vessels bringing supplies from the Soviet Union during their last few miles into port. In June 1937 he was asked to take a merchant vessel, loaded with gun parts, to the Asturias. A Union Jack was painted on the sides. When hailed by a German 'Non-Intervention Control' warship, Cole replied from the bridge, wearing a battered peaked-cap and with a pipe in his mouth. In the Atlantic the Union Jack was painted out and replaced by the French colours. The gun parts were safely delivered in Gijón and the ship, crowded with civilian refugeees, went on to Bordeaux.

Cole then made a quick return to Liverpool and, after speaking at some propaganda meetings, went back to Spain where he was sent to the 129th International Brigade. Wounded, he joined the British Battalion and returned home with them.

Accounts have already been given of the actions of the British Anti-Tank Battery which fought as part of the XVth Brigade on every front from Jarama to Belchite. It was formed in May 1937 from forty men then in training in Madrigueras. The guns, three in the battery, were Soviet made, 45mm calibre, on a light carriage with rubber-tyred wheels. They could fire two types of shell of such high velocity that the trajectory was nearly flat; one was armour-piercing and the other high explosive. This gun was at that time in advance of anything in use in any other army. During the Aragon campaign, the US Military Attaché, visiting the XVth Brigade, spent a long time with the Anti-Tank Battery, not talking to the volunteers but studying the gun itself. After a brief period of training, helped by the attachment for a few days of a young Russian instructor, the gun crews soon became proficient. Later, when half the Battery personnel were Spanish, the expertise in handling and firing the guns was extremely high and the full versatility of the weapon grasped. It was used against armoured vehicles, as close support for infantry, and for engaging fortified machine-gun positions.

Life was not easy and the casualty rate was as high as in the Battalion. However, the Battery enjoyed certain advantages, remaining a cohesive unit with high morale. Each gun-crew was a small team, and at rest – and even sometimes close to action – had certain advantages over the infantrymen. For example, because each gun was towed by a lorry, members of the Battery were able to stow more material among the ammunition boxes than a 'foot slogger' could carry – a few books, writing paper, the simplest things which made life more tolerable.

The Battery gained some fame for activities other than the purely military. At every opportunity a lively social and cultural atmosphere developed. Miles Tomalin was responsible for the bright, lively 'wall' newspaper called *Assault and Battery News* often attached to an olive tree or a pile of ammunition boxes. At rest on the mill island at Ambite, visitors came from all over the Brigade to read the paper in the blue and whitewashed cottage turned into a leisure centre. The 'Beauty Competition' – photos of wives and sweethearts – was voted a tie between one British and one Spanish sweetheart. Tomalin was later made responsible for cultural activities for the whole Brigade.

The British volunteers in the Anti-Tank Battery had a proud record in battle and showed that, despite the brutalizing effects of war, men were still cultured, social beings looking beyond the immediate danger.

In the very first few days of the war the Republic was short of trained pilots and some were hired abroad. A few came from Britain, but all except one were mercenaries flying for financial gain, and were definitely not volunteers. The Republic soon dispensed with their services, some of very questionable value.

At the outbreak of war, the Spanish engineering industry was inferior in general to that of Britain, France or the USA. The aircraft industry in Britain was very much more advanced than in Spain. A request therefore came from the Republican Government to sympathizers in Britain for skilled aircraft workers to go to Spain. Eight carefully chosen, sympathetic, highly-trained and experienced workers went to Barcelona to work in the Hispano-Suiza works, where damaged but badly-needed war-planes were grounded awaiting repairs. The position in the factory was very bad, with intense animosity between the two trade unions. The secretary of the socialist UGT had been shot and the anarchist-oriented CNT was in control. At that stage of the war (1936) the CNT was not cooperating with the Government's drive to increase industrial production, especially in the war industries, and the CNT leaders in the factory resented the presence of socialist foreigners. Half the machines in the machine-shop were standing idle, engines were awaiting overhaul and repair; but, despite pleading from the factory technical director, the British were not allowed to start work. One highly-trained man, with many years experience working with modern British aero-engines, was told to hand-file a test-piece as proof of his competence. After nearly two months of this sabotage of their efforts to work, all the group were brought back, in December 1936, to Britain. Only one other skilled worker, Ernie Woolley, remained in Spain, the only foreign worker in a small factory making shell cases. While this situation continued in the main trade union, no more attempts were made to bring in specialist workers, though the war industry badly needed them. Later, however, skilled members of the International Brigades established workshops to repair motor vehicles and some weapons. Harry Evans, nominally an ambulance driver, assembled abandoned machines and equipment from front-line villages and built up a small but very efficient workshop. Wrecked trucks were collected, broken-down vehicles were cannibalized, and new parts were made, and his workshop kept most of the XVth Brigade's vehicles on the road.

The Republic faced a flood of hostile propaganda from all quarters of the world which aimed to hide the real situation and to allow the fascists to benefit from 'Non-Intervention'. The Government had to counter this, explaining what was really happening in Spain and warning of the consequences to the rest of the world if fascism should win. Several British were involved in the work of propaganda and information. Winifred Bates wrote articles for the Ministry of Information which were sent to English-language papers throughout the world. Ralph Bates, whose novels about Spain were well known, became – after a period of similar work – the first editor of *Volunteer for Liberty*, the journal of the XVth International Brigade. He set the style, carried on by later editors, making it readable and accepted by all the Brigade. Beside reports from the fronts and political news, it carried items from the Battalions, gossip, stories and poems, and information about things at home. Later Bates went on a lecture tour to the United States, alerting the movement there to the threat of fascism in Spain.

Claud Cockburn (writing under the pseudonym Frank Pitcairn) was in Barcelona in July 1936 to report the Workers' Olympiad for the *Daily Worker*. He decided to play a more active part in the struggle, joined the Fifth Regiment and fought on the Sierra Guadarrama where his group held a key pass against the generals' initial drive on Madrid. He went home to Britain to write *Reporter in Spain*, published in October 1936, a moving picture of the bravery and the difficulties of the Republic.

Hugh Slater was in Spain reporting on the political situation for *Inprecorr* (International Press Correspondence, a Communist weekly) when he joined the Brigade. Tom Wintringham was reporting for the *Daily Worker* when he asked and was given permission to change his job and join the British Battalion.

These journalists left their work to become soldiers, but some soldiers became writers. Sam Lesser (who wrote under the name Sam Russell), wounded at Lopera after fighting with the first small group of volunteers, subsequently worked with a Spanish news agency, helping Rust and Kerrigan send regular material to the *Daily Worker* and other English-language journals, and became *Daily Worker* correspondent in Spain after Kerrigan. Ryan, Elliott and Donaldson dropped their military responsibilities and in one month prepared the *Book of the XVth Brigade* a unique record of the experiences of some of the volunteers.

Radio broadcasting was used to help break the web of lies about the situation in Spain. Richard Bennett, who went to Spain with Cornford in July 1936, was employed to broadcast in English on the radio station of the PSUC, the United Socialist and Communist Party of Catalonia. Later, fighters who had been wounded such as Jimmy Shand, a student from Liverpool, and Frank Graham, prepared news stories about members of the International Brigades and messages to relatives, which they then broadcast from Barcelona and

Madrid. At times they wondered if their efforts were even being heard, and they were delighted at any confirmation of news getting through. However, with Hitler and Mussolini having so many wealthy and powerful supporters in the British Government and among influential ruling circles, the Republic's case was no more than a still small voice.

Chapter 18
The Medical Services

During the first week of the fascist rebellion the Republican Government made an international appeal for medical assistance. The reaction in Britain was swift: a meeting was called, at forty-eight hours notice on 8 August 1936, and the Spanish Medical Aid Committee was set up. Dr Charles Brook, Labour London County Councillor, was appointed Secretary. Isabel Brown, a well-known Communist speaker, attended from the National Joint Committee for Anti-Fascist Relief. The meeting sent out a call for funds and £1,500 (a big sum when £3 a week was a good wage) was raised in three days. Vehicles, supplies and personnel were rapidly assembled, and the first medical unit left London for Spain on 23 August 1936. This was the start of a continuing supply of vehicles, medical equipment and of trained people: doctors, nurses and drivers. This help continued until the very last days of the Republic.

In late autumn the same year, another organization, a Scottish Ambulance Unit, was set up under the wing of Sir Daniel Stevenson, a Scottish mine-owner with interests in the Rio Tinto mines in Spain. The motives of some of those organizing and directing this venture were very doubtful: Stevenson had an autographed photograph of Hitler in his study. When the convoy of about twelve vehicles containing medical supplies arrived in Valencia, with Stevenson's secretary in charge, the leaders were dined in the British Embassy itself. The Chargé d'Affaires (Sir Ogilvie Forbes) asked the group to send him reports and information on the situation in Republican zones. The convoy then went to Madrid and established itself in a very large house, an annexe of the British Embassy, where several fascists had taken refuge. Very little medical work was done, food was sold on the black market, and ambulances were used to smuggle civilians on to British naval ships. Reports were made to the Spanish Government that some of the drivers had looted valuables, an offence which carried the death penalty. Seeing the state of affairs, Len Crome, the Unit Medical Officer, Roderick McFarquhar, a railway clerk from Inverness, Maurice Slinden, and one or two more drivers who had joined the unit in good faith, walked out of it and linked up with the International Brigades. Shortly afterwards what was left of the unit was ordered out of Spain and sent back to Britain.

The appeal of the Spanish Medical Aid Committee was on humanitarian grounds alone, but its practical aid was of immense help to the Republic, and many of its contributors and supporters gained a wider understanding of the issues at stake. A strenuous, imaginative campaign to raise money was conducted all over Britain. Circles far wider than the left were involved; for instance, a one-day sale of works by Augustus John, Eric Gill, Jacob Epstein, Barbara Hepworth and other British artists raised enough money to buy a new lorry.

The Spanish Medical Aid Committee – from its address at 24 New Oxford Street in London – acted as the organizing centre for the personnel who went to Spain – about twelve doctors, forty-four nurses, and more than a hundred ambulance drivers and other personnel. Some ambulances were bought from general collections, others were given by trade unions. The ambulance of the Society of Lithographic Artists, Designers and Engravers, suitably inscribed, had a long useful life and, like all the medical services, showed the Spanish people they were not alone. The supplies included the most advanced surgical equipment but also had to include the most elementary necessities of which there was a dearth in Spain, such as bandages and cotton wool. They filled only a small gap in the horrifying shortages but they saved many lives and eased much suffering.

Most of the Spanish doctors in the Republican zone worked devotedly and with high skill, but some doctors had gone over to Franco or were trapped in fascist territory at the outbreak of the rebellion. An enormous extension of the medical services was called for to cope with casualties from the fronts and the civilian victims of bombing; a big expansion of the surgical services was especially urgent. So every doctor and surgeon arriving to help the Republic was highly valued.

Nursing in Spain had been practised very largely by nuns – some of whom continued with this work in the Republic. But they had little training in modern techniques and were unused to the heavy demands of treating the wounded after major surgery. The nurses from Britain made an immeasurable contribution, not only by their own assiduous work but also by training Spanish women as auxiliaries. Their standards of organization, cleanliness, and techniques saved the lives and limbs of many wounded, captured fascist soldiers as well as Republicans. Often working in harsh conditions, and in all-male surroundings, they did something to break down traditional Spanish attitudes to women.

The British ambulance drivers set very high standards not only in bravery but also in keeping their vehicles going despite atrocious conditions and continuous use. It was a feature of the organization that the traditional hierarchical divisions in British medicine tended to disappear in the grim realities of war. Ambulance drivers had to work as mechanics and as general labourers in the preparation of hospitals, but also to serve as anaesthetists in emergency. Wogan Philipps, just out from London with a truck, was put into an operating theatre near Arganda in the Jarama battle, carrying out amputated limbs, even administering an anaesthetic on a sponge while the surgeons worked. He was made a sergeant for his efforts. Doctors not only had to work in specialized fields outside their previous studies or experience, but also to organize, to drive ambulances and even to clean their own hospitals. Nurses performed minor operations, acted as administrators, and took critical decisions about treatment. The medical personnel became adept at working in any situation, and living 'out of a suitcase', in primitive conditions.

The relationships between the Spanish Medical Aid Committee in London, the personnel in Spain, the Republican Government and the International Brigades were not clearly defined, and there were a few difficulties. Some of the Committee in London did not wish to be fully identified with the International Brigades. One or two of its administrative personnel in headquarters at Barcelona and Valencia carried on dubious activities, selling food and supplies on the black market. Viscount Churchill, the Secretary, boasts in his autobiography that he illegally smuggled people out of Spain.

At first the British personnel and resources were not directly under the control of the Republican authorities: there were difficulties over rations and pay, as well as problems of location and role. However, most of the medical personnel – doctors, nurses and ambulance drivers – wanted to work with the International Brigades because, generally, they were in the heaviest actions with high casualty rates, and the language problem was not so acute. Some of the British personnel remained as civilians, but most moved into the military organization with the pay, rations and acceptance of discipline. In any case the difficulties had been made more apparent in the rear, and in London. At the fronts, the work was too compelling and the morale too high to encourage much discussion of administrative rules. When casualties – civilian or military from both sides – reached the dressing-station or the base, no one asked their unit or required their credentials: they received immediate attention from the personnel and the available facilities of the medical services.

Like the Battalion, the British Medical Unit included many from other countries. The first unit sent from London included Dr A.A. Khan, an Indian, and Dr Randall Sollenberger, an American studying in Britain. Dr Jolly came from New Zealand. Seven nurses and two ambulance drivers came from Australia. As the war extended, more and more of the English-speaking personnel changed teams, hospitals and responsibilities. It became impossible to speak of a purely British medical unit or hospital. A British surgeon might work with a team of Hungarian or Czech nurses, with the casualty brought in by a Spanish ambulance, or a Spanish doctor might have a group of British and Australian nurses. But the campaign and the Committee in London continued to provide invaluable supplies, food and equipment which was used where the need was greatest.

The campaign to raise funds for Medical Aid was helped by visits to Spain by public figures who carried out propaganda activity on their return. The writers Sylvia Townsend Warner and Valentine Ackland went in October 1936 and suggested that a group of fifty 'experienced in First Aid' should go to help. The Duchess of Atholl (the Tory MP), Carmel Haden Guest (mother of Angela who was working in the medical services, and of David in the Battalion), Lady Christina Hastings, George Jeger, and many others visited Spain and then wrote and spoke about the medical needs of the Spanish people.

The system of medical organization developed in the First World War was of limited use in handling heavy casualties from a moving battle-front. New styles of organization were improvised and developed to deal with the wounded in action, as well as with the ordinary ills that affect a Battalion. The Battalion doctor was with the unit all the time. Out of action he looked after the earaches, boils, and bad feet, and advised on hygiene, though little could be done about the ubiquitous hungry lice. He handed out the enormous kaolin and opiate pills – the only 'stopper' for the general dysentery brought on by the inadequate and often contaminated water. Most important, he trained the first-aid stretcher-bearers who collected the wounded from the actual battlefield. When fighting began, the Battalion doctor was close behind the front line organizing the stretcher-bearers. He looked at the casualties, gave emergency treatment, and then organized their evacuation, if possible by ambulance, further to the rear where more treatment could be given.

The first of the British Battalion doctors was Colin

Bradsworth, a general practitioner from Birmingham. Plunged into the battle at Jarama, regardless of danger, he coped with the flood of casualties. He was wounded but returned to the front. Later, at Jarama, he faced much ribald chaffing when, relieving himself, he was hit in a sensitive place by a spent, stray bullet.

The next Battalion doctor was Randall Sollenberger, who joined it by 'deserting to the front' from a convalescent home. He was killed while bandaging the wounded in the front line at Brunete. He was succeeded by Dr Robbins, an American, also killed at Brunete. Then Dr Johnny Simon, originally with the Lincoln Battalion, transferred his services to the British, until he was promoted away from the XVth Brigade. After this the system of one doctor for each Battalion often broke down; as there were not enough, one doctor had to be responsible for several Battalions.

The first-aid men and stretcher-bearers in the Battalion were part of the military organization. When the Battalion was not in action they received specialist training in elementary first-aid and techniques of moving the wounded. However, in critical battle situations they often joined in the fighting. Equally, ordinary soldiers might be detailed to take wounded to the rear. At first everyone carried a field-dressing for immediate use. They were in short supply, like so many things, and could not be replaced when used. Being a 'sanitario', first-aid man, was not easy, and often involved great physical strain and danger. In the first days of heavy fighting at Jarama, the wounded had to be carried on stretchers, and then, when the supply ran out, on blankets, more than a mile over steep rocky slopes. Only later did Bradsworth and his orderlies fashion a rough path. At Jarama the British 'sanitarios' established a tradition which was rarely broken of never letting a wounded comrade fall into enemy hands.

The stretcher-bearers could not move fast or take cover when bringing out a casualty by day. At night they scoured the forward areas between the lines, often unsure of the fascist positions and liable to attract fire from both sides. In the

Brunete campaign they faced new difficulties: every forward medical post was subjected to heavy shelling and air attack. In the intense heat the wounded called incessantly for water. But for a stomach wound, which often provokes great thirst, water is utterly forbidden, and for any casualty the contaminated water was a danger.

When the wounded had been collected from the battlefield and received what immediate treatment was possible, they were ferried, by ambulance, further to the rear for surgical and other treatment. Experience showed that treatment at the earliest possible moment drastically cut the number of deaths and improved the rate of recovery. The ambulance service, drivers and vehicles, were under great stress during heavy battles. There were never enough ambulances; the necessary travel across rough country played havoc with springs and engines. The drivers often faced distressing choices – which wounded men to take, which to leave. They were a target for fascist planes and artillery: the Red Cross emblem drew their attention. The strain and demands of driving were heavy. At night, for example, they had to move without lights; by day they were often chased by attacking fascist planes. Yet they dared not drive fast for fear of inflicting further pain and injury on their human cargo.

Several drivers themselves became casualties. On the long, straight, totally exposed road which led from the front at Brunete to the comparative security of the mountains, a bomb hit the ambulance driven by Julian Bell, the poet, nephew of Virginia Woolf, killing him instantly. He had just applied to become a stretcher-bearer, which he considered would give him a more active part in the war. Anthony Carritt, a farm manager from Oxford, was killed when he went forward under heavy shelling and bombing to recover a group of wounded left on the Brunete-Villanueva road.

Workers in some West London factories made some motorcycle ambulances with the stretcher on a side-car chassis, but they proved unsuitable for the very rough terrain. After this factories and trade unions concentrated on raising money to buy trucks and motor ambulances.

Away from the front the casualties were collected at a clearing centre and then sorted by medical personnel into groups. These sorting stations retained the name 'triage' given by the French medical personnel in the very early days. The less serious wounds were treated there by cleaning and bandaging. The more serious injuries – limb, chest and abdominal wounds which needed surgery – were immediately operated on and, if possible, given a blood transfusion. The third group were the cases of extremely severe head and abdominal wounds where nothing could be done; they could only be given morphine to ease their agonies while awaiting death.

These casualty clearing stations had to be established in any available building at a reasonable distance from the front, beyond artillery range but not requiring too long a journey by ambulance.

Reginald Saxton, a GP from Reading, set up a classifying and operating centre for the Jarama battle in Villarejo de Salvanes, where he commandeered the biggest building – a bar. Three bar table-tops became the operating table, and benches tied in pairs were used as beds. In the Brunete offensive Crome had more time to choose and organize the 35th Division centre in a large mansion near El Escorial. Chris Thorneycroft, the last of the British remaining with the German Thaelmann Battalion, transferred his engineering skills to the medical services and, by arranging an electric generator, provided light for the medical teams to work twenty-four hours a day, and deal with the flood of casualties. A number of British personnel were in the teams; Tudor-Hart and Jolly were surgeons, Saxton gave blood transfusions, Archie Cochrane worked as anaesthetist. Among the nurses were Ann Murray from Edinburgh and Margaret Powell from London.

At Teruel the first surgery was performed in farm buildings of such poverty that the glassless windows had to be covered with blankets to keep out the intense cold. Alcohol had to be burnt to give some heat and the only light came from car batteries.

In the Ebro offensive the casualties were treated in caves on or near the river banks. The main forward operations took place fifteen yards inside a railway tunnel at Val de Falset. Though the entrance was bombed, operations continued. Light was provided by a small mobile generator. Instruments were sterilized in a kettle over a primus-stove. Those too ill to be moved after surgery were nursed further back in the tunnel. Patience Darton from London, Joan Purser from Worcester, Ann Murray, and the other nurses needed all their trained skills and long war experience to overcome the difficulties.

In Britain, engineers built and equipped an 'auto chir', an operating-theatre in a lorry. However, this innovation was not successful because the space was too limited for major operations.

From the clearing-stations the lightly wounded often returned to the front still with their bandages. Those casualties needing further treatment were sent, if possible by train, to base hospitals in the rear.

The first British medical group was sent to Grañen, behind the Huesca front in northern Aragon, and early in September 1936 took over an old dilapidated farmhouse. It had to be cleaned and converted into a hospital even while the wounded were streaming in. The 'Hospital Inglés' treated 800 cases in the first month, but later the front became quiet and most of the work involved treatment of local civilian ills, occasionally helping at a birth. Most of the British wanted to be of greater use, and at the end of 1936 they went to hospitals serving the International Brigades on the Madrid front.

After this the British medical personnel were spread over many hospitals; there were no specifically British establishments (though the London Committee was anxious for one). Everywhere the drill was the same: finding a large building appropriately situated for the needs of the military situation, cleaning and adapting it for use as a hospital. At Huete and Uclés old monasteries were turned into hospitals. Organizing a hospital was easier at Benicasím, where large villas on the sea-front were used, and at Mataró, where a big empty school provided large, well-lit rooms. But Nan Green, as administrator, and Frank Ayres, as Political Commissar, had to organize the Valdeganga convalescent centre in the bath house and buildings around hot springs.

The methods of handling casualties developed in Spain – rapid evacuation, classification and treatment as near as possible to the front – were widely adopted in the Second World War. Dr Jerry Steel, writing under the name G.B. Shirlaw, described the systems employed in Spain in a book – called *Casualty – Training, organization and administration of civil Defence Casualty services* – later widely used by the ARP and wartime medical services in Britain.

The organization of the Army medical services, in which Crome played a big part with his experiences as a Battalion doctor, then in charge of the medical services in the 35th Division, and the XVth Army Corps, were studied and followed by many armies from 1939-45. Tudor-Hart's methods of dealing with complex wounds and bone fractures after surgery opened new fields of technique. Saxton, though he had only carried out one blood transfusion before going to Spain, grasped the need for massive prompt transfusions. With the help of Norman Bethune, the Canadian expert, he organized a very efficient service, grouping the blood of every potential donor within reach. There were often fears among the local people about giving blood but they were slowly broken down. Winifred Bates wrote articles about blood transfusions in the local papers, Spanish and Catalan, after which blood supplies became more plentiful. Saxton experimented in taking blood from corpses, but this was never used in transfusions. Lilian Kenton, nursing in the Huete hospital, realized the importance of physiotherapy in the recuperation of the wounded. She developed new exercises and mechanical devices to help the recovery of shattered limbs and wasted muscles. Sinclair Loutit and Cochrane had not completed their medical studies when they went to Spain with the first Medical Aid group. For months they dressed wounds, administered anaesthetics, and organized, before they were sent back, with reluctance, to complete their professional training. The British nurses by example and training showed that the final success of the surgeon's skill rested on modern nursing techniques. At Teruel, when the hospitals were full of frostbite cases the nurses' perceptive care saved many from losing limbs from gangrene. Throughout the war cases of typhoid were common; the British had not acquired immunity. In 1938 there was a major epidemic and the hospital at Vich was crowded with cases. Mary Slater, Janet Robertson, and other nurses showed that with courageous, devoted care men could be pulled through this 'killer' disease, for which there was then no treatment.

Britain made a significant contribution to the Republican medical services. The supplies were invaluable. The courage and devotion of all the personnel, backed by their professional expertise, saved the lives and eased the suffering of many soldiers and civilians of the Republic.

Chapter 19

Getting Home

As we have seen, to enter Spain had not been easy for most of the volunteers. For some, on occasion, it proved equally difficult to leave.

At first there were no problems, except money. In August 1936 Cornford returned home and went back to Spain within a few days. Ovenden, Romilly, and other volunteers went to the frontier, walked across to France and caught the train back to Britain. But with the establishment of the Non-Intervention Agreement, crossing the border into France became more difficult, and at Newhaven and Dover the Special Branch questioned and harassed anyone they thought was returning, not from a Paris weekend, but from Spain.

The medical service personnel, who retained their passports, were able to travel freely to and fro provided their papers were in order. Many went home for short leaves and for propaganda tours, while the drivers often returned to ferry out new ambulances and supplies.

The French Government was as obstructive to those leaving Spain as it had been to those attempting to enter. However, this was counterbalanced in both cases by the active help of the French people – workers on railways and on ships, trade unionists in Paris, the ordinary people everywhere.

Many of those who, despite incapacitating wounds, could still walk, were led on some dark night to a point on the French frontier where there was a gap in the boundary wire only a few yards from the French frontier post. Unchallenged they would walk down the hill into the French town of Cerbère to food, lights and a welcome.

Not everyone was so lucky. Mildwater, wounded at Fuentes de Ebro, was loaded onto a train packed with 'inutiles' of all nationalities, men so badly wounded as to be unfit for further fighting. The train stopped in the tunnel under the frontier between Port Bou and Cerbère because the French authorities refused to let it through. For two hours the tunnel filled with smoke and fumes. They waited. Then all who could walk got out of the train. The French were put in front. On crutches and sticks, with arms in plasters and bandages, the procession moved slowly down the dark track. At the very exit, in the light, was a semi-circle of armed French troops. The party kept moving. The line of troops wavered, then broke and parted. The wounded walked through.

The train with leg and stretcher cases was then allowed to pass. Then after coffee and rolls ('I can still remember the taste,' says Mildwater), they came home through Paris, were interrogated by plain-clothes policemen at Dover, and received treatment in the Middlesex Hospital.

On 21 September 1938 when Prime Minister Negrín announced the Republic's intention to repatriate all foreign volunteers in the vain hope that world opinion would then force the withdrawal of the German and Italian military units, he asked the League of Nations to supervise the withdrawal. The League of Nations duly set up a Commission to check the withdrawal of the volunteers on the Republican side, and a Brigadier Molesworth was appointed as a member from Britain.

However the British Battalion, aware of the impending withdrawal, had still to fight its last bloody battle in the Sierra Pandols. It came out of the line on the early hours of 24 September and when a muster was made in Marsa on 27 September, only seventy-four British volunteers answered the roll.

The League of Nations Commission arrived in the Republic on 16 October. The volunteers expected to be home within a few days. But it was not to be.

Volunteers began to be collected from wherever they were in Spain. Twenty British were still in the south, cut off by the fascists, but they travelled to Catalonia by sea. Those who were reasonably fit were brought in from the hospitals – Vich, Mataró and Santa Columna.

A parade of the XVth Brigade was held in Marsa, with the British, as the oldest Battalion, forming on the right. Major Valledor, Brigade Commander, recalled the Brigade's efforts and sacrifices in the many battles. All the Internationals then withdrew from their formations and Spanish soldiers, officers and men took their places. The XVth Brigade, now all Spanish, moved back into action across the Ebro on 5 October.

On 17 October, two years after the formation of the International Brigades, all the foreign volunteers in the 35th Division – British, American, Canadian, Germans, Poles, Yugoslavs and many other nationalities – paraded and were reviewed. On the reviewing stand were Lt.-Col Tagueña, commander of the XVth Army Corps, André Marty and Luigi Longo, key figures in the International Brigades, as well as trade unionists and other civilians. They were loudly cheered. To mark the occasion a number of promotions were announced, including Dunbar and Wild to Major and John Power, from Waterford – who had taken over the command of his company in the last battle – to Captain.

After this parade the British were now moved north to the small town of Ripoll in the foothills of the Pyrenees, not far from the French frontier. As a result of the gathering-in from hospitals and outlying places, the numbers had reached nearly two hundred.

Then on Saturday 29 October 1938 the International Brigades had their farewell parade in Barcelona. This was a deeply moving event, etched into the memories of the Brigaders. The skies were patrolled by Republican planes, for Franco had declared his intention to destroy the volunteers before they left Spain and indeed bombed many towns and trains during their final withdrawal. The Diagonal, the main street of Barcelona, was thronged deep with many, many thousands – mainly women and children – who expressed with tears, flowers and embraces their feelings towards the Brigades. Negrín and la Pasionaria expressed their gratitude for the help Spain had received.

Addressing the Brigaders, La Pasionaria said:

> Comrades of the International Brigades! Political reasons, reasons of state, the welfare of that same cause for which you offered your blood with boundless generosity, are sending you back, some to your own countries and others to forced exile. You can go proudly. You are history. You are legend. You are the heroic example of democracy's solidarity and universality. We shall not forget you, and when the olive tree of peace puts forth its leaves again, mingled with the laurels of the Spanish Republic's victory – come back!

The Brigaders then marched past Manuel Azaña, President of the Republic, while military bands played. The British were led by the six-foot-tall Jim Brewer (one of the original members of the Anti-Tanks) carrying the Battalion banner. There had been no opportunity for barrack-square training, but the Battalion marched with a dash and a swing. However, the parade was by no means a formal military exercise: the people of Barcelona had their own part to play. Girls would break into the ranks to kiss individuals, in gratitude and in memory. Children joined the ranks and marched holding a volunteer by the hand. Bunches of flowers were offered and carried.

Yet everyone, volunteers and civilians alike, knew very well the terrors and trials still to be faced by the people of Barcelona. The volunteers knew they were leaving unfinished the task they had undertaken. The emotions of the parade ran very deep.

Everyone expected to leave Ripoll for home within a few days but the supervising Commission took its bureaucratic time. The volunteers were comfortably housed; they had concerts, fiestas and sports to amuse them; they dug trenches to protect the local people in case of air-raids. But they were playing no active role. They wanted to get home. In Britain pressure was brought by MPs and others to speed things up. In Ripoll the Battalion, though formally no longer a military unit, took a hand. An elected delegation went to lobby the British Consul in Barcelona much to the consternation of the Consulate butler who tried to shoo them off the patio.

At last on 6 December 1938 the main party of 305 men travelled by train out of Spain. At Puigcerda, just over the French side of the frontier, they were given a simple meal of bread, ham and butter; but their stomachs were not accustomed to such food and their bodies rejected it almost immediately. The French Government routed the train round Paris and the main towns to avoid demonstrations of support and welcome. However, on the outskirts of Paris the Government arranged for the Salvation Army to provide tea and sandwiches. This was regarded as charity by the volunteers and rejected.

Unlike the Canadians, the British Government did pay the cost of the journey to Britain; but then proceeded to send bills to individuals for some years afterwards. The Under Secretary of State for Foreign Affairs wrote: 'The sum of £2-4-11 has been expended from public funds in connection with your repatriation from Spain.' There is no record of anyone paying though, after the second request, Bobby Walker indicated his willingness to pay if all the British soldiers paid the cost of their evacuation from Dunkirk in 1940.

The party got to Victoria Station on the evening of 7 December 1938, to a rousing emotional welcome from a crowd of many thousands. Families, supporters well-wishers and Labour movement personalities filled the whole station and lined the surrounding streets. Wives and children met their men – some so thin and changed that recognition was not immediate. Major C.R. Attlee, leader of the Parliamentary Labour Party, Sir Stafford Cripps, William Gallacher and Will Lawther, President of the National Union of Mineworkers, all spoke in welcome. Wild replied on behalf of the volunteers:

We intend to keep the promise we made to the Spanish people

before we left – that we would only change our front and continue
to fight in Britain for the assistance of Spain.

The *News Chronicle*, reporting the welcome at Victoria next
day, quoted an old porter: 'I have seen nothing like it – not
even at the end of the last war.'

The Brigaders were then fed in the Co-op Hall in
Whitechapel. Many were fitted out with more adequate
clothes, provided at cost by the Co-operative Wholesale
Society, and given their fares home. Flags were out, and there
were welcoming parties in Tonypandy and Clydach Vale in
the Rhondda, in Newcastle, and in many other localities. A
group was entertained in the House of Commons. The South
Wales Miners' Federation laid on a meal and reception for the
Welsh volunteers in the Grand Hotel, Cardiff.

In the next few weeks smaller parties arrived home – those
who had been away from the main group or in hospital. Mary
Slater and other nurses travelled on a hospital train bringing
sixty-nine wounded who were unable to walk. Ten of these
were stretcher cases; three were too ill for the Channel
crossing and had to go into hospital in Paris until they were
stronger.

There were many who still needed treatment for wounds
which had not fully healed. In particular the Middlesex
Hospital gave outstanding help and services. The volunteers
found the regime there a little strange and the staff found the
patients unusual. In Spain they had been encouraged to take
an interest in their own cases, to study the temperature chart,
to discuss symptoms and the purpose of operations, and, if
possible, to help the other patients in the ward. The regime at
the Middlesex was occasionally startled by such participation.

Before the return, the Dependants' Aid Committee had
begun to tackle the problem of jobs – not easy, at a time of
high unemployment. The Committee had written to trade
unions and to some employers who might be helpful. Many
Brigaders had made arrangements with friends, or by sending
money home to keep their union cards paid up, while in other
cases the branch took on the responsibility. A few Brigaders

needed grants from the Dependants' Aid – 14/- a week. However, the employment position became easier as the war industries expanded in 1939.

The Dependants' Aid Committee had been strengthened to face its heavy responsibilities. Charlotte Haldane continued her work as honorary secretary, Fred Copeman and Bill Rowe from Spain went to work in the office with Agnes Aitken, wife of George Aitken, responsible for organization. The big problem was to provide something for the wives and children whose men had not returned, and for the very badly disabled who were unable to work. A National Memorial Fund Appeal for £50,000 was launched, with an extremely wide body of sponsors – political figures like Attlee, Ellen Wilkinson, Wilfred Roberts (Liberal leader), Harry Pollitt; trade-union leaders like Harry Adams (AUBTW), J.C. Little (AEU), Will Lawther (NUM), J. Rowan (ETU); and religious and public figures such as the Canon of Westminster and the Dean of Canterbury, Maude Royden, Sean O'Casey, Paul Robeson, H.G. Wells, Victor Gollancz and Harold Laski. The immediate, and generous response to the Appeal showed the standing of the Brigaders in Britain.

The fund and the campaign were given fresh impetus when a packed meeting at the Earls' Court Exhibition Centre paid tribute to the dead and applauded the surviving volunteers who marched in. Isabel Brown collected £3,800 in twenty minutes – industrial earnings averaged then only £3-90 and unemployment benefit seventeen shillings a week.

Similar meetings, large and small, were held in many places. In Mountain Ash, South Wales, 5,000 people, a significant part of the entire population, packed the Pavilion. In Newcastle the City Hall was packed to overflowing for the Memorial Meeting for the twenty-four men who had died out of the hundred who went from the north-east.

Charlotte Haldane, Agnes Aitken and Bill Rowe visited all the widows and families, to ensure that they knew of their pension rights and benefits, and to help them with their claims. In some cases children were helped to start apprenticeships and training. In addition, grants were made from the fund to help families in their new circumstances without a breadwinner. The grant was usually between £80 and £100; the highest was £150. These were inadequate, it is true, but in those times of public assistance and dole they could be considered reasonable.

The Committee and the fund were then wound up.

Chapter 20

At Home – But Not to Rest

The return of the volunteers to the normality of Britain sharpened their understanding of the threat to Britain should war and fascism spread. All were deeply conscious that the war and the suffering still continued in Spain. Moreover, warmed by their own welcome home, they felt for those volunteers from Germany, Italy and other reactionary states who could enjoy no such welcome.

In the final days in Spain all had pledged:

> We are returning to our respective countries not for celebrations in our honour, not to rest, but to continue the fight we helped to wage in Spain. We are merely changing the fronts and the weapons.

Throughout the years, in differing ways, individually and through the International Brigade Association, the great majority of the volunteers have kept this pledge. A few gave interviews or wrote material which concentrated only on the difficulties and mistakes of the war. Some lost heart and faith and dropped out of activity. But there has been a wide and continuing record of anti-fascism and work for democracy and peace in Spain, Britain and throughout the world.

Their record of activity in the labour movement as individuals, demonstrates the calibre of the volunteers and confirms their high standing and esteem. A very high proportion took office in the trade unions at branch, area or national level. Bill Paynter, Jack Jones (Rhondda), Tom

Degnan (Yorkshire), Lance Rogers (South Wales), Bob
Condon (Cannock) among the miners; J.L. Jones and Tom
Jones in the Transport Union, Lionel Jacobs in ASTMS, Bob
Doyle in the Paperworkers Union, Jack Coward in the
Seamens Union and Jim Prendergast in the NUR: these are
but a few of the well-known names. The activity of the
Brigaders at all levels in most of the unions helped to maintain
a flow of support to the Spanish refugees and to the families of
those in Franco's jails. The unions kept up a continuing
protest against Franco's persecution of the workers and trade
unionists in Spain, and each Trade Union Congress, almost
without exception, denounced his regime.

In the party political field Peter O'Connor in Waterford,
Don Renton in Edinburgh and Jim Brewer in the Rhymney
Valley became Labour Councillors. Michael O'Riordan
became Secretary of the Communist Party of Ireland, Ezekias
Papaioannou the Secretary of AKEL in Cyprus. In Britain,
Harry Bourne, Peter Kerrigan, Bill Rowe, Sam Lesser, Bill
Alexander, Tony Gilbert and Dave Goodman all held
responsible positions in the Communist Party.

When the Second World War began, as the volunteers had
prophesied and feared it would, there was official opposition
to the employment of Brigaders in the forces, despite their
experience in fighting the military units of Hitler and
Mussolini. The opposition had to be overcome by political
pressure at all levels. It was never completely broken. Some
were not allowed into the forces at all. Malcolm Dunbar and
Clive Branson, whose personal backgrounds would have
gained them commissions without question had they not
fought in Spain, were never allowed to rise above the rank of
sergeant. In the House of Commons Aneurin Bevan
demanded why Dunbar, the man who had been highly
influential in the strategy which had sent an army successfully
across the Ebro, was not acceptable in the British Army as so
much as a second-lieutenant. But Cooney, Rosenfeld and
others were several times removed from drafts about to go
overseas.

However, despite this high-level opposition, many

Brigaders forced their way into the war effort. Tony Gilbert and Dougal Eggar, the youngest and oldest prisoners in the San Pedro Concentration Camp, became 'Bevin Boys' in the pits. George Fletcher commanded the Home Guard in the key Rolls-Royce factory; Joe Latus commanded a boat running supplies to the liberation forces in Greece; Tom Wintringham and Hugh Slater advised in Home Guard training. Jack Coward trained units of the Palestine Navy in gunnery. Gilchrist, O'Daire, McFarquhar, Alexander, Longstaff and many others in the army found that, once in a fighting unit, respect took the place of prejudice. Many of the medical people gave invaluable service in the forces and in ARP air-raid precautions units. Tudor-Hart, Crome, Cochrane, Saxton and Jolly were among those who found their war experiences in Spain were welcomed and studied. However, there were still people in influential positions in Britain who had backed the appeasement of fascism and 'Non-Intervention' in Spain, and they blocked the Brigaders from using their abilities and experience to the full in the armed forces.

From their return until the present time the volunteers have played their part in the wide, progressive movements. However, throughout the years their special concern, their distinctive contribution, has been to help the Spanish people in their struggles.

When the volunteers got home, the war in Spain was still going on; the Republic could still defeat fascism but only if it could get arms. The urgent need was to stimulate a new wave of support for the Republic and renewed attacks on Chamberlain's support for Franco. The volunteers inspired activity wherever they lived or worked. Early in 1939 two trucks took Brigaders all over Britain to speak at meetings, factories and clubs to urge political and material support for Spain. From Southampton to Aberdeen every meeting was packed to overflowing; the division of opinion between the British people and the British Government was thus clearly displayed. A group of nurses went to see Mrs Chamberlain at Chequers only to find the gates barred. The campaign continued to the very last days of the Republic but was not strong enough to change Chamberlain's policies. A lorry carrying food, driven by Lou Kenton, dispatch rider with the medical services, organized by the Printers' Anti-Fascist Movement, crossed the border as Catalonia was falling. Its crew was only able to hand this food to the refugees fleeing towards the Pyrenees, and then ferried women, children and old people towards what was hoped to be the safety of the French border.

Immediately after their return the British volunteers had to campaign to prevent reactionary states venting their spite on Republican fighters. In addition, the British had to add to the pressure on the Canadian Government who only reluctantly allowed the Mac-Paps to return home on 3 February 1939. The French Government treated the flood of refugees who crossed into France to escape the fascist terror – civilians, Republican soldiers, International Brigaders from countries to which they could not return – with the utmost callousness. They were herded into camps, at first on the bare sand-dunes, guarded by French colonial troops. British volunteers were in the forefront of activity exposing these conditions, denouncing the French Government and demanding that the British Government give active help. Wogan Philipps chartered a ship, paid for by British donations, normally used to take pilgrims to Mecca, to transport 5,000 Republicans from Southern France to Mexico. Nan Green went on the boat, helping to feed the many children. Winifred Bates helped in the camps themselves.

In the last days of the Republic, in March 1939, it was decided to form an International Brigade Association. Its agreed aims were:

> To carry on in Britain the spirit and tradition of the International Brigade as front-line fighters for defence and advance of democracy against fascism, for the rapid development of common action and purpose among all anti-fascist people to spread the truth about the struggle of the people, Army and Government of Republican Spain and to win all necessary support for the Spanish Republic.

Full membership was limited to those who had served democracy in Spain; next of kin were enrolled as associate members. An attempt to limit membership only to those 'with a clean record in Spain' was rejected. Membership cards, with details of military service in Spain, were issued and branches established in all the main localities in Britain.

A small group of Brigaders formed themselves into an International Brigade League. Its brief activities, aiming to discredit the Brigade, received considerable publicity in the *Sunday Dispatch* and other newspapers. Out of its ten members all but three had deserted from Spain; several had promoted themselves in fanciful accounts of their battle experiences. The organization and its members soon vanished from the scene.

In 1950 the Association changed its name to the 'International Brigade Association and Friends of Republican Spain' to reinforce the dwindling ranks of the Brigaders with people who were active in the cause of Spain but had not actually fought there.

The International Brigade Association has, with a few divergences, confined its activity to its declared aims. Throughout the war and immediately afterwards a main concern was to protect and help those Brigaders who were in danger. Shortly after the internment in France, the authorities separated the International Brigaders from the Spanish, placing them in separate camps, at Gurs and Vernet les Bains where conditions were harsh and primitive. In January 1940 the IBA sent £500 to the volunteers. There were extreme difficulties in getting funds to the camps during the Nazi occupation of France, but by 1949 a total of £18,000 had been sent – little enough but it showed the men inside that they were not forgotten. While demanding the release of all the Brigaders in the camps, arrangements were made to get some out by sponsoring their reception in Britain. Hans Kahle, the German Commander of the 45th Division, was brought out in this way, but was later arrested on arrival and shipped off to Canada by the British authorities along with proven Nazi supporters. Another campaign was needed to secure his return to Britain.

When France collapsed in June 1940 and Hitler's forces occupied half the country, the prospects for the Brigaders in the camps became even more sombre. The Gestapo and the OVRA, Hitler's and Mussolini's political police, took away many to torture and death. Others were coerced into joining the French Foreign Legion; some were sent to labour camps in the French Sahara. Others escaped and found their places in the European resistance movements, where their experience often brought them positions of leadership.

In 1941 Jack Brent became Secretary of the International Brigade Association, a responsibility he held until 1943. Jack, from Whithorn, Scotland, after service with the Cameron Highlanders and a period of odd jobs and unemployment, had been shot through the spine while fighting with the Lincolns at Jarama. His wound never healed; he lost one leg and lived in continuous pain with severe disabilities but led the Association in powerful and often successful campaigns. Appeals were made to President Roosevelt (the United States had diplomatic relations with the Vichy French Government) to get Luigi Longo (Gallo) Pietro Nenni, Franz Dahlem, Heinrich Rau and other leaders of the International Brigades out of the camps and save them from the Italian and German fascists. When Longo was handed over to Mussolini's political police, the IBA inspired and organized appeals from 275 leading figures in Britain to the Pope. Longo's life was saved.

Later, when the allied forces began to advance in Europe, North Africa and the Middle East, Brigaders from many countries were released and picked up by the allied armies. A great conference in London, attended by five ministers of allied governments in exile, demanded that these men be given help and their rights as nationals. Many Brigaders were brought to London and handed over to the care of the IBA who then pressed the many governments in exile to accept their citizens.

There was constant activity on all these campaigns. Three full-time workers were reinforced by the unskilled but immensely valuable clerical assistance of Brigaders from the American, French, Canadian and other Allied Forces in

Britain during the war. Ten thousand copies of every issue of *Volunteer for Liberty* were sold until paper-rationing compelled a reduction.

The Association began to produce *Volunteer for Liberty* in 1939. The first few issues contained much personal information about Brigaders – their whereabouts, jobs, marriages, and then, after a respectable interval, their offspring. But increasingly it was used to develop the campaigns for help to the Brigaders in the camps and Spanish Republican supporters in exile. During the war it carried articles and analysis of the course of the fighting, military techniques, use of weapons and air-raid precautions. Hans Kahle (after his release) and J.B.S. Haldane were regular contributors.

With the defeat of the fascist powers the IBA could extend its efforts to help the Spanish Republicans in exile and step up its demand for political and economic measures to defeat the remaining fascist dictator: Franco. A conference in 1945, 'For a Democratic Spain', well attended and backed by many leading personalities, urged such actions. The American and the British Labour governments, however, took no action hostile to Franco and even helped his regime. In Spain the opposition forces, encouraged by the defeat of Franco's fascist backers, increased their efforts to end his dictatorship. Franco stepped up his terror, with more executions, more torture, and more imprisonment for any one who showed the slightest opposition. The IBA kept up a steady campaign exposing conditions in Spain and trying to help Franco's victims. In 1945 Prime Minister Attlee and Foreign Secretary Bevin joined in the protest to save the lives of Alvarez and Zapirain, facing death for anti-Franco activities.

Volunteer for Liberty – the name was changed in 1946 to *Spain Today* – provided regular information about the situation and protests inside Spain, provoking angry denunciations from Franco's radio in Madrid. Pamphlets and leaflets were produced to meet the demands of the situation. *How they Fight Franco* described the guerrilla struggle inside Spain. In 1950 the pamphlet *Who are the Friends of Franco?* exposed the pro-

Franco group of Tory and Labour MPs. Gordon Schaffer wrote *No Pact with Franco* and a folder *Franco means War – Do you want him as an Ally?* These and other pamphlets opposed the attempts to whitewash the regime.

The IBA organized, collected money and helped many observers to attend the trials of Franco's opponents in Spain. Margaret Richards, Secretary of the National Union of Students, went to Madrid in 1946 for the trial of fourteen students attempting to reform the Students Federation. She was not allowed into the courtroom. The students received sentences varying from one to eight years imprisonment. However, the presence of foreign observers, sometimes allowed in court sometimes not, showed the Spanish people that they were not alone, and may have mitigated, in a minor way, the barbarities of Franco's regime. Dr Hugh Faulkner, sent in 1963 by the IBA and the Socialist Medical Association to attend the trials of Dr Antonio Gutiérrez, a paediatrician, and five others accused of organizing a military rebellion, wrote in his report:

> In my conversations with the representatives of the Embassy and the press there was clearly general agreement that the presence of foreign observers at these military trials serves a very useful purpose, even if it is not possible to claim any specific improvement in the conditions and sentences given.
>
> There can be no question that men and women on charges of conspiracy against the Government are subjected, in very many instances, to brutality, beating up and probably torture, during the first few days following their arrest, by police officers.

Mark Hewitson, MP, was sent to observe the trial in 1954 of José María Sendros and thirty-seven other people, who, on completing their sentences imposed by Court Martial, were rearrested, retried and sentenced to another twenty years imprisonment. He also visited nineteen freemasons who had spent two years awaiting trial in the Carabanchel Jail, Madrid. One, Señor Bayona Zaragoya, said to him: 'I am overjoyed that somebody is at last taking an interest in what is happening to us. We are filled with fresh hope.'

Many trials were held secretly or without notice, but whenever warning of an important trial was received, the Association tried to send an observer. Observers attended trials of all groupings – Communists, Socialists, Anarchists, Basque and Catalan nationalists, ordinary workers and trade unionists, doctors and intellectuals. From Britain, MPs, lawyers, doctors, trade-union leaders, well-known figures, all readily went to Spain to try to break through the secrecy and bureaucracy surrounding the trials of all opponents of Franco's regime. On their return the observers wrote and spoke of the realities of the regime, so misnamed by Franco himself, as 'Social Justice'.

This work rested on continuous activity by the Association, in which the Secretaries, Nan Green, and Alec Digges, who followed Jack Brent, played a leading part. Members spoke at conferences, national and local, there was a generous response to appeals for money, especially from trade unions. A succession of meetings was held at trade-union branches, at clubs and factories; a wide distribution took place of leaflets, pamphlets, *Spain Today*; and an exhibition 'Spain Fights for Freedom', was held in London and Wales. All this helped to reinforce public opinion against those in Britain who wanted to ignore Franco's past and present and bring his regime into a respectable international community.

The barbarity of Franco's rule did not lessen over the years. In 1962 Julian Grimau García, a Communist, was arrested when he returned illegally to Spain. After 'interrogation' he was thrown out of a window of police headquarters in Madrid. He survived, though – as the medical report described – the left side of his face was shattered, the frontal bone had collapsed, there was a large cavity in the right frontal lobe, his jaw was misshapen, there were fractures to both wrists, and his arms and spine were affected.

The IBA sent Gavin Freeman, a barrister, who managed to gain personal access to Manuel Fraga Iribarne, Minister of Information, and to the judge who was conducting an inquiry into the circumstances of how Grimau received his injuries. On his return Freeman's report was widely circulated. When

Grimau, still crippled, was brought to trial in 1963, there was a storm of protest all over Britain. During the trial there were continuous demonstrations outside the Spanish Embassy and the Consulates, with resolutions and deputations going from influential quarters. A wave of protest arose throughout the world. The protests increased after Grimau's execution. Harold Wilson, condemned it in the House of Commons as 'an act of vindictiveness ill-befitting a Government claiming to observe civilized standards. We call upon all to demand an amnesty and the restoration of civil rights in Spain.' Freeman, who had gone to Grimau's trial, said: 'I cannot come to any other conclusion than that his conviction and execution were political and not judicial acts.' The IBA, active in all the demonstrations, published five thousand copies of a hard-hitting pamphlet, *Murder in Madrid*. Later, when Fraga Iribarne arrived in London on a week's visit to promote the virtues of fascist Spain, he was followed by demonstrations, outside the Embassy, the Royal Opera House, everywhere he went, and had a cool or hostile reception from the British press.

The British people never accepted Franco and never forgot his treatment of the Republicans, workers and democrats. His terror against trade unionists and democratic people continued. Bill Paynter attended the trial at the end of 1973, of the ten leaders of the illegal trade unions, the Workers' Commissions, known as the 'Carabanchel Ten' after the jail in which they were held. He reported to meetings and to a conference called by the Scottish Brigaders protesting at the sentences of ten to twenty years' imprisonment for the crime of being trade unionists.

After Franco's death the Spanish people were prepared to struggle for democracy under a constitutional monarchy. Broad solidarity committees were formed in London, Manchester, Scotland, and elsewhere, with Brigaders playing leading roles. They demanded that the new Spanish Government release all political prisoners and, through an amnesty, allow all political exiles to return.

It is significant that more than forty years after the British volunteers fought in Spain, memorials are now being placed in honour of their dead in Glasgow, Dundee, Kirkcaldy, Edinburgh, Swansea, and at the NATSOPA Convalescent Home in Brighton. Thus local authorities, labour and trade union organizations and many, varied groups of people have decided to commemorate the struggle and sacrifices of so long ago by permanent tributes to the British volunteers for liberty.

Chapter 21

Was It All Worth While?

The thoughts of the majority of the volunteers, weighing up their Spain days in retrospect, run in three directions: their impact on the world, on Spain, and last of all, on themselves personally.

The fascist victory in Spain encouraged the dictators to extend their conquest and even envisage world hegemony. The defeat of the Republic therefore brought world war much nearer.

Every achievement of the German and Italian military machines in Spain – the blitzkrieg in Aragon, the effectiveness of the 88mm gun, the impact of the Condor Legion and its war planes – all strengthened the influence of the most bellicose groups in their governments. Every retreat by the British and the French governments – 'Non-Intervention', the Anglo-Italian Mediterranean Agreement, the betrayal of Czechoslovakia at Munich – all these emboldened Hitler and Mussolini to increase their demands and to expect no resistance.

War extended step by step. The month of Franco's victory, March 1939, saw Hitler's occupation of all Czechoslovakia and of Memel. That April Mussolini invaded Albania. Only five months after the defeat of the Republic the Second World War began.

It was precisely the British volunteers in Spain, and their supporters in Britain, who had maintained that to fight for the Spanish Republic was to fight for peace, and who understood that if the Republic was defeated in the war 'it will be our turn next'. It was the Spanish people who had blazoned the slogan 'Bombs on Madrid and Barcelona today can bring bombs to London and Paris tomorrow'. It was the volunteers derided as 'romantic visionaries' fighting in a war 'not their own' who had understood that fascism led to war. Their aim and their efforts were arms in hand, to prevent war and secure peace.

Their cause had been defeated and their words had been proved true. But all had not been lost. The three-year resistance of the Spanish people gave time for people everywhere to learn lessons and to prepare themselves for their own struggle against fascism. Even some people living under dictatorships derived new hope and courage to resist.

The governments of Britain and France did not even try to learn the military and political lessons of the Spanish war. But the British and the French people learned. From the bombing and shelling of the civilians of Madrid and Barcelona, from the wanton destruction of Guernica, from the massacre in the bullring at Badajoz of everyone who had resisted the fascist advance, they learnt the bestial, brutal character of fascism. From the vast numbers in Britain who had in one way or another given active support to the Spanish Republic – the trade-union branch which had donated to Dependants' Aid, the Welsh housewife who had sent the Spanish children a tin of milk from her own almost bare shelves – from all these had arisen a movement strong enough finally to overcome the official approval of appeasement and reaction: a movement which grasped the two great principles of the Spanish people's struggle – 'Resist and Unite'. These lessons influenced people's minds and actions and brought them together in the great anti-fascist war. Would this have happened, would fascism have been defeated, without the Spanish people's fight?

The British International Brigaders have been criticized as 'premature anti-fascists'; it is said that, although it was correct and laudable to fight fascism after 1939, it was not commendable to do so before. The lesson of Spain, and indeed of modern history, is that fascism must be exposed and fought as soon as it appears: it can only be defeated by struggle. The policies of appeasing Hitler and Mussolini did not bring peace: on the contrary, they made war more likely. If the Republic had been helped to win its fight, been given the right to buy arms, and if Germany and Italy had been condemned for their intervention, democracy would have been strengthened and fascism undermined. The course of history would have been different. The act of the volunteers in taking up arms was not premature; the tragedy was that the Republic had to call for such help.

It has been said that the progressive movement in Britain paid too heavy a price in supporting the Republic – that the volunteers should not have gone to Spain. It is true that 526 volunteers were killed, among them the finest of working people, many of whom, at an early age, had already shown high ability in the labour movement and the intellectual world. In addition, many returned disabled and lived the rest of their lives in pain and discomfort, unable to fulfill their potential.

However, would the movement for Spain, with its wide, catalytic effect on the anti-fascist struggle, have arisen without the focus of the volunteers actually there, taking part in the fighting? Could the British people have remained spectators on the sidelines, only applauding the anti-fascist struggle in Germany, Italy and Spain from outside? On the contrary, the sacrifices and losses of the British volunteers were suffered precisely in that wider struggle for democracy and peace and against fascism and war.

The Spanish people carried the brunt of the struggle during the war itself. Then, after Franco's victory, they endured the cruelties when the flower of the nation was eradicated or crippled by execution or by long imprisonment. For forty years the Spanish people suffered poverty, terror and tyranny under Franco. However, despite their defeat, Franco's terror, and the indifference of much of the world, the continuing struggle inside Spain showed that the heart of the Spanish people still clung to La Pasionaria's call: 'Better to die on your feet than to live for ever on your knees.'

A handful of volunteers, unable to put the difficulties of the Republic in perspective and failing to grasp that individuals react in different ways to exceptional strain, saw only the darker side of the war. In the changing political climate, a few have apologized for their 'youthful escapades', their 'gullibility' and 'naive enthusiasm' for Spanish democracy. Their views have been welcomed and peddled by those still wanting to denigrate the memories and the lessons of the Spanish struggle.

However, the overwhelming majority of the volunteers are proud of the part they played. March 1939, the defeat of the Republic, was not the end but a stage in their activity for democracy. They were angry and frustrated at the official, suspicious reluctance to use their experience of modern war, which could have lessened the hardships brought to their people. But they welcomed every opportunity to take on responsibilities in the labour movement.

The last thought of the volunteers would be the impact of their experiences on themselves personally. However, there is a general feeling of personal pride in having stood up at a critical point in history. In Spain there developed a tolerance and warmth for people, workers and intellectuals, all with their particular strengths and weaknesses, but all capable of infinite change and all with a place in the struggle. Experience of fighting alongside the Spanish people weakened old ideas of national superiority. Above all we grew in confidence that ordinary people had infinite potential which could be realised in a truly free and democratic society.

There are occasional thoughts – *'If only* we had reached the top of Mosquito Ridge … *If only* we had been braver and better soldiers … *If only* we had changed the attitude of the TUC … ' These do not lessen our pride and conviction that the British volunteers in Spain helped the onward march to democracy and peace for all mankind.

Roll of Honour

Note: the Roll of Honour contains five hundred and twenty-six names of volunteers who died in Spain between August 1936 and January 1939, or, in a few cases, who died of wounds shortly after evacuation. The information has been collected from the files of the Dependants' Aid Committee, supplemented and checked with the list given in Bill Rust's *Britons in Spain* (1939), and the very incomplete records sent back by the Republican Ministry of Defence. The list has been scrutinized by several volunteers, but there are still gaps in some details – inevitable in the prevailing conditions of recruitment, fighting and documentation. The places given in the centre column are those in the Dependants' Aid Committee records and represent birthplace, workplace or place of departure for Spain.

Roll of Honour

M. Aaronberg, Sheffield, February 1937, Jarama
N. Abramson, London, April 1938, Gandesa
Harry Addley, Folkestone, December 1936, Boadilla
Frank Airlie, Newcastle, July 1938, Ebro
John Alexander, Dundee, July 1937, Brunete
G. Allstop, Rotherham, August 1938, Ebro
J. Alwyn, Bolton, February 1937, Jarama
Antonis Anastasius, London-Cyprus, March 1938, Caspe
Alexander Armstrong, Manchester, February 1937, Jarama
F. Ash, Glasgow, March 1938, Aragon
J. Atkinson, Hull, February 1937, Jarama
C. Avgherinos, London-Cyprus, April 1937, Jarama
Sidney Avner, London, December 1936, Boadilla

William Bailey, Harwood, Lancs., June 1937, Jarama
W. Ball, Reading, February 1937, Jarama
W. Banks, Manchester, March 1938, Ebro
William Barry, Dublin, December 1936, Boadilla
N. Baxter, Leeds, February 1937, Jarama
R. Beadles, Birkenhead, February 1937, Jarama
W. Beales, Newport, Isle of Wight, August 1938, Ebro
John W. Beaton, Glasgow, August 1938, Ebro
William Beattie, Belfast, July 1937, Brunete
Clem Beckett, Oldham, February 1937, Jarama
R. Beckett, London, July 1938, Ebro
Julian Bell, London, July 1937, Brunete
C.A. Bennett, Walsall, July 1938, Ebro
Albert Bentley, London, November 1936, Casa de Campo

J. Bentley, Hull, March 1938, Aragon
John Berry, Edinburgh, February 1937, Jarama
L. Bibby, London, February 1937, Jarama
Lorrimer Birch, London, December 1936, Boadilla
A.E. Bird, London, July 1937, Brunete
John Black, Dover, July 1937, Brunete
R.C. Blair, London, April 1938, Gandesa
W. Bogle, Liverpool, February 1937, Jarama
R. Bolger, London, May 1937, Jarama
Henry Bonar, Dublin, December 1936, Córdoba
Hugh Bonar, Dungloe, Ireland, February 1937, Jarama
Kenneth P. Bond, London, July 1938, Ebro
Alex Bonner, Glasgow, February 1937, Jarama
H.T. Bosley, Stoke, July 1938, Ebro
Bruce Boswell, Coventry, July 1938, Ebro
William G. Boyce, Bristol, January 1938, Teruel
Dan Boyle, Belfast, July 1938, Ebro
Kenneth Bradbury, Oldham, January 1938, Teruel
Thomas Brannon, Blantyre, Scotland, February 1937, Jarama
S.A. Breedon, London, July 1938, Ebro
William Brent, Barnsley, March 1938, Ebro
Robert Bridges, Leith, February 1937, Jarama
George Bright, Thornbury-on-Tees, February 1937, Jarama
William Briskey, London, February 1937, Jarama
Clement Broadbent, Dewsbury, Yorks., September 1938, Ebro
Thomas Bromley, Southwick, Durham, April 1938, Gandesa
N. Brookfield, Maidstone, September 1938, Ebro
H.M. Brooks, London, July 1938, Ebro
Frank Brown, Prestwich, July 1938, Ebro
George Brown, Manchester, July 1937, Brunete
W. Brown, Stockport, Killed – whereabouts unknown
W.J. Brown, Newmilns, Ayrshire, February 1937, Jarama
Felicia Browne, London, August 1936, Aragon
John Bruce, Alexandria. February 1937, Jarama
Dave Buffman, Leeds, September 1938, Ebro
E. Burke, London, January 1937, Córdoba
T. Burke, Glasgow, July 1937, Brunete
J.P., Burley, Stoke, March 1938, Ebro
J. Burton, Bristol, February 1937, Jarama
H. Byrom, Manchester, March 1938, Ebro

D. Cameron, Glasgow, February 1937, Jarama

J. Campbell, London, February 1937, Jarama
Ralph Campeau, London, February 1937, Jarama
Ahillea C. Canaris, London-Cyprus, July 1937, Brunete
Ralph Cantorovitch, Manchester, July 1937, Brunete
Phil Caplan, London, July 1937, Brunete
A. Capps, London, January 1938, Teruel
H. Carass, ?, Killed – whereabouts unknown
Antony Carritt, Oxford, July 1937, Brunete
T.J. Carter, West Hartlepool, February 1937, Jarama
James Cassidy, Glasgow, February 1937, Jarama
Payaniotis Catsaronas, London-Cyprus, February 1937, Jarama
P. Charlton, Leeds, February 1937, Jarama
W. Clasper, London, July 1938, Ebro
Lewis Clive, London, August 1938, Ebro
James Cockburn, London, January 1937, Córdoba
S. Codling, South Shields, March 1938, Caspe
Denis Coady, Dublin, January 1937, Las Rozas
William Coles, Cardiff, February 1937, Jarama
J. Connolly, Glasgow, February 1937, Jarama
Frank Conroy, Kildare, December 1936, Córdoba
Kit Conway, Tipperary, February 1937, Jarama
Jim Coomes, London, October 1937, Aragon
Charles E. Cormack, London, August 1938, Ebro
John Cornford, Cambridge, December 1936, Córdoba
G. Corry, Cleckheaton, Yorks., March 1938, Caspe
R. Coutts, North Shields, February 1937, Jarama
M. Cox, Dundee, March 1938, Aragon
Ray Cox, Southampton, December 1936, Boadilla
William Cox, London, February 1937, Jarama
A. Craig, Glasgow, February 1937, Jarama
George Craig, Ulmanston, February 1937, Jarama
C.W. Cranfield, London, January 1938, Teruel
William J. Crawford, Glasgow, February 1937, Jarama
W.E. Crispin, London, April 1938, Gandesa
Fraser Crombie, Kircaldy, July 1937, Brunete
Ed Cross, London, April 1938, Gandesa
R. Cruickshanks, Glasgow, April 1938, Gandesa
Alec Cummings, Cardiff, September 1938, Ebro
James Cunningham, Glasgow, August 1938, Ebro
Pat Curley, Dumbarton, February 1937, Jarama

J. Dalglish, Leigh, Lancs., February 1937, Jarama

Peter Daly, Enniscorthy, Ireland, September 1937, Quinto
M. Davidovitch, London, February 1937, Jarama
Thomas Davidson, Aberdeen, April 1937, Gandesa
Adam Davie, Glasgow, February 1937, Jarama
Harold Davies, Neath, South Wales, February 1937, Jarama
William J. Davies, Tonypandy, South Wales, July 1937, Brunete
William Davies, Dublin, July 1937, Brunete
G. Deegan, Balloch, Ireland, January 1938, Teruel
Vincent Deegan, Brighton, March 1938, Ebro
Archibald Dewar, Aberdeen, March 1938, Ebro
P. Dewhurst, Oxford, July 1937, Brunete
E.A. Dickinson, London, February 1937, Jarama, Shot while prisoner
W.J. Dickson, Prestonpans, July 1937, Brunete
Harry Dobson, Rhondda, July 1938, Ebro
Walter Dobson, Leeds, August 1938, Ebro
Frank Docherty, Glasgow, July 1938, Ebro
John Dolan, Glasgow, February 1937, Jarama
Thomas Dolan, Sunderland, February 1937, Jarama
Charles Dolling, London, July 1937, Brunete
James Domegan, London, September 1938, Ebro
J. Donald, Methill, March 1938, Belchite
W. Donaldson, Glasgow, January 1938, Teruel
S. Donnell, Glasgow, April 1938, Calaceite
Charles Donnelly, Tyrone, February 1937, Jarama
A. Doran, Weston-super-Mare, February 1937, Jarama
J. Douglas, Glasgow, February 1937, Jarama
F. Drinkwater, Burnley, July 1937, Brunete
G.N. Drury Fuller, Maidstone, September 1938, Ebro
James Duffy, Glasgow, April 1938, Ebro
A. Dunbar, London, July 1937, Brunete
Richard Duncan, Tillicoultry, Scotland, September 1938, Flix
Thomas Duncombe, Wotton, Glos., April 1938, Gandesa
Martin Durkin, Middlesborough, August 1938, Ebro
W.F. Durston, Wembley, September 1938, Ebro

Sydney Edelman, London, April 1938, Aragon
Phillip Elias, Leeds, February 1937, Jarama, Shot while prisoner
Robert S. Elliott, Blyth, Notts., July 1937, Brunete
Thomas Elliott, Worthing, June 1937, Jarama
Victoriano Esteban, Abercrave, South Wales, Killed – whereabouts unknown

Edwin A. Evans, Glasgow, March 1938, Aragon

J. Fairchild, London, March 1938, Ebro
J. Fellingham, Bury, January 1938, Teruel
R. Felton, Rochester, February 1937, Jarama
John Ferguson, ?, Killed – whereabouts unknown
Sydney Fink, Salford, March 1938, Aragon
A. Finnan, Dundee, March 1938, Belchite
H.D. Fisher, Romsey, Hants., July 1938, Ebro
Thomas Flecks, Blantyre, April 1937, Chimorra
J.F. Flynn, Glasgow, April 1937, Córdoba
Tony Fox, Dublin, December 1936, Córdoba
Ralph Fox, Halifax, December 1936, Córdoba
William Fox, Blantyre, February 1937, Jarama
C.L. Foxall, Sale, Cheshire, February 1937, Jarama
Archibald (Josh) Francis, Reading, March 1938, Aragon
S. Francis, London, January 1938, Teruel
F.Freedman, London, January 1938, Teruel
George Fretwell, Penygroes, South Wales, February 1937, Jarama
Harold Fry, Edinburgh, October 1937, Fuentes de Ebro

Michael Gallagher, Wigan, July 1937, Brunete
P. Garland, Glasgow, July 1938, Ebro
T. Gaunt, Chesterfield, March 1938, Aragon
W. Gauntlett, Glasgow, July 1938, Ebro
Thomas Gibbons, London, July 1937, Brunete
W.J. Giles, Liverpool, February 1937, Jarama
J. Gilmour, Prestonpans, February 1937, Jarama
Pat Glacken, Greenock, January 1938, Teruel
Ben Glaser, London, September 1938, Ebro
Pat Glasson, Redruth, Cornwall, July 1937, Brunete
R. Glen, Alexandria, July 1938, Ebro
A. Gold, London, February 1937, Jarama
H. Gomm, London, February 1937, Jarama
Charles Goodfellow, Bellshill, Scotland, July 1937, Brunete
Michael Goodison, Salford, April 1938, Ebro
R. Goodman, Nottingham, February 1937, Jarama
W.R. Goodman, Salford, February 1937, Jarama
George Gorman, Derry, September 1938, Ebro
William J. Gough, Luton, December 1936, Boadilla
R.A. Grant, London, March 1938, Calaceite

T. Grant, Nottingham, March 1938, Aragon
George Green, Stockport, September 1938, Ebro
Leo Green, Dublin, February 1937, Jarama
M. Green, Manchester, March 1938, Aragon
R. Grierson, Annan, March 1938, Aragon
Henry Gross, London, July 1937, Brunete
D. Grossart, Glasgow, April 1937, Jarama
E. Guerin, London, August 1937, Quinto
David Guest, London, July 1938, Ebro
Mark Gura, London, February 1937, Jarama

Alex Hall, Plymouth, August 1938, Ebro
John Hall, Rutherglen, March 1938, Belchite
David Halloran, Middlesborough, February 1937, Jarama
T. Hamill, Glasgow, February 1937, Jarama
Sid Hamm, Cardiff, July 1937, Brunete
James Harding, Stockton-on-Tees, September 1938, Ebro
George Hardy, London, April 1938, Aragon
James Harkins, Clydebank, July 1938, Ebro
A. Harris, Liverpool, July 1937, Brunete
T.J. Harris, Llanelly, February 1937, Jarama
Alex Harvey, Glasgow, February 1937, Jarama
Martin Hempel, London, July 1938, Ebro
David Henderson, Glasgow, February 1937, Jarama
James Henderson, London, July 1937, Brunete
Richard Henderson, Kircaldy, April 1938, Ebro
William Henry, Belfast, February 1937, Jarama
Ivor Hickman, Petersfield, Hants., September 1938, Ebro
Robert M. Hilliard, Killarney, February 1937, Jarama
S. Hilton, Newhaven, July 1938, Ebro
Arnold Hoare, Leeds, August 1938, Ebro
Albert Hobbs, Chelmsford, September 1938, Ebro
G. Hollanby, Liverpool, April 1938, Gandesa
Roger Hone, Hammersmith, August 1938, Ebro
D. Horradge, Huddersfield, July 1937, Brunete
J. Howarth, Manchester, July 1938, Ebro
William Hudson, Newcastle, October 1936, Chapineria
V.J. Hunt, London, July 1937, Brunete
W. Hunter, Glasgow, March 1938, Aragon
Leslie Huson, Bristol, May 1938
C. Hyman, Glasgow, March 1937, Jarama
James Hyndman, Glasgow, January 1937, Las Rozas

E. Jackman, Liverpool, February 1937, Jarama
George Jackson, Cowdenbeath, Scotland, August 1938, Sierra Pandols
William Jackson, Oldham, April 1938, Gandesa
Sydney James, Treherbert, South Wales, July 1938, Ebro
W.E. Jasper, London, February 1937, Jarama
Arnold Jeans, Manchester, December 1936, Boadilla
Wilf Jobling, Blaydon-on-Tyne, February 1937, Jarama
Thomas Johnson, London, July 1938, Ebro
W. Johnson, Newcastle, December 1936, Córdoba
D.E. Jones, London, July 1938, Ebro
D.J. Jones, Rhondda, February 1937, Jarama
E. Jones, ?, December 1936, Madrid
H. Fred Jones, London, November 1936, Madrid
James Jones, Harrow, July 1938, Ebro
T. Howell Jones, Aberdare, August 1938, Ebro
L. Jordan, Manchester, July 1937, Brunete
R.P. Jordan, Wembley, March 1938, Caspe
Emmanuel Julius, London, November 1936, Aragon

W. Keegan, Glasgow, July 1937, Brunete
F. Keery, ?, July 1938, Ebro
G. Kelly, Greenock, July 1938, Ebro
Michael Kelly, Ballinsaloe, Ireland, July 1937, Brunete
W. Kelter, Glasgow, March 1938, Gandesa
A. Kemp, Glasgow, January 1938, Teruel
W. Kenny, Manchester, February 1937, Jarama
J. Kent, New Zealand, June 1937, Drowned S.S *City of Barcelona*
J. Keogh, Ashton under Lyne, March 1938, Calaceite
James Kermode, Milngavie, Scotland, January 1937, Las Rozas
Thomas Kerr, Belfast, October 1938, (of typhoid in Vich hospital)
A Kerry, London, July 1937, Brunete
T.F. Killick, Southport, February 1937, Jarama
R. Kirk, Liverpool, February 1937, Jarama
James Knottman, Manchester, January 1937, Córdoba
W. Knowles, London, February 1937, Jarama

Clifford Lacey, London, September 1938, Ebro
G. Lamb, London, April 1938, Gandesa
James Langham, Motherwell, July 1937, Brunete
W. Langmead, London, July 1937, Brunete

L.G. Large, London, April 1938, Died as prisoner of war
C.A. Larlham, London, October 1937, Fuentes de Ebro
William Laughlin, Belfast, July 1937, Brunete
James Laughran, Motherwell, July 1937, Brunete
J. Lawrie, London, August 1938, Ebro
Harold Laws, Southampton, February 1938, Teruel
Clifford Lawther, Hexham, Northumberland, February 1937, Jarama
D.A. Ledbury, Swansea, July 1938, Ebro
Samuel Lee, London, February 1937, Jarama
Joseph Lees, Oldham, July 1937, Brunete
Alexander Leppard, London, February 1937, Jarama
G.S. Leslie, London, July 1937, Brunete
Ariel Levine, London, March 1938, Aragon
S. Lewis, London, July 1938, Ebro
A. Lichfield, London, July 1938, Ebro
M. Livesay, London, June 1937, Segovia
Sidney Lloyd Jones, Wales, October 1936, Chapineria
T.C. Loader, Bexley, Kent, December 1937, Died of fever, whereabouts unknown
J. Lobban, Alexandria, September 1938, Ebro
R.K. Lomax, Shrewsbury, February 1937, Jarama
W.E. Lower, Sunderland, June 1937, Drowned in S.S. *City of Barcelona*
James Lyons, Glasgow, February 1937, Jarama

Albert McCabe, Bootle, Lancs., August 1937, Quinto
F. McCabe, Dundee, July 1937, Brunete
B. McCafferty, London, July 1938, Ebro
F. McCulloch, Glasgow, October 1937, Aragon
Alex McDade, Glasgow, July 1937, Brunete
Donald McDonald, Brighton, April 1938, Gandesa
R. McDonald, Glasgow, June 1937, Drowned in S.S. *City of Barcelona*
James McElroy, Wishaw, Scotland, February 1937, Jarama
G. McEwen, Liverpool, June 1937, Jarama
D. McGower, Glasgow, March 1938, Aragon
H. McGrath, Belfast, September 1938, Ebro
Alex McGregor, London, January 1938, Teruel
William S. McGregor, Dublin, September 1938, Ebro
Eamon McGrotty, Derry, February 1937, Jarama
E. McGuire, Dundee, February 1937, Jarama
W. McGuire, Dundee, February 1937, Jarama

James McHugh, Dundee, March 1938, Gandesa
David McKay, Milngavie, Scotland, April 1938, Gandesa
David McKay, Glasgow, August 1938, Ebro
McKenzie, Glasgow, March 1938, Aragon
A. McKeown, Glasgow, July 1937, Brunete
G. McKeown, Liverpool, June 1937, Jarama
R.H. Mackie, Sunderland, July 1937, Brunete
William Mackie, London, August 1938, Ebro
J. McKissock, Glasgow, April 1937, Jarama
J. McLanders, Dundee, April 1937, Jarama
J. McLannaghan, Greenock, September 1938, Tarragona
F. McLaughlin, Newmains, Lanarkshire, Killed – whereabouts unknown
G.C. McLaurin, Cambridge and New Zealand, November 1936, Madrid
Charles McLeod, Aberdeen, August 1938, Ebro
T. McLeod, Liverpool, March 1938, Aragon
Tim McManus, London, Killed – whereabouts unknown
James McMorrow, Glasgow, July 1938, Ebro
W. McMullen, Belshill, Scotland, January 1938, Teruel
A. McNally, Birmingham, March 1938, Aragon
Thomas McWhirter, Glasgow, March 1938, Caspe
A. Madero, Louth, Lincs, April 1938, Died in hospital
M. Mandell, London, July 1937, Brunete
A. Marks, London, July 1937, Brunete
Inver A.R. Marlow, (John Scott), London, February 1937, Jarama
James Marshall, Clydebank, August 1938, Ebro
Bert Maskey, Manchester, February 1937, Jarama
N. Mason, Carshalton, Surrey, March 1938, Aragon
Robert Mason, Edinburgh, February 1937, Jarama
Sam Masters, London, July 1937, Brunete
H. Matthews, Cuffley, Herts., April 1938, Gandesa
Leslie Maugham, London, January 1938, Teruel
Michael May, Dublin, December 1936, Córdoba
John Meehan, Galway, December 1936, Córdoba
Cecil Mennel, London, January 1938, Teruel
W. Meredith, (Bob Dennison), Glasgow, July 1937, Brunete
Martin Messer, Glasgow, December 1936, Boadilla
George Middleton, Reading, November 1936, Casa de Camps
J. Miller, Glasgow, March 1938, Aragon
Morris Miller, Hull, August 1938, Ebro
James Moir, Perth, July 1937, Brunete
J.A. Moore, Portsmouth, January 1939, Died of wounds
Thomas Moore, Manchester, January 1938, Teruel

Ken Morrice, Aberdeen, July 1938, Ebro
A. Morris, Cardigan, 1937, Madrid
William Morris, Llanelly, July 1937, Brunete
Phil Morriss, London, February 1937, Jarama
Sam Moriss, Ammanford, South Wales, July 1937, Brunete
Christos Mortakis, London-Cyprus, April 1938, Gandesa
R. Moss, London, April 1938, Gandesa
J.D. Mudie, Dundee, March 1938, Caspe
Alexander Muir, London, February 1937, Jarama
Dan Murphy, Cardiff, April 1938, Gandesa
James Murphy, Glasgow, March 1938, Caspe
Ben Murray, Belfast, March 1938, Aragon
James Murray, Glasgow, July 1937, Brunete
James Murray, Dundee, March 1938, Caspe
Joe Murray, London, March 1938, Aragon
William Murray, Glasgow, July 1937, Brunete

Jack Nalty, Dublin, September 1938, Ebro
Max Nash, London, July 1938, Ebro
George Nathan, London, July 1937, Brunete
J. Ness, Dundee, July 1938, Ebro
F. Newbury, Manchester, February 1937, Jarama
J. Newman, Liverpool, February 1937, Jarama
Arthur Newsome, Sheffield, January 1937, Córdoba
Demidrus Nicolaou, London-Cyprus, March 1938, Gandesa
Michael Nolan, Dublin, December 1936, Córdoba
J.T. Norbury, Liverpool, February 1937, Jarama
Frank Norton, Liverpool, February 1937, Jarama
M. Nuns, (Emile Pezaro), London, March 1938, Aragon

Francis Duffy O'Brien, Dundalk, January 1938, Teruel
Thomas T. O'Brien, Liverpool, February 1937, Jarama
Peter O'Day, London, March 1938, Aragon
T. Oldershaw, London, March 1938, Aragon
Dick O'Neill, Belfast, February 1937, Jarama
L. O'Nichen, Stoke, June 1938, Ebro
Loukas Orfanides, London-Cyprus, March 1938, Belchite
Paddy O'Sullivan, Dublin, July 1938, Ebro
Bert Overton, Stockton, July 1937, Brunete
Ruth Ormesby, ?, April 1938, Barcelona
Frank Owen, Mardy, South Wales, July 1937, Brunete
J.D. Owens, Liverpool, February 1937, Jarama

George Palmer, London, January 1937, Las Rozas
J. Palzeard, South Shields, February 1937, Jarama
Spiros Pantelides, London-Cyprus, March 1938, Belchite
Alec Park, Glasgow, March 1938, Aragon
A. Parkes, Manchester, July 1937, Brunete
Tom Patton, Mayo, December 1936, Madrid
Edward Paul, London, February 1937, Jarama
Henry Pearson, London, July 1937, Ebro
Nikos Perdicos, London-Cyprus, February 1937, Jarama
Leonard Perry, London, April 1938, Gandesa
Arthur Perryman, London, April 1938, Died in hospital
J. Peterson, Liverpool, April 1938, Gandesa
E. Petrie, London, August 1937, Brunete
Thomas Picton, Rhondda, April 1938, Killed while prisoner
J. Pitman, London, April 1937, Chimorra
F.A. Plumb, Luton, February 1937, Jarama
A. Porter, Manchester, February 1937, Jarama
Frank J. Procter, Liverpool, August 1938, Ebro
Lawrence G. Pryme, London, August 1938, Ebro
A. Purvis, Edinburgh, April 1938, Gandesa

Maurice P. Quinlan, Waterford, Ireland, February 1937, Jarama
Frank Quinton, London, June 1937, Morata

James Rae, Glasgow, February 1937, Jarama
Harry Rawson, (Heap), Oldham, December 1936, Córdoba
K. Rebbechi, Melbourne, Australia, January 1939, Vich hospital
J Redhill, Glasgow, October 1937, Aragon
J. Redmond, Liverpool, March 1938, Aragon
H. Reynolds, Newcastle, February 1937, Jarama
John Rickman, London, February 1937, Jarama
J. Riddell, Glasgow, October 1937, Aragon
John Riley, Glasgow, January 1938, Teruel
J-E. Riordan, London, April 1938, Ebro
J. Roach, Leeds, March 1938, Gandesa
Victor Robilliard, Dagenham, October 1938, Ebro
A. Leonard Robinson, Blackhall, Durham, October 1937, Fuentes de Ebro
Joseph C. Roche, Leeds, February 1937, Jarama
Román Rodríguez, Dowlais, South Wales, July 1937, Brunete
John Ross, Edinburgh, March 1938, Aragon
George Rossides, London-Cyprus, April 1938, Gandesa

W.C. (Maro) Rowney, London, February 1937, Jarama
James Rutherford, Edinburgh, April 1938, Shot while prisoner
Maurice Ryan, Tipperary, August 1938, Ebro
Edward Ryder, London, June 1938, Died of wounds while prisoner

D. Samson, Dundee, July 1937, Brunete
Scott, ?, April 1937, Chimorra
C.J. Scott, London, August 1938, Ebro
H.G. Scott, London, February 1937, Jarama
James Scott, Swansea, March 1938, Caspe
William Seal, London, February 1937, Jarama
Nathan Segal, London, December 1936, Córdoba
Vic Shammah, Manchester, March 1938, Aragon
D. Sheehan, Brighton, July 1938, Ebro
Jack Sherpenzeel, London, July 1938, Ebro
B. Shields, Clydebank, March 1938, Caspe
J. Shields, Glasgow, February 1937, Jarama
R. Shields, Glasgow, September 1938, Ebro
Thomas Silcock, Liverpool, February 1937, Jarama
Ernest Sim, Aberdeen, September 1938, Ebro
C.J. Simmons, Portsmouth, February 1937, Jarama
A.C. Smith, Manchester, August 1938, Killed while prisoner
David Smith, Glasgow, February 1937, Jarama
H.J. Smith, Gateshead, February 1937, Jarama
John Smith, Irvine, Scotland, September 1938, Ebro
Malcolm Smith, Dundee, August 1938, Ebro
W. Smith, Birkenhead, March 1938, Aragon
Randall Sollenberger, London and USA, July 1937, Brunete
F. Spencer, Pontefract, February 1937, Jarama
Christopher St. John Sprigg, (Caudwell), London, February 1937,
Jarama
Walter Sproston, Manchester, March 1938, Calaceite
Ken Stalker, London, February 1937, Jarama
John Steele, Falkirk, May 1937, Jarama
Nathan Steigman, London, February 1937, Jarama
T.E. Stephens, Bristol, July 1938, Died in hospital
John Stevens, London, February 1937, Jarama, Shot while prisoner
J.E. Stevens, London and Australia, July 1937, Brunete
Joseph Stevenson, Belshill, Scotland, February 1938 (typhoid)
J. Stewart, ?, February 1937, Jarama
George Stockdale, Leeds, July 1938, Ebro
Maurice Stott, Rochdale, February 1937, Jarama
James Straney, Belfast, July 1938, Ebro

Jim Strangward, Onllwyn, South Wales, August 1938, Ebro
L.R. Strickland, London, February 1937, Jarama
James Sullivan, Glasgow, July 1938, Ebro
Eddy Swindells, Manchester, February 1937, Jarama
Fred Sykes, Leicester, February 1937, Jarama
Jack Sylvester, London, February 1937, Jarama
Ronnie Symes, London, November 1936, Madrid

John Tadden, Dundee, February 1937, Jarama
H. Tagg, Doncaster, February 1937, Jarama
W. Tallis, London, April 1938, Gandesa
Louis Tanklevitch, Liverpool, July 1938, Ebro
Walter Tapsell, London, April 1938, Calaceite
Edward Tattam, Whitburn, Scotland, March 1938, Aragon
William Tattam, Whitburn, Scotland, July 1937, Brunete
G. Taylor, Cardiff, April 1938, Calaceite
J. Taylor, London, February 1937, Jarama
Terry, ?, July 1937, Brunete
Brazell Thomas, Llanelly, July 1938, Ebro
J.G.C. Thomas, Gillingham, February 1937, Jarama
A. Thompson, Durham, January 1938, Teruel
Robert Traill, London, July 1937, Brunete
A. Trauber, London, September 1938, Ebro
Liam Tumilson, Belfast, February 1937, Jarama
F. Turnhill, Worksop, Notts., January 1938, Teruel

J. Unthank, Middlesborough, February 1937, Jarama

David Walshe, Ballina, Ireland, January 1938, Teruel
J. Walsh, Liverpool, February 1937, Jarama
S.E. Walsh, Newcaste-on-Tyne, July 1937, Brunete
Thomas Walsh, Dublin, February 1937, Jarama
F. Warbrick, London, March 1938, Aragon
R. Ward, Manchester, June 1937, Jarama
R. Wardell, Hull, April 1938, Gandesa
J. Wark, Airdrie, February 1937, Jarama
J. Watson, Leicester, February 1937, Jarama
William Watson, Glasgow, July 1938, Ebro
James Watt, Swansea, August 1938, Ebro
Roy Watts, Leicester, September 1938, Ebro
W.A. Webb, London, February 1937, Jarama

G. Westfield, Liverpool, October 1937, Aragon
Eric Whalley, Mansfield, October 1937, Fuentes de Ebro
John Whalley, London, March 1938, Aragon
James Wheeler, London, February 1937, Jarama
Fred White, Ogmore Valley, South Wales, July 1937, Brunete
J. White, London, February 1937, Jarama
F. Whitehead, Manchester, February 1937, Jarama
E.F. Wilkinson, Sunderland, February 1937, Jarama
Norman Wilkinson, Manchester, February 1937, Jarama
E. Williams, Swindon, March 1938, Caspe
J.E. Williams, Ammanford, South Wales, July 1937, Brunete
W. Williamson, London, July 1938, Ebro
Bernard Winfield, Nottingham, January 1938, Teruel
A. Winter, Glasgow, July 1937, Brunete
H. Wise, London, January 1937, Córdoba
Clifford Wolstencroft, Oldham, March 1938, Aragon
Thomas Woods, Dublin, December 1936, Córdoba

Anthony Yates, Glasgow, February 1937, Jarama
Stephen Yates, London, November 1936, Madrid
W.J. Young, Sydney, Australia, July 1938, Ebro
Francisco or Frank Zamora, Abercrave, South Wales, January 1938, Teruel

Select Bibliography

1. Books and pamphlets written by or about British volunteers in Spain. These are mainly personal accounts. Most are out of print and difficult to find. They are all in the International Brigade Archives, Marx Memorial Library, Clerkenwell Green, London.

Cook, Judith, *Apprentices of Freedom*, Quartet Books, 1979. An account using taped interviews with some Brigaders.

Copeman, Fred, *Reason in Revolt*, Blandford Press, 1948. An autobiography which includes an account of his service in Spain.

Corkhill, D., Rawnsley, S., (eds), *The Road to Spain*, Borderline Press, 1981. Taped interviews with some Brigaders.

Coward, Jack, *Escape from the Dead, Daily Worker*, pamphlet, date unknown, probably 1940. An account of his adventures after capture and how he made his way from prison back to Britain.

Cronin, Sean, *Frank Ryan*, Repsol, Dublin, 1980. A biography covering Ryan's life in the Irish nationalist movement, in Spain and his last days in Germany.

Cunningham, Valentine (ed.), *The Penguin Book of Spanish Civil War Verse*, Penguin, 1980. A very full collection of poetry and some prose, much of it written by volunteers; marred by the political bias of the introduction.

Deegan, Frank, *There's No Other Way*, Toulouse Press, 1980. An autobiography of his life as a docker in Liverpool and member of the British Battalion.

Felstead, Richard, *No Other Way*, Alun Books, Port Talbot, 1981. An account, written by his grandson, of the activity of Jack Roberts as a miner in South Wales, in Spain and as a Communist councillor.

Frow, R. and E. (eds), *Bill Feeley, Singer, Steel Erector, and International Brigader*, AUEW (Construction Section) pamphlet, 1978. Tributes to his life and work.

Gillan, Phil, *The Defence of Madrid*, Communist Party pamphlet, 1937. The impressions of a young member of the 'first few' of the early fighting in November and December 1936.

Gurney, Jason, *Crusade in Spain*, Faber and Faber, 1974. A highly fanciful account of his period in Spain.

Haden Guest, C. (ed.), *David Guest – a Scientist Fights for Freedom, 1911-1938*, Lawrence and Wishart, 1939. A memoir covering his life as a student, scientist, Communist and fighter in the British Battalion.

Haldane, Charlotte, *Truth Will Out*, Weidenfeld and Nicolson, 1949. The writer of this autobiography was Secretary of the Dependant's Aid Committee. Her son was a volunteer and her husband – J.B.S. – was closely associated with the Brigades.

Harrison, Stanley, *Good to be Alive*, Lawrence and Wishart, 1954. A biography of Jack Brent covering his fighting in Spain and as Secretary of the International Brigade Association.

Horner, Arthur, (foreword), *They Fought in Franco's Jails*, Communist Party pamphlet, 1939. A description of conditions and life in Franco's prisons and how the British prisoners organised.

Jenkins, Mick, *George Brown – Portrait of a Communist Leader*, North West Communist Party History Group pamphlet, 1972. The story of Brown's life in Manchester as a Communist organiser and then in the British Battalion until his death July 1937.

Kisch, Richard, *They Shall Not Pass*, Wayland, 1974. His experiences in the unsuccessful attack on Mallorca in 1936, and other material on Spain.

Lehmann, John, Jackson, T.A., Lewis, C. Day (eds), *Ralph Fox – a Writer in Arms*, Lawrence and Wishart, 1937. Includes a tribute by Harry Pollitt, extracts from Fox's letters from Spain, and an account of his death by Hugh Slater, followed by a selection from his writings.

O'Riordan, Michael, *Connolly Column*, New Books, Dublin, 1979. An account of the Irish fighters in Spain written by a volunteer.

Palmer, Nettie, *Australians in Spain*, Spanish Relief Committee, undated pamphlet, Sydney, probably 1938. An account of the Australians – fighters, nurses and ambulance drivers – their background and their experiences in Spain.

Paynter, William, *My Generation*, Allen and Unwin, 1972. His life as a miners' leader and his experiences as British Political Commissar at the Albacete Base.

Pitcairn, Frank (Claud Cockburn), *Reporter in Spain*, Lawrence and Wishart, 1936. An account by the *Daily Worker* correspondent of his part in the fighting in the Sierra Guadarrama in 1936.

Romilly, Esmond, *Boadilla*, Hamish Hamilton, 1937; new edition, with introduction and notes by Hugh Thomas, Macdonald, 1971. An account of his part in the actions up to December 1936.

Rust, William, *Britons in Spain*, Lawrence and Wishart, 1939. A history of the British volunteers based on the then current material and on close contact with the Battalion.

Sloan, Pat (ed.), *John Cornford, A Memoir*, Cape, 1938; reprinted Borderline Press, 1978. Contains letters and poems from Spain and reminiscences from his comrades.

Sommerfield, John, *Volunteer in Spain*, Lawrence and Wishart, 1937. A personal account of the early battles in University City, Madrid and Boadilla.

Stansky, Peter and Abrahams, William, *Journey to the Frontier*, Constable, 1966. A joint life of John Cornford and Julian Bell, both killed in action in Spain.

Toynbee, Philip, *The Distant Drum*, Sidgwick and Jackson, 1976. A selection of prose writing about the Spanish war including five contributions by British volunteers.

Wintringham, Tom, *English Captain*, Penguin, 1941. A detailed and graphic account of the Jarama battle.

Clem Beckett – Hero and Sportsman, Manchester Dependants' Aid Committee pamphlet, probably May 1937. The story of his life as a speedway-rider and anti-fascist, and his death at Jarama.

And After, Dependants' Aid Committee pamphlet, 1939. The story of the work of the Dependants' Aid Committee on behalf of the wives and families of the volunteers.

2. *Books about the International Brigades. This list is mainly limited to studies in English dealing with those units closely associated with the British volunteers.*

Bessie, Alvah, *Men in Battle*, Charles Scribner, New York, 1939; Seven Seas Books, Berlin, 1960. Bessie was a volunteer himself and tells of the fighting by the Lincolns in the Aragon and in the Ebro offensive.

Brome, Vincent, *The International Brigades*, Heinemann, 1965. A superficial, inaccurate attempt at a history.

Castells, Andreu, *Brigadas Internacionales de la Guerra de España*, Ariel, Barcelona, 1974 (in Spanish). This book uses extensive material and records of the International Brigades captured by Franco's forces. It is a serious study and not without some respect for the International Brigades.

Cox, Geoffrey, *Defence of Madrid*, Gollancz, 1937. The author was Madrid correspondent of the *News Chronicle* and tells of his contacts with the British group there.

Diamint, David, *Combattants Juifs dans l'Armée Républicaine Espagnole*. Editions Renouveau, Paris, 1979 (in French). The author, himself a volunteer, describes the contribution of Jewish fighters in the International Brigades.

Elliott, Lon, Nesterenko and others (eds), *International Solidarity with the Spanish Republic*, Progress Publishers, Moscow, 1975. Accounts, written by responsible leaders, of the part played in Spain by volunteers from twenty-one nations.

Hoar, Victor, *The Mackenzie-Papineau Battalion*, Copp Clark, Canada, 1969. An account of the Canadian fighters in Spain. A new history of the Mac Paps is being prepared.

Horner, Arthur, *Incorrigible Rebel*, Macgibbon and Kee, 1960. Includes accounts of his two visits, as leader of the South Wales Miners' Federation, to Spain and contacts with the British volunteers.

Landis, Arthur, *The Abraham Lincoln Brigade*, Citadel Press, New York, 1967. A detailed history of the activity of all the Americans in various units and their contact with other nationalities. The author was himself a volunteer.

Mahon, John, *Harry Pollitt – A Biography*, Lawrence and Wishart, 1976. Includes descriptions of Pollitt's visits to the British fighters in Spain and his activities in support of the Republic.

Nelson, Steve, *The Volunteers*, Masses and Mainstream, New York, 1953. An account of his personal experiences in the American labour movement and as a political commissar of the XVth Brigade.

Ryan, Frank (ed.), *Book of the XVth Brigade*, War Commissariat, Madrid, 1938; reprinted by Frank Graham, Newcastle, 1975. An illustrated compilation including reportage and profiles written by members of the XVth Brigade.

3. Book in English on the general history of the Civil War period.

Brenan, Gerald, *The Spanish Labyrinth. An Account of the Social and Political Background of the Spanish Civil War*, Cambridge University Press, 1943; paperback reprint, 1960. An account of Spanish history from 1874 written to explain the background and the causes of the war.

Fraser, Ronald, *Blood of Spain. An Oral History of the Spanish Civil War*, Allen Lane, 1979; Penguin edn, 1981. An extensive account, using interviews with Spanish participants in the war, as well as written sources.

Jackson, Gabriel, *The Spanish Republic and the Civil War, 1931-1939*, Princeton University Press, 1965. A valuable, sympathetic and fair account.

Landis, Arthur, *Spain: the Unfinished Revolution*, Camelot, California, 1972. The author fought in the Lincoln Battalion and wrote a history of the American volunteers. Polemical and strongly committed to the Republic.

Mitchell, Sir Peter Chalmers, *My House in Malaga*, Faber and Faber, 1938. A personal account of the fall of Malaga to the fascists (including the capture of Arthur Koestler).

Sandoval, José and Azcárate, Manuel, *Spain 1936-39*, Lawrence and Wishart, 1963. A brief history of the war by two senior members of the Spanish Communist Party.

Thomas, Hugh, *The Spanish Civil War*, Eyre and Spottiswoode, 1961; revised Penguin edn, 1965. This widely-read work must be studied with caution. The author does not see the war in the context of the general struggle against fascism, and is unsympathetic to the Republican cause.

Tisa, John (ed.), *The Palette and the Flame*, Collet's, 1980. Coloured reproduction of posters printed during 1936-39 compiled by a member of the Lincoln Battalion. They illustrate, in a powerful way, many of the aims, military and social, of the Republic.

Selected Name Index
including all volunteers mentioned